Growing Old in an Older Brazil

Growing Old in an Older Brazil

Implications of Population Ageing on Growth, Poverty, Public Finance, and Service Delivery

Michele Gragnolati
Ole Hagen Jorgensen
Romero Rocha
Anna Fruttero

THE WORLD BANK
Washington, D.C.

© 2011 The International Bank for Reconstruction and Development / The World Bank
1818 H Street NW
Washington DC 20433
Telephone: 202-473-1000
Internet: www.worldbank.org

1 2 3 4 14 13 12 11

ISBN: 978-0-8213-8802-0
eISBN: 978-0-8213-8803-7
DOI: 10.1596/978-0-8213-8802-0

Cover design: Quantum Think
Cover photo: © World Bank/Scott Wallace

Library of Congress Cataloging-in-Publication Data

Growing old in an older Brazil : implications of population aging on growth, poverty, public finance and service delivery / Michele Gragnolati ... [et al.].
    p. cm. — (Directions in development)
    Includes bibliographical references.
    ISBN 978-0-8213-8802-0 (alk. paper) — ISBN 978-0-8213-8803-7 (ebk)
    1. Older people—Brazil. 2. Old age assistance—Brazil. 3. Older people—Brazil—Economic aspects. 4. Aging—Brazil. I. Gragnolati, Michele, 1968- II. World Bank.
    HQ1064.B7D57 2011
    305.260981—dc22

                                                                    2011016220

Contents

Figures

Tables

Foreword

This report addresses population aging, one of the most fundamental issues to the development of Brazil, which could define whether the country will enter a cycle of sustained and inclusive development, or at the other extreme, fall into a fiscal trap with a lack of socioeconomic opportunities for youth.

Population aging traditionally was not a top concern in a country that is seen as synonymous with youth. But this has been changing drastically in the last few decades. Brazil embarked on a process of development that has led to the country's social and demographic indicators approaching those of developed countries, but with systems and institutions inherited from a different context.

There has been little debate about this transition until now, especially from a broader perspective that seeks to understand the complex and interconnected dimensions of the relationship between demographic change and socioeconomic development. This report seeks to reduce this gap and encourage the debate on public policy options in this relatively new field. It will become clear to the reader that this debate can no longer be delayed.

Above all, the current rapid demographic changes in Brazil represent a great opportunity to boost social and economic development and growth. Brazil is going through a short "demographic bonus," unique to each nation, when the labor force is much larger than the dependent population. This is an inflection point that will last only until 2020, but will have far reaching impacts.

Because of this, it is impossible to overstate the importance of the moment. Today's policy decisions in terms of education, health, and social welfare will determine the country's ability to invest in its youth and provide good and long lives to its elderly. These decisions will also have a profound impact on economic growth, government services, and Brazil's international competitiveness, at a moment when Brazil is committed to achieving "developed" status.

The current framework for social policy was developed after Brazil passed its current constitution in 1988 in a young demographic context, with much poverty, recently created institutions, and high inflation. The policy favors public transfers for the elderly over transfers to children. This model has been very efficient in reducing poverty and inequality, but it has led to OECD-level costs, even though Brazil's population is still relatively young. This has resulted in lower investments in youth and much higher average benefits to the elderly (66.5 percent of the average wage in Brazil versus 30.4 percent of the OECD average).

Brazil is moving into a fundamentally different demographic context, in which the increasingly older population will place an extra burden on the system if new policies are not introduced. The country will have to make difficult choices, with consequences for the poor and vulnerable groups and long-term economic growth.

Brazil needs to take advantage of the current opportunity and prepare for the structural changes in the coming decades. For example, the labor market needs to create enough opportunities for the working-age population in the short term, but to sustain productivity growth Brazil will also have to encourage women and other groups to participate further in the economy. Moreover, it will be necessary to stimulate efficient ways to finance the fiscal expenses related to an older population and to stimulate savings and growth. In this way, population aging may lead to a large accumulation of capital and an increase in incomes, wealth, and well-being.

However, institutional changes are usually difficult to negotiate with the many stakeholders of a society as complex as Brazil, and they have long transition periods. International experience shows that the longer reforms are delayed, the greater the need for them, and the more drastic they must be. At the same time, the report points out that the ongoing and future demographic change itself reveals opportunities for gains and improvements. For example, as fewer students enter the system due to a lower birth rate, more resources are available for key investments, such as increasing the quality of education or the reach of early childhood development programs.

This report is a result of more than two years of work by the World Bank's Brazil Human Development Team, led by Michele Gragnolati. We are certain that it will contribute to the debate on the issues outlined here and help Brazil face this new challenge, which by itself attests to the country's progress on the path to equitable and sustainable development and poverty reduction.

Makhtar Diop
Director for Brazil, World Bank

Keith Hansen
Director for the Human Development Department of the Latin American and Caribbean Region, World Bank

Acknowledgments

This report was written by Michele Gragnolati, Ole Hagen Jorgensen, Romero Rocha, and Anna Fruttero, with help from Carla Zardo, Mariane Brito, and Marize de Fatima Santos. It was requested and financed by the World Bank Brazil Country Unit to deepen the Bank's knowledge in strategic areas of human capital formation in Brazil, including population aging, early child development, education quality, and job quality. The team is grateful for the support and guidance received from Makhtar Diop, Helena Ribe, and Tito Cordella.

The report builds on the findings of the background papers listed below, most of which were presented at the Workshop on Aging in Brazil organized by the World Bank in Brasilia, April 6–7, 2010.

1. Kaizo Beltrao and Sonoe Sugahara: "Mortality Estimates with Emphasis on Old Age"
2. Kaizo Beltrao and Sonoe Sugahara: "Demographic Transition in Brazil"
3. Ana Amelia Camarano: "Options for Long-Term Care in Brazil: Formal or Informal Care?"
4. Ole Hagen Jorgensen: "Macroeconomic and Policy Implications of Population Aging in Brazil"

5. Alexandre Kalache: "Implications for the Health Sector of the Aging Process in Brazil"
6. Tim Miller and Helena Castanheira: "Public Finance Implications of Population Aging in Brazil: 2005–50"
7. Bernardo Queiroz and Moema Figoli: "The Social Protection System for the Elderly in Brazil"
8. Romero Rocha: "Aging, Productivity, and Wages: Is an Aging Workforce a Burden to the Firms?"
9. Rodrigo Soares: "Aging, Retirement, and the Labor Market in Brazil"
10. Paulo Tafner: "Public Expenditure Review for Health, Education, and Social Security in the Context of Population Aging in Brazil"
11. Cassio Turra and Romero Rocha: "Public Transfers among Dependent Age Groups in Brazil"

Abbreviations and Acronyms

AEPS	*Anuário Estatístico da Previdência Social*—Statistical Yearbook of the Social Security
BEPS	*Boletim Estatístico da Previdência Social*—Social Security Statistical Bulletin
BPC	*Benefício de Prestação Continuada*—Benefits of Continued Provision
CELADE	*Centro Latinoamericano de Demografia*—Latin American and Caribbean Center of Demography
CENSUS	Program for Evaluations and Experiments (individual enumeration, universality within a defined territory, simultaneity, and defined periodicity)
CEPAL	*Comissão Econômica para a América Latina e o Caribe*—Economic Comission for Latin America and the Caribbean
CIAPE	*Centro Interdisciplinar de Assistência e Pesquisa em Envelhecimento*—Interdisciplinary Center of Assistance and Research in Aging
CVD	cardiovascular disease
DLAs	daily life activities
DALYs	disability-adjusted life years lost
EC	*Emenda Constitucional*—Constitutional Amendment

GDP	gross domestic product
IBGE	*Instituto Brasileiro de Geografia e Estatística*—Brazilian Geographical and Statistical Institute
IHD	ischemic heart disease
IMF	International Monetary Fund
INPC	*Índice Nacional de Preços ao Consumidor*—National Consumer Price Index
INPS	*Instituto Nacional de Previdência Social*—National Institute of Social Welfare
INSS	*Instituto Nacional de Seguridade Social*—National Institute of Social Security
IPEA	*Instituto de Pesquisa Econômica Aplicada*—National Institute for Applied Economic Research
LAC	Latin America and the Caribbean
LCH	Life Cycle Hypothesis
LE	life expectancy
LEB	life expectancy at birth
LOAS	*Lei Orgânica da Assistência Social*—Organic Law of Social Assistance
LOC	length of contribution
LOS	length of service
LTC	long-term care
MDS	*Ministério do Desenvolvimento Social e Combate à Fome*—Ministry of Social Development and Fight Against Hunger
MOH	Brazil Ministry of Health
MPS	*Ministério da Previdência Social*—Ministry of Social Security
NCD	noncommunicable disease
NTA	National Transfer Accounts
NPV	net present value
OECD	Organisation for Economic Co-operation and Development
OLGs	overlapping generations
OLS	ordinary least squares
PAYG	pay as you go
PC	period of contribution
PE	partial equilibrium
PHC	primary health care
PIA	Annual Industrial Survey
PLOC	Propositional Length of Contribution
PNAD	*Pesquisa Nacional por Amostragem a Domicílios*—Brazilian Household Survey

POF	*Pesquisa de Orçamentos Familiares*—Brazilian Family Budget Survey
PPP	purchasing power parity
PRP	Professional Recycling Governmental Program
PSF	*Programa Saúde da Família*—Family Health Program
RA	retirement age
RAIS	Annual Relation of Social Information Survey
RGPS	*Regime Geral de Previdência Social*—General Regime of Social Security, Private Workers Social Security
RMV	*Renda Mensal Vitalícia*—Lifelong Monthly Income
RPPS	*Regime Próprio de Previdência Social*—Public Employee Pension System
Senac	*Serviço Nacional de Aprendizagem Comercial*—Commercial Learning National Service
SES	State Health Secretariat
SMS	Municipal Health Secretariat
SP	social protection
SSW	social security wealth
SUR	seemingly unrelated regression
SUS	*Sistema Único de Saúde*—Unified Health System
SVS	Secretariat of Surveillance, Ministry of Health
TFR	total fertility rate
UN	United Nations
UNESCO	United Nations Educational, Scientific and Cultural Organization
VAR	vector auto-regression
WB	World Bank
WEO	World Economic Outlook
WHO	World Health Organization

Key Findings

The Facts

1. Brazil is in the middle of a profound socioeconomic transformation driven by demographic change. Mortality started declining, mostly at young ages, around 1940. Infant mortality decreased from 135 to 20 per thousand live births between 1950 and 2010, and life expectancy at birth increased from about 50 to about 73 years over the same period. The change in fertility has been even more spectacular and has more dramatic implications. The average Brazilian woman had more than six children in the early 1960s and currently has fewer than two. Over time these changes in mortality and fertility alter the population age structure.

2. Brazil is currently in the so-called "demographic bonus," that is, a period in a nation's demographic transition when the proportion of population of working-age group is high. This period is characterized by a smaller dependency ratio (ratio of dependents to working-age population). The dependency ratio, which has been declining since 1965, will reach its bottom value in 2020 and then will start increasing.

3. The speed of population aging in Brazil will be significantly faster than that experienced by more affluent societies over the last century. For example, it took more than a century for France's elderly population, aged 65 and above, to increase from 7 percent to 14 percent of the total population. In contrast, the same demographic change will occur in the next two decades in Brazil (2011–31). The elderly population will more than triple within the next four decades, from less than 20 million in 2010 to approximately 65 million in 2050.

4. The elderly population will increase from about 11 percent of the working-age population in 2005 to 49 percent by 2050, while the school-age population will decline from about 50 percent of the working-age population in 2005 to 29 percent by 2050. These shifts in population age structure will lead to substantial additional fiscal pressure on publicly financed health care and pensions, along with substantial reductions in fiscal pressures for publicly financed education.

5. Per capita public transfers to the elderly compared to transfers to the children are much larger in Brazil than in any OECD or other LAC country with similar welfare systems. Brazil's public sector spending in education and pensions (as a percentage of GDP) is similar to that of OECD countries. However, given Brazil's much younger population age structure, this results in markedly lower public education investment in youth (9.8 percent of average wages in Brazil vs. 15.5 percent in the OECD) and markedly higher average public pension benefits (66.5 percent of average wage in Brazil vs. 30.4 percent in the OECD). Aggregate public health care expenditures in Brazil are much below the OECD average, and average health benefits are somewhat lower as well.

6. The increasingly smaller size of the school-age population provides a unique opportunity to increase per student investment to OECD levels without adding much burden on public finance. An ambitious expansion of educational spending to reach OECD levels per student within a decade would require an increase of education spending of little more than 1 percent of GDP by 2020. After that, the share of GDP devoted to education would gradually decline as the school-age population drops, and investment levels per student would be maintained at OECD levels.

7. Heath care expenditures are likely to increase substantially. Indeed, health care is likely to emerge as a major fiscal challenge in the coming decades in Brazil. There are two driving forces behind the projected increase in health expenditures: the increasing proportion of elderly in the population and a growing intensity of formal health care use among the elderly.

8. It is also anticipated that the number of elderly people generating a demand for formal long-term care will increase because of two factors. First, the dramatic increase in the number of the very old over the next 30 years will result in a larger number of frail old people at any given time, even despite a reduction in the proportion of frail old people as a result of improvements in health care and postponement and better administration of disabilities. Second, the changing status of women and of family and social values will continue to decrease the availability of family caregivers. Projections for Brazil estimate that compared to 2008, twice as many people will be cared for by non-family members in 2020, and five times as many in 2040.

9. Public transfers in Brazil have been very effective in reducing poverty among the elderly. In particular, the pension system extends benefit coverage to most of the elderly population and provides protection to the poorest segments of society. Indeed, the programs have contributed to reducing poverty and inequality, particularly in rural areas. However, this has come at high cost, with sharp increases in expenditures of the social security system. Without substantial changes, the aging of the population will put a strain on the current system that will result in some critical trade-offs with consequence for poverty among other vulnerable groups and for the growth prospects of the country.

10. The current pension system creates negative incentives for labor market participation and social security contribution behavior. The low age limit and the existence of a length of service without minimum age eligibility result in a population that retires early. Thus a system meant to sustain the income of individuals who are unable to work ends up doing so for a longer period of time than those individuals contributed. Moreover, early retirement implies that a portion of the productive labor force is not being used or that they continue working in the informal sector.

11. The rules of the pension system incentivize informality, especially for low-skilled workers. The availability of a non-contributory program that transfers a benefit equal to the minimum income in the contributory program (equivalent to the minimum wage) reduces the incentives for low earners to contribute. Thus, a large proportion of the population does not contribute to the social security system while in the working age, but will benefit in old age. As the population in Brazil ages, the need to ensure that a larger part of the population contributes to the system will become more and more pressing.

12. The pension reforms of 1999 and 2003 were successful in slowing the expansion of pension costs. Without these reforms, spending for pensions would rise from 10 percent of GDP in 2005 to an astounding 37 percent in 2050, because of the mere increase in the number of eligible pensioners associated with population aging. The recent set of pension reforms more than halved the projected costs. However, with pension expenditures projected to more than double to 22.4 percent of GDP by 2050, the problem of affordability of pension expenditures will urgently need to be solved. Even under more optimistic scenarios, increases in pension expenditures dominate the fiscal outlook for Brazil.

13. Given the strong association between people's economic behavior and the life cycle, changes in the population age structure have a major impact on economic development. Brazil's current favorable age composition provides opportunities for higher economic growth through various channels, often referred to as "demographic dividends." The labor supply increases as generations of children born during periods of high fertility enter the labor force (first demographic dividend), and at the same time, as fertility declines, women's labor force participation is also likely to increase. Savings are likely to increase too as the number of individuals of working age who are expected to live longer increases. This leads to an increase in physical capital, the second demographic dividend. Investment in human capital may also increase as lower fertility leads to healthier women and parents have more resources to invest in education.

14. Over the medium term, however, the expected changes in labor force composition due to population aging will pose challenges to economic growth. After the mid-2020s, the growth rate of the 15–59 age

group will turn negative and population growth will be driven only by the increase in the number of the elderly. Moreover, at the micro level, there may be negative effects on productivity as a larger share of the labor force will be beyond its peak in productivity. The negative economic impact is likely to be amplified because the same decreasing age profile observed for productivity is not observed for wages in the formal sector, which tend to increase with seniority (and age). This, in turn, is likely to affect firms' competitiveness, profitability, and investment negatively.

15. Targeted training programs can be effective in softening or halting any age-related decline in the ability to learn new skills. Until now, however, all evidence indicates that access to training decreases substantially through one's working life. In the future, firms will have no choice but to expand their training programs to invest more in older employees and to reorient the programs to meet the needs of those workers.

16. It is the conventional view that aggregate saving will be reduced by population aging. However, this may not necessarily be the case in Brazil. This is because elderly generally save to a high extent out of their gross income, which remains high in Brazil mainly thanks to public transfers. So, when population aging leads to a higher fraction of elderly, the average saving rate may increase, or at least not fall. However, households' saving behavior (and Brazil's aggregate saving rate) will be affected by how the increasing costs of pension and health expenditures associated with an increasing older population will be financed.

The Policy Implications

1. Brazil needs to seize the current opportunity and prepare for the structural changes of the coming decades. The prospect of population aging in Brazil, as for most middle-income (and even more so for most low-income) countries, is a source of concern for two reasons: (1) it might obstruct fiscal sustainability and hinder further economic growth and (2) it might put a strain on existing institutions.

2. There is urgency in putting in place the right institutional and policy framework for two main reasons: (1) institutions are slow to change

and (2) those who will be the elderly in 2050 are already entering the workforce today and the rules of the current system are shaping their choices. Decisions they make over their entire adult life will be framed by the social and economic institutions, actual and expected, that influence economic security in old age. In addition, political realities typically impose a long transition period until a new regulatory framework is fully implemented. The longer a reform is postponed, the greater the need for it, and the more drastic it will have to be.

3. As more resources per student become available, it is important that they be used to improve the effectiveness of the education system. Brazil has made impressive progress in basic education over the past 15 years, but the country is still far from its goal of OECD-level educational quality by 2021. The key to accelerated progress in basic education is a mix of continuity in key areas where substantial progress has been achieved (financing equalization, results measurement, and conditional cash transfer programs) and further progress in four areas: (1) improving teachers, (2) reaching the poorest children with quality early child education, (3) raising quality in secondary education, and (4) maximizing the impact of federal policy on basic education. In addition, there is a clear need for reform in tertiary education, which the Ministry of Education has been moving slowly but steadily to address.

4. The organization of the health care system needs to be adjusted for the different demographic and epidemiological profile of the increasing older population in Brazil. The magnitude of the health care spending increases associated with an older population will depend crucially on whether the longer life span mean more healthy years or added years of illness and dependency. Prevention and postponement of disease and disability and maintenance of health, independence, and mobility in an aging population will be the major health-related challenges of population aging.

5. Policy alternatives to home care need to be developed to address the long-term care demand of an increasing number of elderly who will receive support by family members. Strengthening the capacity of the Family Health Program may be a possible strategy, but it will require additional focus and resources.

6. The pension system should be made more efficient, especially in reevaluating the incentives that lead to retirement at a very young age, excessively high replacement ratios, and receipt of multiple benefits. For example, a structural policy response of linking mandatory retirement (or entitlement) ages to increasing life expectancy could be considered. Such a reform has already been implemented in various OECD countries (Denmark, for example). This would boost labor supply and reduce the fiscal costs of aging. This reform should be implemented promptly so younger generations have time to adjust their saving behavior.

7. The government should increase coverage and improve incentive-compatibility of social insurance for old age. Indeed, it faces a big challenge in avoiding the consolidation of a bi-polar social protection system, where poor families are limited to non-contributory programs and unable to benefit from the more generous formal sector social insurance programs.

8. Economic policies should be directed toward capturing the demographic dividends. For example, the labor market needs to create enough opportunities for the growing working-age population in the short term. To sustain aggregate output growth over the medium and long term, however, Brazil will have to stimulate participation in the economy of groups such as women and to support productivity growth. On the one hand, to boost productivity of the existing labor force, Brazil needs to invest in incentives and means for skills upgrading of current workers, for example, through training and retraining of mature workers and lifelong learning programs. On the other hand, to boost the productivity potential of future generations, it needs to invest in better public education. In particular, increasing coverage and improving quality of education at early stages is likely to be among the most important determinants of a more productive labor force in the future. And this will make retraining more efficient and more effective at later stages of working-age life.

9. Moreover, government policies formulated appropriately, adequately, and in a timely way to meet aging-induced fiscal costs are needed in order to stimulate endogenous increase in savings and, thus, growth. By such means, population aging is likely to lead to substantial capital accumulation and increases in lifetime income, wealth, and welfare.

For example, refraining from increasing contributions to social security while, instead, allowing replacement rates to gradually adjust downward when the share of elderly per worker increases would keep pensions from further crowding out private saving—thus promoting capital accumulation and economic growth. Policies to enhance the financial market capacity to turn savings into investments are also key to achieving the demographic dividend from private saving.

CHAPTER 1

Introduction and Overview

Motivation for the Study

Brazil is undergoing a profound socioeconomic transformation driven by demographic change. Mortality started declining, mostly at young ages, around 1940. Infant mortality decreased from 135 per 1,000 births to 20 per 1,000 between 1950 and 2010, and life expectancy at birth increased from about 50 to about 73 years over the same period. Even more spectacular, and with more dramatic implications, has been the change in fertility. Brazilian women on average had more than six children each in the early 1960s and today have fewer than two. The large birth cohorts generated at the onset of the demographic transition had, and continue to have, dramatic effects on the population age structure. First, the population of working age, between 15 and 59 years old, started to increase rapidly. Second, the older age population then began to increase, a trend that will become increasingly powerful.

Between 1950 and 2010, the Brazilian population grew at an average annual rate of 2.2 percent. In the same period, the elderly population 60 years of age and older grew at an average annual rate of 3.4 percent, about 1.5 times as high as the total population. In the next 40 years, the Brazilian population is expected to grow less than 0.3 percent annually, while the elderly population will grow 3.2 percent annually, that is, almost 12 times as high. As a result, the elderly population, which represented 4.9 percent and 10.2 percent of the total population in 1950 and 2010, respectively, will represent 29.7 percent of the total population in 2050—that is, a proportion close to the 30 percent of present-day Japan (today's "oldest" country) and considerably above the "old continent" of Europe, where the average proportion is currently 24 percent. In absolute numbers, the elderly population will increase from 2.6 million in 1950 to 19.6 million in 2010 and to 64.0 million in 2050. Moreover, the working-age population will start declining in 2025, after which population growth in Brazil will be entirely due to increases in the older population (the youth population started declining in the early 1990s).

The prospect of population aging in Brazil, as for most middle-income (and even more so for most low-income) countries, is a source of concern both because it may (1) hinder further economic growth and (2) put a strain on existing institutions. On the first point, achieving high-income status may be more difficult for countries with large elderly populations. Developed countries, by and large, first become rich and then become old. Brazil and other countries at a similar stage of socioeconomic development are becoming older at a much faster rate than occurred in countries that developed in the past. Indeed, most of the more developed nations have had decades to adjust to this change in age structure (figure 1.1). For example, it took more than a century for France's elderly population, 65 and above, to increase from 7 percent to 14 percent of the total population. In contrast, many less developed countries are experiencing rapid increases in the number and percentage of older people, often within a single generation. The same demographic aging process that unfolded over more than a century in France will occur in two decades in Brazil.

On the second point, the strain on institutions, meeting the needs of a large elderly population requires rethinking the economic and social institutions needed to realize income security and provide adequate health care and other services for an aging society. Moreover, there is a certain urgency to putting in place the right institutional and policy framework, because institutions are slow to change and the people who will be elderly in 2050 are entering the workforce today, and the rules of the current system are shaping their choices. Decisions over their adult lifetime will be framed by the social and economic institutions, actual and expected, that influence economic security in old age. In addition, political realities typically impose a long transition period until a new regulatory framework can be fully implemented. The longer a reform is postponed, the greater the need for it and the more drastic it will need to be.

Figure 1.1   The Speed of Population Aging

years for population 65+ to increase from 7% to 14%

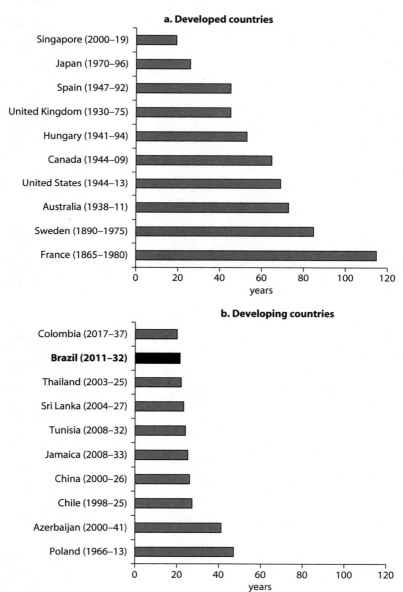

a. Developed countries

b. Developing countries

Source: National Institute on Aging 2009 (updated with status changes for several countries as of 2011).

As a result, the cost of existing programs (relative to GDP) may continue to rise for a number of years along the transition period before the stabilizing effects of a reform are felt.

As mentioned, the speed of the demographic transition in Brazil will be significantly faster than that experienced by more affluent societies over the last century: the elderly population will triple in the next four decades. Hence the policies and solutions sought by these societies are of limited relevance. The fast pace of aging will affect all aspects of society—from health care and social security to urban planning, education, and the job market. What, for instance, are the implications of population shrinkage in an emerging market economy? Germany, Japan, and Spain are already struggling with population loss. However, those countries can compensate by importing labor. Worldwide today some 240 million legal immigrants have left their poorer home countries in search of opportunities in richer ones. Will this be an option open to Brazil in the future when long-term low fertility rates have led to an inevitable population decline?

Introducing pro-natal policies and increasing retirement age may be unavoidable necessary steps. However, the debate about the catastrophic consequences of population growth has prevailed for so long that the public at large and many professionals are still under the impression that this remains a central issue. Yet, discussion about the need to boost fertility rates in Brazil is likely to be at the forefront of the political agenda soon. Delaying retirement age to increase the working-age population and reducing the pressure on the social security system may be difficult to achieve. Europe's experience is not encouraging. General strikes erupted in France in 2011 in opposition to the extension of the pensionable age by only two years, to a still early 62 threshold. In addition, for this option to be feasible, it is imperative to ensure that the future cohorts of older people will stay healthy for many years beyond the 60 or 65 "old age" starting point.

The crucial bottom line is that Brazil cannot afford simply to emulate the policies adopted by richer countries that have aged over a much longer period within a context of relative wealth and which themselves are still struggling to address the same issues. Solutions will have to be developed from within Brazilian society. Certainly, the experiences of other countries need to be observed—particularly those of other developing countries also experiencing a fast population aging—but the devised solutions need to be coherent with the country's history, culture, resources, and values.

Several articles have analyzed demographic trends and their implications on different dimensions of Brazilian economy, public policy, and society. However, no report has yet presented these questions in a comprehensive and systematic way that captures the broad complexity of issues—from economic growth to poverty, from public financing of social services and transfers to savings, from employment to health and long-term care, and their interrelations. This study aims to fill this gap by providing an overview of past and future demographic dynamics, analyzing their effect on social and economic development in Brazil, and discussing public policies to address opportunities and challenges associated with population aging.

This chapter introduces the main issues associated with population aging, many of which will be investigated in detail throughout the volume. The next section describes the demographic transformation that Brazil has been experiencing and highlights its specific features, including a very rapid population aging process in the next few decades. Then the main economic framework behind this work—the life cycle theory according to which individuals' economic behavior varies according to their age—is discussed. The section after that introduces the first and second demographic dividends associated with the changing population age structure that accompanies the demographic transition of any country. Next covered is how poverty is linked to the life cycle in Brazil and the role of public transfers in reducing poverty among different age groups, followed by an investigation of how public expenditures vary across age groups and generations and what makes Brazil distinct from comparable OECD (Organisation for Economic Co-operation and Development) and Latin American countries. Concluding the chapter are the main findings of the report.

Demographic Change in Brazil

Demographic patterns in Brazil are characterized by five features: (1) the demographic transition is advanced compared to other Latin American countries, but Brazil is still a relatively young country compared to OECD countries; (2) fertility rates have declined rapidly; (3) reduction in mortality has not been as rapid and profound as that of fertility; (4) population age structure has been changing rapidly; and (5) the current age structure is very conducive to economic growth.

First, Brazil is at an advanced phase of the demographic transition (compared to other Latin American countries) but not as advanced as most European and other OECD countries where mortality and, most importantly, fertility decline started much earlier (figure 1.2a). Although the average number of children Brazilian women have in 2005–10 (1.9) is smaller than the average number of children of all Latin American

Figure 1.2   Life Expectancy at Birth and Total Fertility Rate (TFR), 2005–10

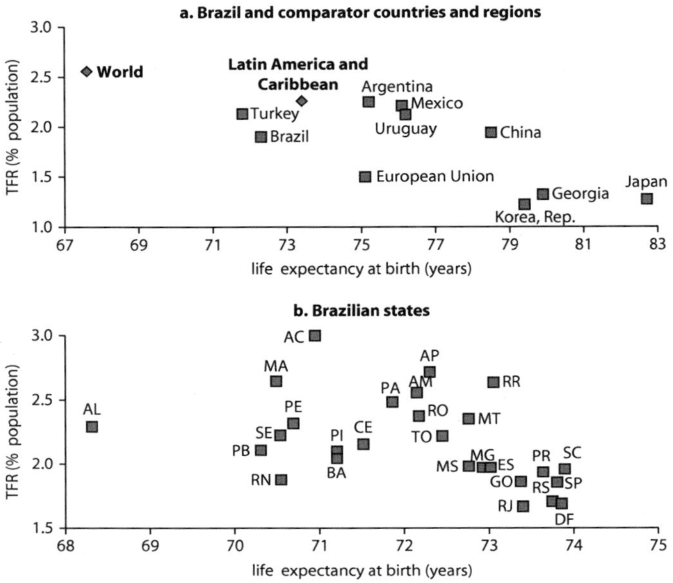

a. Brazil and comparator countries and regions

b. Brazilian states

AC: Acre	AL: Alagoas	AM: Amazonas	AP: Amapá
BA: Bahia	CE: Ceará	DF: Distrito Federal	ES: Espírito Santo
GO: Goiás	MA: Maranhão	MG: Minas Gerais	MS: Mato Grosso do Sul
MT: Mato Grosso	PA: Pará	PB: Paraíba	PE: Pernambuco
PI: Piauí	PR: Paraná	RJ: Rio de Janeiro	RN: Rio Grande do Norte
RO: Rondônia	RR: Roraima	RS: Rio Grande do Sul	SC: Santa Catarina
SE: Sergipe	SP: São Paulo	TO: Tocantins	

Sources: United Nations 2008; IGBE 2009.

countries, with the exception of Cuba (1.5), it is still higher than the corresponding number for the average European woman (1.5). Among comparator countries and regions, the lowest Total Fertility Rate (TFR) is
found in Republic of Korea (1.2). At the same time, life expectancy at
birth of the average Brazilian in 2005–10 is lower than that of the average
Latin American person (72.3 and 73.4 years, respectively) and much
lower than that observed in Japan, the country where currently people
live longest (almost 83 years).

As expected in such a large and heterogeneous country, demographic
indicators in Brazil vary considerably across geographic areas, even though
a robust pattern of convergence, described in more detail in chapter 2, has
been observed during the past three decades. Figure 1.2b shows that the

lowest and highest life expectancy at birth are found in the states of Alagoas and Santa Catarina (68.3 and 73.9 years, respectively) and the lowest and highest TFRs are found in Rio de Janeiro and Acre (1.6 and 3.0 children, respectively).

The second change in demographics is that fertility is low and its decline was very fast (figure 1.3). For example, among comparator countries, with the exception of Republic of Korea, Brazil has experienced that fastest transition from a TFR of 3 to a TFR of 2 (19 years). It took almost 60 years for the average European country to experience such a change. This rapid decline in fertility has resulted in rapid population aging, that is, old people representing an increasing share of the population, which is described briefly below and in more detail in chapter 2.

The third demographic shift is that the reduction in mortality has not been as rapid and profound as that of fertility, and life expectancy at birth is still considerably lower than in other Latin American countries—notably Argentina, Chile, Costa Rica, Cuba, and Uruguay—indicating that there is much room for improvement. Furthermore, the latest figures (United Nations 2008) indicate that life expectancy at birth for a female child, 76.7 years, is 7.6 years higher than for a male child (69.1 years). This reflects higher male mortality rates at all ages, particularly those of young adults, due to exceedingly high death rates from accidents and violence. If even some of these deaths could be prevented, a significant

Figure 1.3   Years to Reduce Fertility (TFR) from 3 to 2 and Increase Life Expectancy from 50 to 70[a]

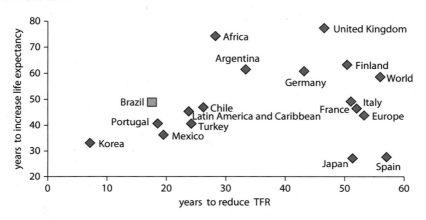

Source: United Nations 20008.
a. The actual time these changes took place in each country varies: for example, the United States life expectancy increase from 50 to 70 took place 1842–1963, while in Brazil the period was 1951–2000.

increase in overall life expectancy at birth would be achieved. As mortality at adult ages continues to improve, the proportion of old (and very old) population will increase at a faster rate. Chapter 4 presents an in-depth description of mortality patterns and their implications for health and long-term care.

Fourth in the demographic factors, the population age structure has been changing rapidly. Each stage in the transition corresponds to a shape in the population distribution: Countries in the early stages of the transition display an age-sex distribution as a large base pyramid with narrow top. As countries advance in the transition process, the base (young population) narrows and the top (elderly population) increase. In the later stages, countries would display a pillar-shaped age-sex distribution. In the extreme cases of negative growth it could eventually lead to an inverted pyramid. The whole movement is called from-pyramid-to-pillar and is described in figure 1.4 for Brazil.

It is clear from these figures that the Brazilian population will experience, as is the case for most of the already aged world, a feminization of aging, that is, many more women than men reaching older ages. This has important implications for health and long-term care as well as for employment policy. The longer lives of these women are often marked by poor health and frailty. They are particularly prone to nonfatal but debilitating conditions. A frequent addition is loneliness—as they more often than not survive their male partners, ending their lives in widowhood commonly accompanied by poverty. At the same time, although there has been a substantial increase in female labor force participation since at least the early 1970s, early retirement is still common among women. This has important consequences for economic production; duration of life after retirement; and duration, cost, and financing of pension benefits. These questions are investigated in chapters 2 (labor market) and 4 (health and long-term care).

Changes in the population age structure are well summarized by changes in the aging index, which is the number of people aged 65 and older per 100 youths under age 15 (figure 1.5). The Brazil aging index showed only a small increase between 1980 and 2000 (from 10.5 to 18.3). Since then it has increased, again, by a small amount, 8.4. This helps to explain why attention to population aging has only recently started to grow in Brazil. Until then, it was simply not that obvious to the public that the country was aging. However, from now on, much more substantial increases in the aging index are expected: close to 20 by 2020, 28.5 from then to 2030, some 40 more between 2030 and 2040, eventually reaching

Figure 1.4   Brazil: A Century of Changes in the Population Age Structure, 1950–2050

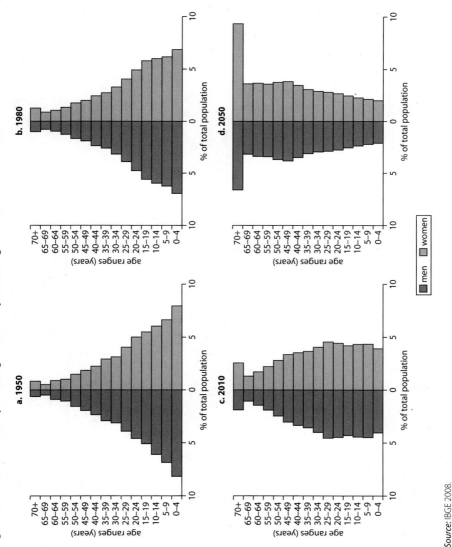

Source: IBGE 2008.

9

Figure 1.5   Brazil: Aging Index, 1980–2050

no. people 65 and older per 100 youths under age 15

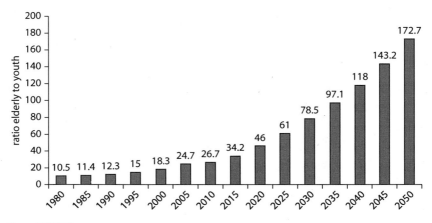

Source: IBGE 2008.

172.7 by 2050; that is, an increase of 146 points within the next 40 years, compared to only 16.2 over the previous 30.[1]

As the fifth demographic factor, Brazil is currently enjoying a favorable age structure, with the largest share of its population in working ages. This is often referred to as a "demographic bonus." During the demographic transition, not only for Brazil but for all countries, there is a period when the proportion of people of potentially productive age grows steadily in relation to potentially inactive ages. In that period, when the dependency ratio—which relates the number of people in dependent age groups (children under age 15 and persons over age 59, in this study) to that of people in the working-age group (aged 15–59)—drops to record lows, the situation is particularly conducive to development, as there are more possibilities for saving and investment leading to capital accumulation and economic growth, while there is also reduced pressure on education spending. In Brazil, the dependency ratio will reach its bottom value in 2020 and will be increasing after that (see figure 1.6).

The Economic Life Cycle

Changes in the population age distribution matter because individuals vary their economic behavior according to their age. The life cycle theory helps explain labor income, consumption, and saving patterns of

Figure 1.6   Brazil: Total, Child, and Old-Age Dependency Ratio, 1950–2050

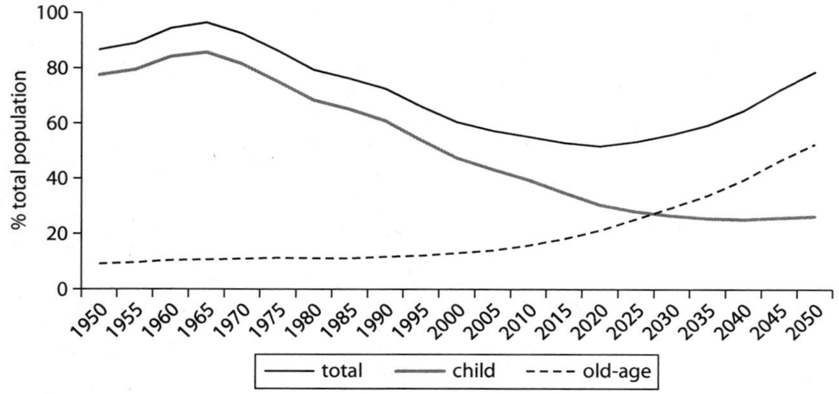

Source: United Nations 2008.

individuals across their life span. The simple idea is that people make choices about how much to spend on the basis of their permanent lifetime rather than current income (Modigliani and Brumberg 1954; Modigliani 1988). Indeed, individuals start consuming at the moment they are born and never cease until death. However, they start working only later in life and, at some point, may have to stop or decide to stop. Indeed, the life cycle can be divided into three stages: pre-work, work, and post-work.

During the first and the last stage, individuals consume more than they produce, whereas in the second stage, they produce more than they consume. The length of each stage differs across individuals and is affected by many factors beyond biology: economic structure of society, educational opportunity, family needs and expectations, and health, among others. The existence of public programs, the level of wealth, the availability of financial institutions, and cultural expectations are all important drivers of the leisure-work trade-off. Likewise, the relative level of consumption across the life cycle combines biological needs, living arrangements, public programs for children and the elderly, fertility rates among the poor and the non-poor, and other factors (World Bank 2011).

Private consumption and labor income represent a standard relationship in Brazil; consumption increases and is relatively smooth over time, while labor income shows a steep increase as young adults enter the labor market and a much slower reduction as the elderly start exiting it (figure 1.7). As discussed above, during the first and last stage, individuals represent a

Figure 1.7   Brazil: Income and Private Consumption, 2008

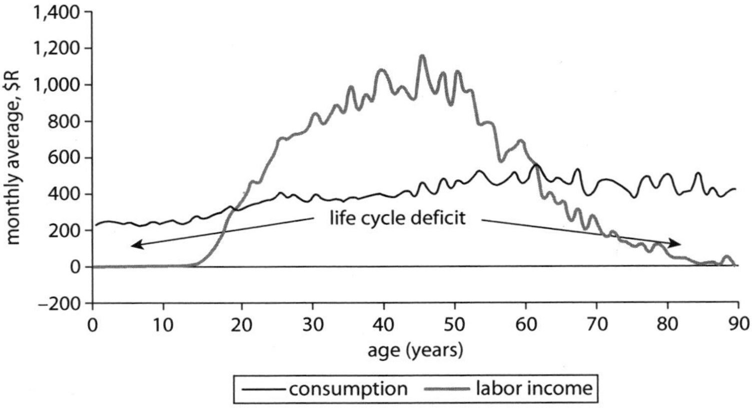

Source: Authors' calculations based on IGBE 2010.

"life cycle deficit" as their consumption is higher than their labor income. During these periods, consumption is financed mainly by private or public transfers. Indeed, intergenerational transfers play a major role in redistributing resources from people of working age to children and the elderly. Whereas the elderly generally receive substantial support through social insurance programs, family transfers are the main support for children (Lee 2003).

Average labor income becomes higher than average consumption around age 20, and then low again around age 62. These thresholds would be different if privately and publicly funded education and health consumption were included. The individual's withdrawal from the labor market is slow and there is no total exit—labor income remains significant even at age 80-plus. The average 60-year-old earns about two-thirds of what the average adult age 30–49 earns, and the average 70-year-old earns about 25 percent of what prime-age adults earn.

The relationship between labor income and consumption differs across countries. Turra, Lanza, and Rios-Neto (forthcoming) use the estimates produced under the National Transfer Accounts (NTA) project (box 1.1) to compare Brazil with other countries.[2] Their analysis of consumption includes publicly and privately provided education and health. Figure 1.8 shows the normalized life cycle deficit, that is, the difference between labor income and consumption divided by the average labor income at ages 30–49. Three features differentiate Brazil from the other

Box 1.1

National Transfer Accounts

In all societies, intergenerational transfers are large and have an important influence on inequality and growth. The development of each generation of youth depends on the resources it receives from productive members of society for health, education, and sustenance. The well-being of the elderly depends on familial support and a variety of social programs. The National Transfer Accounts (NTA) system provides a comprehensive approach to measuring all reallocations of income across age and time at the aggregate level around the world. It encompasses reallocations achieved through capital accumulation and transfers, distinguishing those mediated by public institutions from those relying on private institutions (Mason and Lee 2010).

NTA is a system for measuring economic flows across age at the aggregate level in a manner consistent with National Income and Product Accounts, the national income measurement system that is the main source of data on general economic activity in the United States. These flows arise primarily because of a fundamental feature of the economic life cycle, that is, that children and elderly consume more than they produce through their labor. NTA provides estimates of the components of the economic life cycle and the inter-age flows that inevitably arise. The accounts distinguish the economic form of flows, transfers, asset-based flows, and the institutions that mediate the flows (government and private institutions). Currently, 33 countries from the Americas (10), Europe (9), Asia-Pacific (9), and Africa (5) are participating in the project. (For detailed methodology and other information see www.ntaccounts.org.)

Source: Masow and Lee (2010).

countries under examination: (1) the relatively advanced age at which consumption is lower than income, (2) the early age at which it returns to being high,[3] and (3) the imbalance between the accumulated deficit in the first and last stage and the period of positive production in the second stage.

While the international comparison shown in figure 1.8 has limitations due to the different years of reference, it is still informative. The Brazilian surplus stage lasts about 20 years, starting between ages 30 and 35 and ending between ages 50 and 55. The old-age life cycle deficit turns negative at an early age and is very large. Thus, Brazil presents the shortest second stage among all the countries considered, and old-age dependency

Figure 1.8   Normalized Life Cycle Deficit in Brazil vs. Other NTA Countries, 1996

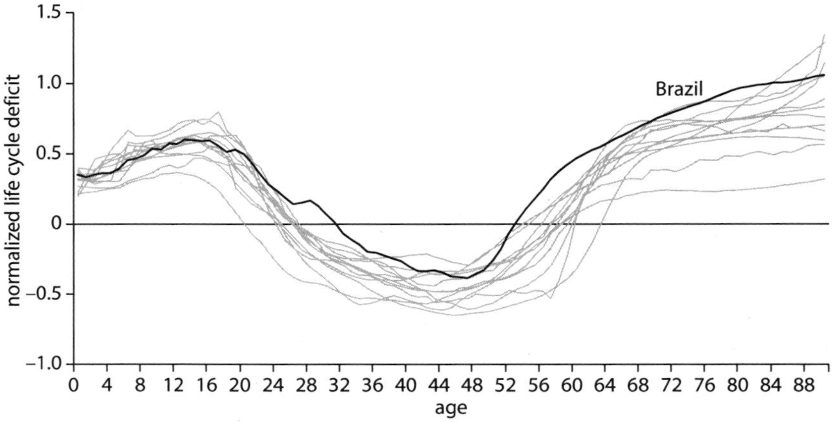

Source: Turra, Lanza, and Rios-Neto forthcoming.
Note: NTA = National Transfer Accounts.

stands out as a long stage of the Brazilian life cycle. In some countries, surpluses start as early as around age 20 (China) and end as late as around 64 (Sweden). Brazil also stands out as the country with the highest levels of deficits in old age, along with low surpluses.

It is possible that the shape and location of both labor income and consumption curves in any country could be unchanged while the number of people in each stage could differ. The aggregate deficit thus depends on the number of individuals at each stage. Keep in mind that the previous analysis does not account for the stock of people in each stage. For example, for a given relationship between labor income and consumption, such as the one in figure 1.7, the stock of people in each stage may be very different across countries and points in time. And the stock is what determines the total "deficit" faced by the economy. With an aging population, a higher number of individuals in the third stage would be expected.

The Economic Implications of Demographic Change

Changes in age structure tend to have a major impact on economic outcomes because people's economic behavior changes throughout the life cycle. As we have seen, Brazil currently has a favorable age structure with a large share of the population in working ages, that is, with a positive life cycle surplus. However, the dependency ratio will reach its lowest value in 2020 and then will rise rapidly, resulting in an increasing number of people at any given point in time living in a "life cycle deficit" stage with important consequences on public finance (especially for transfers and services for the elderly), economic growth, and poverty.

Initially, the falling dependency ratio frees up resources for private and public investment in human and physical capital. The entailing economic growth is called the "first demographic dividend." Hence, the GDP growth generated by the additional workers is the measure for the first dividend. While more workers generate more output, with all other things being equal, the same workers generate more savings. To the extent that saving is converted into domestic investment, more capital (human and physical) will be accumulated. As a result, each worker will have more capital to work with in the future and production will rise on account of that—giving rise to the "second demographic dividend." As the aging population in Brazil can expect to live longer, they need to finance a longer period of time in retirement; thus, saving and capital accumulation might increase even further—enhancing the second demographic dividend.

The first dividend typically lasts decades, but it is transitory in nature. A rise in the share of the working-age population is likely to lead to an increase in output per capita, as the labor force used in production simply grows faster than the population as a whole. The first dividend arises to the extent that the economy is able to create productive jobs for the increasingly larger working-age population. It will then turn negative as total population growth outstrips growth in the productive labor force. However, the same demographic forces that produce an end to the first dividend may lead to a second demographic dividend. Unlike the first dividend, the second dividend is not transitory—since aging may produce a permanent increase in capital per worker, thus, in per capita income—and is highly likely to increase further in proportion to increases in life expectancy. The second dividend arises to the extent that the institutional and policy framework induces individuals, firms, and governments to accumulate capital.

The dividends are not automatic, but depend on institutions and policies to transform changes in population age structure into economic growth. Thus, the dividend period is a window of opportunity rather than a guarantee of improved standards of living. In particular, when policies are designed to deal with the economic growth and public finance implications of population aging, it is crucial to consider the effects such policies might have on economic behavior. How exactly might demographic change lead to these two demographic dividends, and what is the implication of alternative policy responses? This question is analyzed in detail for Brazil in chapter 7.

Poverty Across the Life Cycle and the Role of Public Transfers

Over the last three decades, poverty rates decreased more than fivefold in Brazil.[4] The percentage of the population living in poverty declined from about 53 percent in 1981 to 9.5 percent in 2008 (PPP [purchasing-power parity] $2 a day). In addition, extreme poverty (PPP $1 a day) decreased by about 4 percentage points between 2000 and 2007, and the proportion of the extreme poor, about 4 percent, is now significantly lower in Brazil than in many other developing countries.

There have been two distinct periods of poverty decline since the early 1980s: 1980–2000, characterized by moderate reduction, and 2001–08, characterized by a significant acceleration in the pace of poverty reduction. Four factors contributed to poverty alleviation during the first period. First, non-contributory pension benefits were established after the promulgation of the new constitution in 1988, providing income to rural and urban retirees who were unable to fulfill the contribution criteria. Second, the Brazilian government established measures in the early 1990s that helped to stabilize the economy and kept inflation under control with positive effects on real wages mainly for the poorer. Third, demographic transitions reduced family size and the dependency ratio within the families, alleviating poverty through increases in the relative number of adults.[5] Fourth, the progressive and constant increase in human capital (investments in health and education) and in female labor force participation rates helped boost family income across cohorts.

Poverty reduction accelerated in the 2000s. Poverty rates in Brazil are highly correlated with income inequality: the richest 10 percent accounts for about 45 percent of the total income (Barros et al. 2006); thus, policies that improve income distribution also reduce poverty (Barros, Henriques, and Mendonça 2001). Until 2000, despite the increase in GDP per capita (from US$1,800 in 1950 to US$6,000 in 2000), high income inequality (the 2000 Gini coefficient of 0.593 was close to the historical average) prevented faster poverty alleviation. But 2001 marked the onset of a new period characterized by a steady decline in income inequality: between 2001 and 2008 the Gini coefficient decreased from

0.593 to 0.544 and the per capita income of the poorest 10 percent grew by 8 percent, almost three times faster than the national average (Barros et al. 2006).

The government's cash transfer programs and minimum wage policy account for a high share of the reduction in poverty and inequality. In 2008 the percentage of the population living in poverty represented was only a third of the estimate for 2001. Studies based on counterfactual analysis reveal that 48 percent of the decline in income inequality between 2001 and 2005 was due to the development of cash transfer programs (mainly the Bolsa Família program) and to further expansion of the non-contributory pension system (Barros et al. 2006). In addition, the policy of minimum wage increases that favored low-wage workers and pension system beneficiaries lowered inequality and reduced poverty levels.

The impressive reduction in poverty has not been homogenous across groups. Following a seminal study by Preston (1984) of trends in the age profile of well-being in the United States in the 1970s, myriad studies conducted in Brazil, including official reports (Brant 2001), have stressed the importance of public transfers, particularly social security benefits for poverty alleviation within specific age groups. Most of these studies use simple counterfactual analysis to compare poverty rates with and without public benefits. For example, Turra, Marri, and Wajnman (2008) use household data for 2005 to show that poverty incidence among men (women) aged 60 and older in Brazil would have risen from 3.9 percent (15.6) to 63.5 percent (83.8 percent) had these people not received pensions. Cotlear and Tornarolli (2009) compared poverty rates with and without pensions for two large age groups—60 and older and 15 and younger—across several Latin American countries (see table 1.1). Brazil together with Argentina, Chile, and Uruguay are "pro-aging" countries, that is, countries with large and generous pension systems that have relatively greater impact on poverty rates among the elderly. In Brazil, the poverty headcount ratio in 2008 declines from 49.3 percent to 4.2 percent after pensions are taken into account. However, not surprisingly, the authors found that the effect of pensions on poverty among children in Brazil is much smaller (the poverty headcount ratio in 2008 declines from 38.0 percent to only 31.0 percent after pensions are taken into account).

To better illustrate the role of public transfers in reducing poverty among different age groups in Brazil, figures 1.9 to 1.11 compare poverty rates by age for three years, 1981, 1995, and 2008. Poverty rates are

Table 1.1 Headcount Ratio by Age and Region Poverty Line, with and without Pension

PPP US$2.50/day

Country	All With	All Without	60+ With	60+ Without	0–59 With	0–59 Without	65+ With	65+ Without	0–64 With	0–64 Without	0–14 With	0–14 Without	15–24 With	15–24 Without	25–59 With	25–59 Without
Argentina	11.0	18.6	4.9	40.0	12.0	15.1	3.7	46.5	11.8	15.4	19.2	21.9	11.6	15.1	8.0	11.1
Bolivia	35.0	38.1	26.6	48.6	35.8	37.1	25.3	52.8	35.6	37.1	44.5	45.6	28.4	30.1	30.7	31.9
Brazil	18.2	29.2	4.2	49.3	19.8	26.8	3.5	54.9	19.3	27.1	31.8	38.0	18.3	25.5	13.8	21.0
Chile	5.2	9.2	2.5	18.0	5.7	7.9	2.3	20.7	5.5	8.1	8.6	10.7	5.5	8.0	4.2	6.5
Colombia	37.8	40.6	42.2	52.0	37.3	39.2	44.3	54.2	37.3	39.5	46.3	47.5	36.3	38.5	31.0	33.4
Costa Rica	11.6	15.2	17.2	39.0	11.0	12.8	18.7	44.3	11.1	13.2	16.7	18.1	8.7	10.7	8.5	10.5
Dominican Rep.	18.7	19.5	16.0	18.6	19.0	19.6	15.6	18.6	18.9	19.6	26.8	27.4	16.6	17.5	14.0	14.6
Ecuador	17.6	19.1	16.2	23.6	17.7	18.5	17.2	26.3	17.6	18.5	24.0	24.7	15.1	15.8	13.8	14.7
El Salvador	27.1	27.9	20.3	23.9	27.8	28.4	20.7	24.6	27.5	28.2	35.2	35.6	24.9	25.6	22.4	23.1
Guatemala	33.9	36.1	28.2	34.9	34.4	36.2	29.1	37.1	34.2	36.0	42.4	44.0	28.4	30.1	27.6	29.8
Honduras	36.9	37.3	35.6	37.4	37.0	37.2	37.0	38.9	36.9	37.2	45.7	45.8	30.1	30.4	31.3	31.6
Mexico	13.9	15.9	19.9	30.1	13.3	14.5	21.9	33.0	13.3	14.8	18.2	19.1	11.8	13.0	10.2	11.8
Nicaragua	42.7	43.2	32.5	34.5	43.5	43.9	32.5	34.8	43.2	43.7	53.2	53.7	38.5	38.8	36.6	37.1
Panama	22.3	27.9	16.9	36.0	22.9	26.9	18.1	39.3	22.7	27.0	32.4	36.5	21.8	25.6	16.6	20.5
Paraguay	21.4	22.1	16.9	20.4	21.8	22.2	17.2	21.2	21.7	22.1	29.7	30.0	18.1	18.5	16.5	17.0
Peru	21.0	22.0	19.9	23.1	21.2	21.8	20.4	24.2	21.0	21.7	28.9	29.4	21.6	22.3	20.5	21.1
Uruguay	6.7	14.8	1.1	23.5	8.1	12.6	0.9	26.4	7.7	12.7	14.6	19.6	7.2	12.2	4.8	9.0
Venezuela	38.7	41.4	32.9	44.6	39.1	41.2	34.1	46.9	38.9	41.1	49.7	51.1	36.0	38.3	32.2	34.6
Latin America and Caribbean average (Unweighted)	23.3	26.6	19.7	33.2	23.7	25.7	20.1	35.8	23.6	25.7	31.5	33.3	21.1	23.1	19.0	21.1

Source: Cotlear and Tornarolli 2009.

Figure 1.9   Brazil: Poverty Rates by Age with and without Transfers, 1981

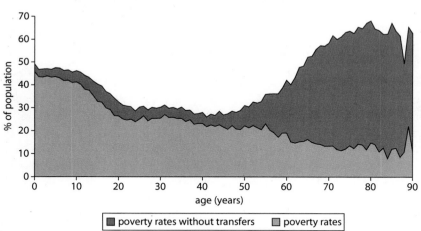

Source: Turra and Rocha 2010.

Figure 1.10   Brazil: Poverty Rates by Age with and without Transfers, 1995

Source: Turra and Rocha 2010.

estimated with and without public transfers, including contributory and non-contributory retirement benefits and conditional cash transfers (CCTs) from Bolsa Família. Data from PNAD ("Pesquisa Nacional por Amostragem Domiciliar") are used (a national representative household survey from Brazil) to measure the percentage of the population living

Figure 1.11   Brazil: Poverty Rates by Age with and without Transfers, 2008

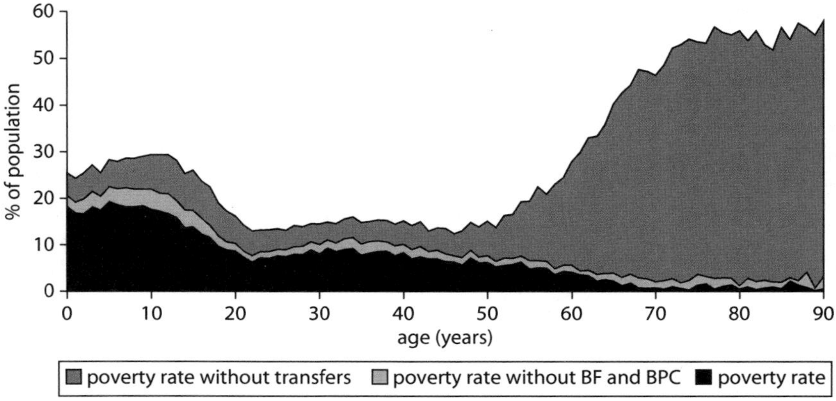

Source: Turra and Rocha 2010.

in poverty according to the World Bank poverty line of US$2 a day at 2005 PPP.

Figure 1.9 shows poverty rates by age in 1981, hence before the 1988 federal constitution and the expansion of social welfare programs in Brazil. On average, 53 percent of the population lived in poverty. The incidence varied little by age, ranging from 65.2 percent among children under 15 to 47.7 percent among adults ages 65 and older. Given that conditional cash transfer programs for poor families had not been established in 1981, it is not surprising that the impact of excluding public transfers on poverty levels would be virtually zero among children. On the other hand, about 25 percent of the population above age 65 did not receive public pensions in 1981; thus, excluding social security benefits would have just a moderate effect on poverty incidence (20 percentage points on average).

A more striking picture emerges in 1995 (figure 1.10). Compared to 1981, the incidence of poverty is much lower among the elderly (13.6 percent) than among children (40.8 percent). The counterfactual analysis suggests that the main factor in the reduction of poverty among the elderly is the expansion of social security benefits; without public transfers, poverty rates would be four times larger. Poverty rates decreased for all ages in 2008 (figure 1.11). The development and expansion of conditional cash transfer programs for poor families (Bolsa Família, BF) would have reduced the percentage of children living in poverty by at least five percentage points (figure 1.11). However, the continuous expansion of social protection to the elderly, particularly through the increase in non-contributory benefits (BPC, *Benefício de Prestação Continuada*, Benefits of Continued Provision), magnified relative differences in poverty incidence by age—for every old person in poverty there were still almost 16 children in the same condition in 2008.

Although these simple counterfactual analyses are instructive, they do not imply causation. In the case of poverty rates, for example, the simulations ignore the possibility that a slower expansion of social welfare programs could have created incentives for increased labor supply and savings, with positive effects on the percentage living in poverty. In addition, many of the counterfactual analyses found in the literature are based on data for a synthetic cohort and, therefore, ignore the historical determinants of poverty trends that are related to period and cohort changes. However, the results are confirmed by an age-period-cohort (APC) analysis of poverty trends (Turra and Rocha 2010).

Among the elderly, period effects have dominated and are probably related to the expansion of social welfare. Indeed, the years of expansion in social security benefits to rural workers (1991–93) and the years of real minimum wage gains (2006–08) coincide with two of the largest period effects of poverty alleviation detected in the model by Turra and Rocha (2010). On the other hand, among children, long-term effects related to gradual changes in the life histories of the cohorts have played a major role during most of the period of observation, which explains why the decline in poverty has been slower for younger ages. It was only in the 2000s that period effects accelerated the process of poverty alleviation. Period effects for children also coincide with real minimum wage gains, and the development and expansion of the Bolsa Família program.

Finally, note that public transfers in Brazil have been effective in reducing poverty among the elderly. Poverty levels for this group are very low by international standards, but would have been very high in the absence of public transfers. However, the same cannot be said about poverty among children. Although programs like Bolsa Família have been successful in reducing child poverty, a greater investment in education is necessary to help the younger generations escape poverty. The next section discusses intergenerational investments, comparing Brazil's lower investment in education and higher investment in pensions to other LAC (Latin America and Caribbean) and OECD countries.

Characteristics of Public Expenditures across Generations and Age Groups

The previous section demonstrated that the expansion of the old-age social protection system over the last several decades was responsible for the largest single improvement in poverty rates in Brazil. Since 1980, socioeconomic conditions have improved significantly for the elderly despite the shift in the population age structure. Therefore, a legitimate question, which has been asked for other countries (for example, Bommier et al. 2010), is whether the elderly in Brazil are benefiting from public transfers at the expense of younger generations. Becker and Murphy (1988) theorize that the timing of creation of public programs for children and the elderly can be optimized. First, the state taxes the working-age population to provide the optimal amount of education for children. Next, to compensate parents for spending resources on the younger generation, the state taxes the children when they become adult workers in order to provide their parents with pensions.

In the case of Brazil, the rise of public expenditures for education started much later than in other nations at similar or higher levels of development. For instance, Bommier et al. (2010) shows that in the United States public expenditures on education started by the end of the 19th century and that the public pension system emerged around the 1930s. The expansion of the Brazilian public pension system occurred after World War II (Queiroz 2008) and has accelerated over the last 20 years, but the consolidation of primary public education did not occur before most of the elderly population had begun receiving retirement benefits (Rios-Neto 2005). Public education was first established in Brazil back in the 19th century, but its expansion was slow until the end of 1980s, when the new Brazilian constitution gave municipalities and state governments greater financial and decision-making autonomy (Fleury and Fleury 2001).

To illustrate this point, figure 1.12 shows the evolution of public expenditures as a percentage of the GDP. Both pensions and public education systems have expanded since 1980 and reached high coverage levels (above 85 percent) in 2000. However, pension expenditures (around 10 percent of GDP) are far larger than public education expenditures (around 4 percent in 2000, increasing to 5.1 percent of GDP in 2007).

Comparing Brazil to other countries in general terms, the reallocation system in Brazil is similar to those in other countries represented in the National Transfer Accounts project. But the elderly in Brazil receive much higher per capita public transfers than children do. Figure 1.13, which compares the ratio of net per capita public transfers for the elderly

Figure 1.12   Brazil: Expenditures on Pensions and Public Education, 1933–2000

Source: Turra and Rocha 2010.

Figure 1.13   Ratio of Net per Capita Public Transfers (Elderly to Children)

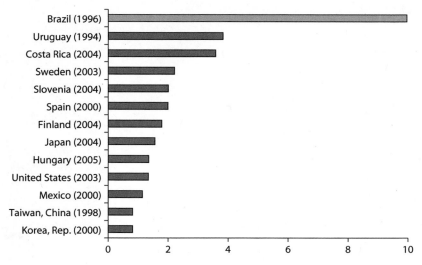

Source: Turra, Lanza, and Rios-Neto forthcoming.

(ages 65+) to net per capita public transfers for children (ages 0–15), shows that the ratio in Brazil of 9.96 is more than seven times that of the United States, about 6.5 times that of Japan, and between 4.5 and 7.5 times larger than ratios in selected European countries. It is also 2.6 times larger than the ratio in Uruguay and 2.78 times larger than that in

Costa Rica—both Latin American countries with social, economic, and institutional arrangements similar to those in Brazil.

Following the work by Bommier et al. (2010), Araujo, Turra, and Queiroz (2010) looked at the effects of the welfare state in Brazil on intergenerational equity. The authors calculated the net present value (NPV) at birth of pensions and public education benefits received minus taxes paid for Brazilian generations born between 1923 and 2000. Figure 1.14 presents their estimates. The creation of the social security system in the 1960s led to financial gains for early participants. The current elderly population in Brazil (cohorts born before 1950) received larger benefits than the taxes they paid to the system. The gains decrease for younger cohorts as the taxes paid over the life course become larger than the benefits received. The NPVs are negative for cohorts born between early 1950s and 1970s; these generations have borne the costs of the expansion in social security benefits after 1992 and they also have paid for the expansion of basic education in the 1990s. Therefore, life cycle results by Araujo, Turra, and Queiroz (2010) show large transfers from younger to older generations in Brazil and corroborate earlier findings based on period data (Turra 2000; Turra, Lanza, and Rios-Neto

Figure 1.14   Brazil: Net Present Value at Birth of Expected Lifetime Total Transfers (Pensions and Education), 1923–2000

by year of birth

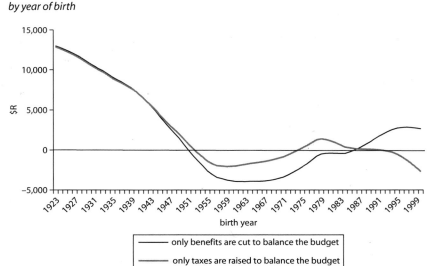

Source: Araujo, Turra, and Queiroz 2010.

forthcoming) showing that the public sector has been generous to the current generations of elderly in Brazil.

In summary, the current generation of adults has borne the fiscal costs of reducing the percentage of elderly currently living in poverty, despite having themselves experienced high levels of poverty and not having received optimal levels of public investment during childhood. These estimates, therefore, appear to contradict the argument by Becker and Murphy (1988) since adults who are now taxed to allow the expansion of both public pensions and public education did not benefit from public transfers at earlier ages.

Despite the significant decline in inequality mentioned above, Brazil remains an unequal country.[6] Figure 1.15 shows an aggregate view of the distribution of social expenditures across income groups and across age groups. The expenditures considered include education, health care, pension benefits, and Bolsa Família. The comparison of income quintiles shows a growing proportion of public expenditures going to each subsequent quintile as income increases. The concentration of public expenditures in the top quintile is particularly striking: they are 3.6 times higher than in the bottom quintile. The shape of the aggregate pattern is driven by the shape of pensions which, at 12 percent of GDP, account for a large part of total public expenditures in the social sectors.

The comparison by age shows a per capita age profile and an aggregate distribution estimated by weighting the per capita profiles by the age distribution. The per capita profiles show a small bulge among children and young adults and then fall to grow steeply at around age 50. The per capita profiles also reflect the weight of pensions; public spending on an individual elderly person is several times higher than public spending on an individual child. When the overall distribution of the population is taken into account, the aggregate public expenditures on the elderly and the young remain strongly biased toward the elderly in Brazil despite a still young population age structure.[7]

This pattern suggests a society where the public sector is responsible for the sustenance of the elderly and where the families remain responsible for the sustenance of children. Other studies of Brazil (Turra 2000; Turra and Rios-Neto 2001; Turra, Lanza, and Rios-Neto forthcoming) have shown that old people's consumption depends largely on public health care services and pensions. Is this perhaps a "normal" pattern found in other regions of the world? To answer this question, Turra and Holz (2010) use data from the NTA project to

Figure 1.15   Brazil: Distribution of Total Public Expenditures by Income and Age Group, 2006

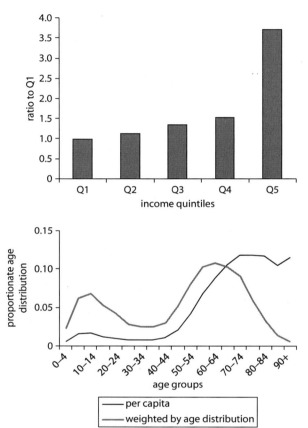

Source: Turra and Holz (2010).

compare the importance of public transfers as a proportion of the consumption by elders and children; these data are shown in figures 1.16 through 1.18.[8]

The importance of public transfers in financing consumption by the young and elderly is found to vary widely across countries and regions. Figure 1.16a shows that, in Europe, a full two-thirds of elderly consumption is financed from public transfers. At the other end of the spectrum, public transfers to the elderly are very small in Republic of Korea and Taiwan, China ("other Asia" in figure 1.16a). Japan is in the

Figure 1.16   Public Transfers as a Percent of Total Consumption

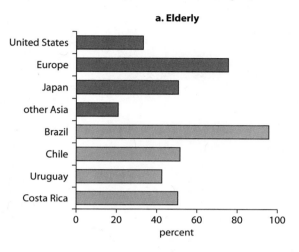

a. Elderly

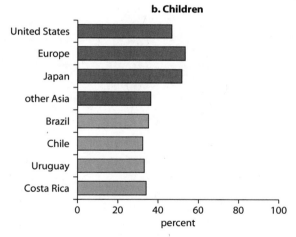

b. Children

Source: Turra and Holz (2010).

middle of the spectrum with about half of elderly consumption financed by public pensions. Data are available for four LAC countries: Chile, Costa Rica, and Uruguay are in the middle of the spectrum, as is Japan. Brazil stands out in LAC and in the world, with pension benefits equivalent to over 95 percent of consumption by the elderly—more than in Europe.

Figure 1.17   Role of Education in Children's Consumption

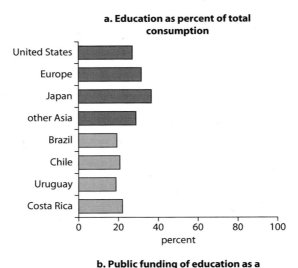

a. Education as percent of total consumption

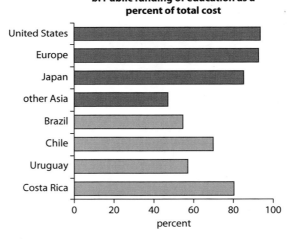

b. Public funding of education as a percent of total cost

Source: Turra and Holz 2010.

Figure 1.16b shows that public transfers also finance a significant fraction of children's consumption through cash transfers and in-kind provision of services such as education and health. Public financing for children is highest in Europe and Japan, where it constitutes over half of children's total consumption. In LAC and Other Asia it is smaller but not insignificant, at about a third of children's total consumption. In all four of the

Figure 1.18   Private Transfers to the Elderly as Percent of Total Consumption

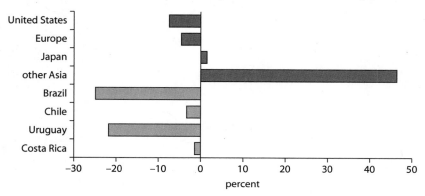

Source: Turra and Holz 2010.

LAC countries, public expenditures finance about a third of children's consumption.

Is the public sector more important to finance consumption by children or the elderly? There is no global pattern. In the United States and Asia, public expenditures finance a larger fraction of children's consumption compared with their importance in elderly consumption. In Europe and the four LAC countries, public expenditures finance a larger fraction of elderly consumption.

Figure 1.17a shows that education is a substantial part of the value of children's consumption. Here, too, there are significant variations across countries. The cost of education (public and private) as a percent of total consumption by children is highest in Japan (37 percent), followed by Europe (about a third), the United States (a bit over a fourth), and Other Asia, with the four LAC countries studied trailing behind all these international comparators. Figure 1.17b shows that most of the cost of education is publicly financed in the richer countries. Other Asia has the lowest public financing of education. Within the four LAC countries, Chile and Costa Rica have relatively higher levels, while Brazil and Uruguay have the lowest levels in the sample.

Figure 1.18 shows familial private transfers as a proportion of consumption by the elderly. It is usually thought that elderly parents are helped by "upward transfers" (private transfers from their children). The NTA data show that this is observed only in Asia. In Europe, the United States, and Latin America and the Caribbean, the pattern observed is of net "downward transfers"—from the elderly to their children and grand-children. These downward transfers are particularly large in Brazil and Uruguay, where the elderly receive significant transfers from public pensions and pass some of these funds to their children and grandchildren. However, as described earlier, public transfers to the elderly have a limited impact on poverty among the young, in large part the result of living arrangements in Brazilian households. In 2008 only 11.7 percent of people younger than 15 were living in households with people older than 60. Chapter 4 presents intra-family relationships and financial flows where family arrangements for the provision of long-term care to the elderly are concerned.

Cross-cutting Issues and Conclusions

Demographic change is one of the most important forces shaping the outcome of social and economic policy, but it cannot be observed in the short term. In the following chapters, this report analyzes the socioeconomic and macroeconomic impacts of demographic change in Brazil under a longer time perspective. The main findings are presented below.

Economic Growth

The size and composition of the workforce in Brazil is changing as a consequence of the demographic transition of the increasing elderly population. The share of the working-age population is expected to increase until 2025. A growing working-age population means more people in the labor force, which, all else being equal, should result in more wealth being generated. Brazil is currently experiencing a very favorable population age structure. While the share of the mature labor force (25–59) is expected to continue growing until the late 2020s, the share of the junior labor force (15–24) has already started declining. As the mature workforce has more overall economic activity and usually generates most of a country's wealth, Brazil has a great opportunity to increase growth, savings, and government revenues.

Over the medium term, however, the expected changes in the labor force composition due to population aging will pose challenges to economic growth. After the mid-2020s the growth rate of the 15–59 age group will turn negative. A shrinking labor force means that Brazil will have to rely more on productivity growth than on new entrants in the labor market to sustain aggregate output growth. Negative effects of population aging on productivity are expected at the micro level, which, in turn, may have important effects on the aggregate economy as a larger share of the labor force would be beyond its peak in productivity.[9]

Brazil needs to seize the current opportunity and prepare for the structural changes it will face over the next decades and beyond. The labor market needs to create enough opportunities for the growing working-age population in the short term. Moreover, to boost the productivity potential of future generations, it needs to invest in better public education, as well as in incentives and means for the education and retraining of mature workers. The implications of a demographic change on the share of working-age population and productivity are discussed in chapters 2 and 5, respectively.

The pension system also needs to be modified to address the perverse effects its rules have on the labor market. The low age limit for retirement and the existence of a length of service without minimum age eligibility result in a population that retires early. Thus a system meant to sustain the income of individuals who are unable to work ends up doing so for a longer period than the time those individuals contributed to the system. Moreover, early retirement implies that a portion of the productive labor force is not being used or that they continue working in the informal sector. The system also incentivizes informality, especially for low-skilled workers. The availability of a non-contributory program that transfers a benefit equal to the minimum wage reduces the incentives for low earners to contribute. This is damaging because a large proportion of the population does not contribute to the social security system during the working age, but expects to benefit from it in old age. As the population in Brazil ages, the need to ensure that a larger part of the population contributes to the system will become more and more pressing. The "inefficiencies" of the old-age social protection system in Brazil are described in chapter 3.

Economic behavior and macroeconomic outcomes change both systematically and endogenously with aging. The impact of population aging on saving (and consequently on growth) is particularly important and is analyzed in depth in chapter 7. It is traditionally believed that aging will reduce saving, and thereby limit growth, because the relative share of "prime" savers in the population will decrease, as implied by the life cycle hypothesis. However, under certain conditions Brazil may not experience a fall in saving and growth. In fact, if government policies are *appropriately*, *adequately*, and *timely* formulated, there is likely to be substantial capital deepening and associated increases in growth, lifetime income, and wealth.

Econometric evidence reveals that an increase in the old-age dependency ratio has led to an increase in the private saving rate—suggesting that aging may lead to higher growth in the future. Ultimately, there is no econometric evidence that suggests that increasing the old-age dependency ratio will lead to reductions in saving and growth. Brazil is not the only developing country that has experienced such unexpected dynamics—several other Latin American and Caribbean countries display similar relationships.

So, under what conditions might saving and growth increase when the population ages, that is, under what conditions will the second demographic dividend materialize? Four issues are likely to boost capital accumulation and thus income per capita over the long term despite aging and as an effect of aging. First, age-specific saving rates in Brazil show a pattern that does not conform to conventional life cycle theory. Saving rates do not fall as people age; in fact, after about age 40 saving rates remain virtually unchanged on average. This is not too surprising if intra-household bequests and the relatively high public pensions in Brazil are taken into account. Also, it is not uncommon for developing countries to feature high old-age saving rates. It is therefore likely that the saving rate will increase in the future since the population structure will comprise a larger fraction of high-saving workers and elderly rather than low-saving young. This depends, of course, on the future structure of the pension system and whether public pensions remain relatively high.

It is important to note that high pensions themselves crowd out saving—if people are sure that they will receive high public pensions, why should they save for their retirement? As a result, the implications of high public pensions must be analyzed jointly with the motive for saving to see which effect dominates. This analysis, also to be done in chapter 7, shows that further increases in public pensions will lead to lower lifetime income per capita and lower (net) capital accumulation—effectively leading to a smaller second demographic dividend. Consequently, there are two counteracting forces. On the one hand, higher pensions could crowd out saving, since there is less incentive to save when retirement consumption is financed by pension. On the other hand, higher pensions could enhance the saving rate because the elderly save a large fraction of their pension. The main finding is that the net effect of higher pensions on the saving rate is negative; that is, if pensions increase, then the positive effect on the saving rate originating from a higher old age income would not outweigh the negative effect originating from reduced incentives to save for consumption in old age. The economic intuition behind this result is that each worker, of which there are fewer, would need to pay higher taxes in order to finance the constant pensions of more and longer-living retirees. Those workers would therefore save much less, and capital accumulation and growth would likely suffer.

A second reason why aging might promote saving is if the reduction in poverty and inequality continues their recent downward trends. In that case, more people are likely to display higher savings—in effect increasing the average saving rate. Third, the first demographic dividend of more prime working-age savers as a share of the population, combined with higher life expectancy, will probably lead to capital deepening and the potential of a non-negligible second demographic dividend. Fourth, there is also a simple, but important, effect on capital deepening of fewer work-ers, which mechanically leads to an amplifying effect on the second demographic dividend. As a result, any potentially negative consequences of aging can be abated to a large extent through prudent fiscal and struc-tural government policies.

Building on the potentially increasing saving rates in the future, a key driver of growth is the endogenous accumulation of capital. The eco-nomic behavior related to consumption and saving over the life cycle is directly affected by taxes, transfers, and debt dynamics. As a result, the capital accumulation that arises due to saving is greatly affected by poli-cies for taxation, transfers, and the issuance of debt in order to postpone the fiscal burden for future generations. Therefore, to analyze the implica-tions for capital accumulation and growth, it is crucial to take into account the financing choices for the aging-induced fiscal costs that the government has at its disposal.

Three scenarios for financing the fiscal costs associated with aging are compared in a general equilibrium setting: *Tax-Financing*, where taxes increase to absorb the costs; *Benefit-Financing*, where social security ben-efits fall to accommodate the fiscal pressure; and *Debt-Financing*, where public debt increases so the government can refrain from changing taxes or benefits. It is found that Debt-Financing is likely to reduce the divi-dend, Tax-Financing will keep it more or less unchanged, while a policy response of keeping taxes and debt constant and allowing pension to adjust (downward) is likely to promote the second demographic divi-dend. As a result, in terms of preferable parametric policy responses, the second demographic dividend will be best promoted by keeping taxes and debt constant while allowing public pensions to adjust downward.

A sensible policy mix would consider the appropriateness of the generosity of the social security system in connection with a reform of entitlement ages to such transfers. A structural policy response of linking mandatory retirement (or entitlement) ages to increasing life expectancy would boost labor supply and reduce the fiscal costs of aging. The international experience, especially from observing Scandinavian countries with longevity-indexed mandatory retirement ages, is ample and thoroughly analyzed. The effective labor supply is likely to increase when the statutory retirement age increases, because people will (ideally) stay in the labor force for a longer period of time. Leisure, however, may also increase when the statutory retirement age increases. This is mainly because there will be less need to save since the retirement period will also be proportionally lower. More resources will be available for working-period consumption, and since leisure could be assumed to be a normal good, labor supply at the intensive margin is likely to fall. The effects that such policy responses have for labor supply therefore ought to be taken into account.

Public Finance and Service Delivery

The impact of population aging becomes readily apparent in long-term projections of public spending on education, health care, and pensions, which are the product of the average generosity of the benefits received by each individual and the age structure of the population. The share of economic output directed toward education, health care, and pensions through the public sector can be decomposed into two multiplicative components. The demographic factor measures the size of the demand for a specific benefit (education, health care, and pension) relative to the working-age population. The economic factor measures the average benefit received per beneficiary.

Each sector will face different challenges and opportunities. Projecting all three expenditure paths with a comparable methodology provides insight into the interconnections and trade-offs available to Brazilian policy makers. Too often, policy reforms of pension, health care, and education systems are debated, analyzed, and implemented in isolation from each other without considering the links among these systems. Such projections are presented in chapter 6. The shifts in population age structure projected for the next four decades are going to lead to substantial additional fiscal pressures on publicly financed health care and pensions, along with some reduction in fiscal pressures for publicly financed education.

With respect to benefit levels, Brazil's public sector spending on education and pensions resembles that of OECD countries (as a percent of

GDP), but its population age structure is much younger. The result is a markedly lower public education investment in youth (9.8 percent of average wages in Brazil vs. 15.5 percent in OECD) and markedly higher average public pension benefits (66.5 percent of average wage in Brazil vs. 30.4 percent of average wage in OECD). Aggregate public health care expenditures in Brazil are much below the OECD average, and average health benefits are somewhat lower.

In 2005, total public spending on education, pensions, and health care amounted to 17.7 percent of Brazil's GDP. Although forecasts of both demographic and benefit change must be interpreted with caveats, a few robust conclusions emerge. The status quo scenario, in which current benefits (for education and pension) and expenditures by age (for health care) are not changed, would result in an increase of total social spending of 14.2 percentage points of GDP in 2050. With regard to education, the increasingly smaller size of the school-age population provides a unique opportunity to increase investment per student to OECD levels without adding much burden on public finance. An ambitious expansion of educational spending to reach OECD levels of investment per student within a decade would require an increase of education spending as a percent of GDP of less than 1 percent by 2020. After that, the share of GDP devoted to education would gradually decline in concert with the decline in the school-aged population—while maintaining investment levels per student similar to those of OECD countries.

Health care is likely to emerge as a major fiscal challenge in the coming decades in Brazil. Indeed, health care expenditures are likely to increase GDP by more than 4 percentage points in 2050. Two driving forces behind the projected increase in health expenditures are the increasing proportion of elderly in the population and the eldery population's growing intensity of formal health care use. In terms of public pensions, without the recent reforms (1999 and 2003), spending on pensions would have risen from 10 percent of GDP in 2005 to an astounding 37 percent of GDP, simply because of the increase in the number of eligible pensioners associated with population aging. Clearly the old support system would have been difficult to afford. Recent pension reforms are estimated to have more than halved the projected costs. However, the problem of affordability of pension expenditures has not yet been solved, and pension expenditures are projected to double to 22.4 percent of GDP by 2050. Even in an optimistic scenario that would bring Brazil pension benefits in line with those of OECD countries, increases in pension expenditures dominate the fiscal outlook for Brazil.

So what policy actions can be taken to help mitigate the unavoidable tension toward increasing social expenditures that is driven by rapid population aging in Brazil? First, as more resources become available per student in Brazil, it is important that such resources be used to improve the effectiveness of the education system. The United States, Japan, Republic of Korea, and European countries have used declines in student numbers to shift resources toward quality. In Brazil, some of the resources saved from primary education could support the expansion of crèche care (daycare) and preschool, which are still far from universal and which research shows are among the best strategies for ensuring that children arrive in primary school ready to learn. It could substantially help finance the expansion of higher quality, full-day schooling at the secondary level. The seven million empty seats in primary school could also finance investments in quality for the 24 million primary students who will remain (World Bank 2011). Moreover, such an ambitious increase in educational investment would likely have profound implications for both economic growth and inequality in Brazil. Indeed, Lee and Mason (2010) present simulation results that suggest that such investments in human capital can offset the costs of population aging.

Second, it is urgent that the organization of the health care system adapt to the different demographic and epidemiological profiles of the increasing older population in Brazil. Despite Brazil's passage through the advanced stages of the epidemiological transition—that is, the shift from infectious to chronic noncommunicable diseases—its medical schools are still training doctors for the requirements of the 20th century. Students are schooled in child care and reproductive health but are presented with little or nothing about aging-related issues. A doctor graduating in 2010, with an average 40 years of medical practice ahead, will witness a three-fold increase in the elderly population, to 63 million people. In whatever specialty they choose, they will be increasingly confronted with older patients regardless of their level of preparedness. Curriculum reform reflecting Brazil's rapid aging is critical if the country is to avoid an epidemic of iatrogenic conditions—and the consequent escalating health care costs. As noncommunicable diseases emerge as the leading cause of disability, morbidity, and mortality, effective programs must be implemented to address their main risk factors: smoking, physical inactivity, alcohol consumption, and unhealthy diet.

The magnitude of the increase of health expenditures associated with an older population will depend crucially on whether longer life spans mean more healthy years or added years of illness and dependency.

Prevention and postponement of disease and disability and maintenance of health, independence, and mobility in an aging population will continue to remain the major health-related challenges of population aging. Recently, a life course framework was proposed to design policies addressing the needs of the elderly. This plan is described in chapter 4. Central to the life course approach to aging is the notion of functional capacity—that is, that individuals reach the peak of their physical functional capacity early in adulthood and then experience a progressive decline throughout the life course that is a natural result of the aging process. Importantly, however, this is not necessarily a problem. Provided that, say at age 85, an individual continues to be independent and capable of performing the activities of daily living, he or she will remain a resource to their family, their community, their society, and the economy. Thus, good policies on aging are those that will help individuals to remain above the disability threshold as they age.

It is anticipated that the number of elderly people generating a demand for formal long-term care will increase because of two factors. First, the numbers of the very old in Brazil will dramatically increase over the next 30 years, and this will result in larger numbers of frail old people at any given point, even if a decrease in the proportion of frail old people is expected as a result of improvements in disease prevention, postponement of disability, and better administration of disabilities. Second, the changing status of women and family and social values will continue to affect the availability of family caregivers. The low birth rates and the complexities of younger peoples' transition into modern adulthood will compound the scenario. Studies from a wide range of developing countries reveal that older people are becoming less confident about receiving family support. The projections in chapter 4 estimate twice as many people being taken care of by non-family members in 2020, and five times as many in 2040, compared to 2008. Strengthening the capacity of the Family Health Program—a government program created in 1994 to bring primary health care closer to Brazilian families—to reach and assist the increasing elderly population at home and in residential institutions would be a possible strategy to address the increasing demand for health and long-term care services.

Third, the pension system will have to be strengthened to become more efficient. The pension system extends benefit coverage to most of the old age population and provides protection to the poorest segments of society. Indeed the programs have contributed to reducing poverty and inequality, particularly in rural areas. However, this has come at an extremely high cost, with sharp increases in expenditures. As chapter 3 will show, these increases are to a large extent a consequence of some characteristic of the pension programs that leads to retirement at a very young age, excessively high replacement ratios, and multiple receipt of benefits. The survivors' pension system, meant to ensure that the dependants of the deceased do not fall into poverty, is exceptionally generous and ends up representing an extremely high share of old-age pension expenditures, with benefits accumulating and being paid to young individuals with a long life expectancy. In light of the aging of the population that is bound to put pressure on social security expenditure, it becomes of utmost importance to address these issues promptly. Without substantial changes to the current system, the aging of the population will put a strain on the system that will result in some critical trade-offs with consequences for the growth prospects of the economy.

Poverty and Redistribution

Brazil has made considerable progress in reducing poverty and inequality. Public transfers have played a significant role in these achievements. The establishment of a non-contributory program and a program for rural workers has extended coverage to some of the usually excluded part of the population. Moreover, the fast growth in the minimum benefit guaranteed equal to the minimum wage has resulted in an increase of the income floor for the elderly that is faster than the growth of the higher retirement benefits, resulting in a reduction in inequality. The pension system is responsible for the almost complete eradication of old-age poverty. However, this has come at a high cost and has resulted in a system with perverse incentives and distortions.

Per capita public transfers to the elderly compared to per capita public transfers to children are much larger in Brazil than in any other LAC and OECD country with similar welfare systems. At the same time, the quality of public education in Brazil has been much worse than in other LAC and OECD countries. Bolsa Família, a federal CCT program, has improved children's social protection, with positive effects on child health and education attainment, but it is insufficient to reduce the gap between human capital outcomes of richer and poorer children and to contribute to include the latter groups in the most productive sectors of the economy.

An important concern is the need to maintain horizontal equity by giving equal consideration to the needs of all groups in poverty—the aging, children, persons with disabilities, and working families with low earnings. Grosh and Leite (2009) observe that in many LAC countries, the total allocation to non-contributory social assistance programs is under 1 percent of GDP; therefore, they emphasize the need to be cautious before defining policies that would allocate a similar or greater amount to a subgroup of the poor. This concern leads to recommending that payments to the elderly be administered as part of the general social assistance system. Although social assistance expenditures (mostly on the Beneficio de Prestação Continuada, non-contributory payments to the elderly, and Bolsa Família) are larger in Brazil than in other LAC countries, resources available are not enough to reach all poor groups. Thus, using an integrated framework to administer all resources for social assistance in Brazil would allow policy decisions to reflect explicit trade-offs among competing priorities and possible groups of beneficiaries.

Notes

1. In 2000, only a few countries (Bulgaria, Germany, Greece, Italy, and Japan) had an aging index above 100 (more older people than youth).

2. The countries are Austria, Chile, China, Costa Rica, Finland, Germany, Hungary, India, Japan, Slovenia, Spain, Sweden, Taiwan, United States, and Uruguay.

3. In other words, the Brazilian surplus stage lasts about 20 years, starting at 30–35 and ending at 50–55. As Mason et al. (2009) point out when describing the life cycle model, the age profiles imply a gradation of dependency. In Brazil, for example, persons aged 70 and older are economically more dependent than those aged 60–69, and youths aged 10–19 are more dependent than young adults aged 20–29.

4. This subsection draws heavily on Turra and Rocha (2010).

5. Recently, Turra, Wajnman, and Simões (2009) used counterfactual analysis to show that 95 percent of the decline in the proportion of the Brazilian population living in extreme poverty 1985–95 was due to changes in dependency ratio within families.

6. This subsection section draws heavily from Turra and Holz (2010).

7. In 2005, 27.6 percent of the Brazilian population was under age 15 and 8.9 percent above age 60.

8. "Consumption" is defined to include in-kind services in education and health care and private consumption of goods and services purchased by the household.

9. The evidence is mixed; for example, see Lindh and Malmberg (1999); Tang and MacLeod (2006); Feyrer (2007). A review of the main findings is presented in chapter 5.

References

Araujo, T., C. M. Turra, and B. L. Queiroz 2010. "Equidad intergeneracional en el Brasil: transferencias de seguridad social y educación pública entre generaciones nacidas en el período 1923–2000." *Notas de Población* 90: 73–85. CEPAL, Santiago, Chile.

Barros, R., M. Carvalho, S. Franco, and R. Mendonça. 2006. "Uma análise das principais causas da queda recente na desigualdade de renda brasileira." *Econômica, Rio de Janeiro* 8 (1): 117–47.

Barros, R., R. Henriques, and R. Mendonça. 2001. "A estabilidade inaceitável. Texto para Discussão," n. 800. IPEA, Rio de Janeiro.

Becker, G. S., and K. H. Murphy. 1988. "Economic Growth, Human Capital and Population Growth." Paper presented at the Conference on the Problem of Development: Exploring Economic Development Through Free Enterprise, sponsored by the Institute for the Study of Free Enterprise Systems, State University of New York, Buffalo, May 1988.

Bommier, A., R. Lee, T. Miller, and S. Zuber. 2010." Who Wins and Who Loses? Public Transfer Accounts for U.S. Generations Born 1850 to 2090." *Population and Development Review* 36 (10): 1–26.

Brandt, R. 2001. "Desenvolvimento social, previdência e pobreza no Brasil." *Conjuntura Social* 12 (2) (abr/jun): 7–63.

Cotlear, D., and L. Tornarolli. 2009. "Poverty, the Aging and the Life Cycle in LAC." Paper presented at the Authors Workshop for the Regional Study on Demographic Change and Social Policy in LAC, World Bank, Washington, DC. July 14–15, 2009.

Feyrer, J. 2007. "Demographics and Productivity." *The Review of Economics and Statistics* 89 (1): 100–09.

Fleury, A., and M. T. L. Fleury. 2001. *Estratégias empresariais e formação de competências*, 2nd ed. São Paulo: Atlas.

Grosh, M., and P. Leite. 2009. "Defining Eligibility for Social Pensions: A View from a Social Assistance Perspective." In *Closing the Gap: The Role of Social Pensions and Other Retirement Income Transfers*, ed. R. Holzmann and D. A. Robalino. 161–186. Washington, DC: World Bank.

IBGE (Instituto Brasileiro de Geografia e Estatística). 2008. "Projeção da População do Brasil por Sexo e Idade—1980–2050," rev. 2008. Estudos e Pesquisas: Informação Demográfica e Socioeconômica 24. IBGE, Rio de Janeiro. http://www.ibge.gov.br/home/estatistica/populacao/projecao_da_populacao/2008/projecao.pdf.

———. 2009. PNAD (Pesquisa Nacional por Amostra de Domicílios) 2008. IBGE, Rio de Janeiro.

————. 2010. POF (Pesquisa de Orçamentos Familiares) 2008–2009. IBGE, Rio de Janeiro.

Lee, R. 2003. "Demographic Change, Welfare, and Intergenerational Transfers: A Global Overview." *Genus* 49 (3–4): 43–70.

Lee, R., A. Mason, and D. Cotlear, D. 2010. "Global Aging and Its Economics Consequences: An Issues Paper for the World Bank." World Bank, Washington, DC.

Lee, R. D. 1994. "The Formal Demography of Population Aging, Transfers, and the Economic Life Cycle." In *Demography of Aging, Committee on Population, Commission on Behavioral and Social Sciences and Education*, ed. L. G. Martin and Samuel H. Preston, 8–49. Washington, DC: National Research Council, National Academy Press.

Lee, Ronald, and Andrew Mason. 2010. "Fertility, Human Capital, and Economic Growth over the Demographic Transition." *European Journal of Population* 26 (2): 159–82.

Lindh, T., and B. Malmberg. 1999. "Age Structure Effects and Growth in the OECD, 1950–90," *Journal of Population Economics* 12 (3): 431–49.

Mason, A., and R. Lee. 2010. "Introducing Age into National Accounts." NTA (National Transfer Accounts) Working Paper, University of California at Berkeley. http://www.ntaccounts.org/web/nta/show/WP10-02.

Mason, A., R. Lee, A. Tung, M-S. Lai, and T. Miller. 2009. "Population Aging and Intergenerational Transfers: Introducing Age into National Accounts." In *Development in the Economics of Aging*, ed. David Wise, 89–126. Cambridge, MA, and Chicago: National Bureau of Economic Research and University of Chicago Press.

Modigliani, Franco. 1988. "The Role of Intergenerational Transfers and Life Cycle Saving in the Accumulation of Wealth." *Journal of Economic Perspectives* 2 (2): 15–40.

Modigliani, Franco, and Richard H. Brumberg. 1954. "Utility Analysis and the Consumption Function: An Interpretation of Cross-Section Data." In *Post-Keynesian Economics*, ed. Kenneth K. Kurihara, 388–436. New Brunswick, NJ: Rutgers University Press.

National Institute on Aging. 2007. "Why Population Aging Matters: A Global Perspective." National Institutes of Health, U.S. Dept. of Health and Human Services, and U.S. Department of State, Washington, DC.

Preston, S. H. 1984. "Children and the Elderly: Divergent Paths for America's Dependents." *Demography* 21 (4): 435–57.

Queiroz, Bernardo. 2008. "Retirement Incentives: Pension Wealth, Accrual and Implicit Tax." *Well-Being and Social Policy* 4 (1): 73–94.

Rios-Neto, E. L. G. 2005. "Questões emergentes na análise demográfica: o caso brasileiro." *Revista Brasileira de Estudos de População, São Paulo* 22 (2): 371–408.

Tang, J., and C. MacLeod. 2006. "Labor Force Ageing and Productivity Performance in Canada." *Canadian Journal of Economics* 39 (2): 582–603.

Turra, C. M. 2000. "Contabilidade das gerações: Riqueza, sistema de transferencias e consequências de mudanças no padrão demográfico." Master's thesis, Centro de Desenvolvimento e Planejamento Regional, Universidade Federal de Minas Gerais. Belo Horizonte, Brazil.

Turra, C. M., and M. Holz. 2010. "Who Benefits from Public Transfers? Incidence across Income Groups and across Generations." Paper presented at author's workshop for Demographic Change and Social Policy: A LAC Regional Study, World Bank, Washington, DC, July 14–15.

Turra, C. M., B. Q. Lanza, and E. L. G. Rios-Neto. Forthcoming. "Idiosyncrasies of Intergenerational Transfers in Brazil." In *Population Aging and the Generational Economy: A Global Perspective*, ed. A. Mason and R. D. Lee. Cheltenham, UK: Edward Elgar Publishing Ltd.

Turra, C. M., I. G. Marri, and S. Wajnman. 2008. "Os argumentos de proteção social e equidade individual no debate sobre previdência e gênero no Brasil." *Mudança Populacional: aspectos relevantes para a Previdência*, vol. 27, 55–69. Brasília, DF: Ministério da Previdência Social.

Turra, C. M., and E. L. G. Rios-Neto. 2001. "Intergenerational Accounting and Economic Consequences of Aging in Brazil." Paper presented at the XXIV IUSSP (International Union for the Scientific Study of Population) General Population Conference, Salvador, Brazil, 2001. August 18–24.

Turra, C. M., and R. Rocha. 2010. "Public Transfers among Dependent Age Groups in Brazil." Background paper prepared for the Workshop on Aging in Brazil, World Bank, Brasilia, April 6–7, 2010.

Turra, C. M., S. Wajnman, and C. Simões. 2009. "The Role of the Demographic Transition to Changes in Income Inequality and Poverty Rates in Brazil." Paper presented at the XXVI IUSSP (International Union for the Scientific Study of Population) Conference. The Hague, The Netherlands, March 26–28.

World Bank. 2011. *Population Aging: Is Latin America Ready?* Directions in Development series. Washington, DC: World Bank.

CHAPTER 2

Population Dynamics in Brazil

This chapter provides an overview of past and future demographic dynamics in Brazil, focusing on the demographic transition as the process by which a population moves from an initial state characterized by high fertility, high mortality, and the preponderance of a young population, to a different state characterized by low fertility, low mortality, and the preponderance of an old population. The intermediate stage is characterized by high rates of population growth, as a result of the gap between the initial fall in mortality and the reduction in fertility.

Brazil has followed the typical phases of the demographic transition (see figure 2.1). During the first (pre-transitional) stage, up to around 1940, the Brazilian population experienced high birth and death rates and consequently low natural growth. However, between 1870 and 1930, an important population increase (above 2.0 percent per year) took place as a result of international migration. Brazil started the second stage of its demographic transition around 1940, which was characterized by sustained mortality decline, mostly at young ages, high fertility, and almost an absence of international migration. The population growth rate increased during this period and reached a plateau of approximately 3 percent between 1950 and 1960. The decline in infant and

Figure 2.1   Demographic Transition in Brazil

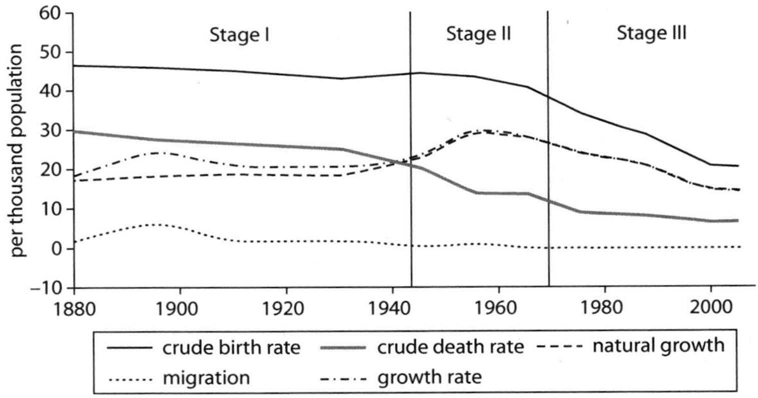

Sources: Merrick and Graham (1979, 37); IBGE (1990, 85); IBGE, Census 2000.

Box 2.1

Source of Demographic Data

Unless otherwise specified, the data used for Brazil and comparator countries in this report are from the United Nations "World Population Prospects: The 2008 Revision" (http://esa.un.org/unpp/index.asp). Given the uncertainty of future demographic trends, the UN usually produces a number of projections based on different assumptions about the future paths of the demographic variables, fertility in particular. This chapter uses the medium-fertility variant, normally regarded as the most likely among the variants. Under the medium-fertility variant, total fertility in all countries is assumed to converge eventually toward a level of 1.85 children per woman. (In the case of Brazil, the UN population projections are slightly more conservative than those prepared by the Brazilian Geographical and Statistical Institute [IBGE] in 2008, which projects that the Total Fertility Rate will continue declining until it reaches a value of 1.5 children per woman in 2030, then it will remain stable at that level.)

Source: Beltrão and Sugahara (2010).

---

child mortality led to a large increase in the number of surviving children and a corresponding rise in the child share of the population.

Brazil entered the third stage of its demographic transition at the end of the 1960s, when fertility began to decline rapidly and at a much faster pace than mortality. From more than 3 percent per year in 1950, the population growth rate slowed to 1.6 percent between 1991 and 2000 and reached 1.4 percent in 2007. Moreover, the changes in the population age structure associated with the demographic transition and a projected sustained decline in fertility for the next 40 years predict an increasingly smaller population growth rate, which eventually will turn negative in 2040–45. The large birth cohorts generated by the onset of the demographic transition will continue to have dramatic effects on the population age structure. First, they increased the share of the population in the working ages, then, as time goes on, they are now increasing the share of population at older ages. A continued decline in death rates reinforces the effects of the fertility decline because the gains in survival are now increasingly concentrated at older ages.

Trends in Mortality, Fertility, and Migration

The crude rates described above do not allow a full understanding of the structural changes in mortality and fertility patterns, since crude rates are heavily dependent on age structure.[1] This section discusses both age-specific mortality and fertility behavior and international migration to better understand the forces behind demographic change observed in Brazil over the past 60 years.

Mortality

During the first half of the 20th century, mortality declined slowly in Brazil. In 1950–55, life expectancy at birth was only 50.9 years, and infant mortality was 134.7 per thousand births (see table 2.1). From then on, life expectancy started increasing, first as a result of the decline in infant mortality—mainly due to improved control over infectious, parasitic, and respiratory diseases—and then as a product of declining mortality across the entire population. As a result, over the last 60 years, life expectancy in Brazil has increased by 21.4 years, reaching an average 72.3 years in 2005–10.

As in almost all societies, male mortality in LAC tends to be higher than female mortality, reflected in longer life expectancy for women. This difference also widened as life expectancy increased over the last half-century, mostly because of the joint effect of reduced mortality from female-specific causes such as those related to reproductive health (for example, pregnancy and childbirth complications) and increased mortality from causes that affect mainly men, such as accidents and violence. Between 1950–55 and 2005–10, the difference

Table 2.1   Brazil: Life Expectancy at Birth by Sex and Infant Mortality Rate, 1950–2050

Five-year period	Life expectancy (years) Both sexes combined	Men	Women	Infant mortality (per 1000 births)
1950–55	50.9	49.2	52.6	123.3
1970–75	59.5	57.3	61.8	76.9
1990–95	67.2	63.5	71.2	36.5
2000–05	71.0	67.2	74.9	23.4
2005–10	72.3	68.7	76.0	19.9
2010–15	73.5	69.9	77.2	16.9
2020–25	75.9	72.5	79.4	11.3
2045–50	79.9	76.5	83.4	5.8

Source: United Nations 2008.

between female and male life expectancy increased from 3.4 years to 7.3 years. Population projections indicate that this difference will remain during the next decades, although a reduction is expected in the future, following a trend currently observed in developed countries.

The pace of mortality decline observed in Brazil during the second half of the 20th century has been faster than the equivalent decline observed in most European countries during the entire 20th century, but has been slower than the equivalent decline observed in many East Asian countries during the same period. For example, it took 50 years (from 1950 to 2000) for life expectancy to increase from 50 to 70 years in Brazil. The same 20-year increase took 60 years in Germany (from 1900 to 1960), but only 27 years (from 1937 to 1964) in Japan and 33 years in Korea (from 1954 to 1987).

Figure 2.2 presents life expectancy at birth for Brazil and a set of comparator regions and countries. In 2010 life expectancy in Brazil was 73.5, that is, 7.0 years shorter than Germany and 10.2 years shorter than Japan. The common behavior is an increasing trend with smaller gains for higher levels. Japan is the uppermost curve from the late 1980s on. Brazil follows a path very similar to Mexico, both countries starting at the same level in the early 1950s, distancing themselves from the world average. Mexico, though, shows a higher rate of increase than Brazil. The fastest average annual growth rate during the 100-year period is projected for Republic of Korea, where life expectancy is expected to increase from 47.9 in 1950 to 83.8 in 2050.

Figure 2.2 Life Expectancy at Birth, 1950–2050

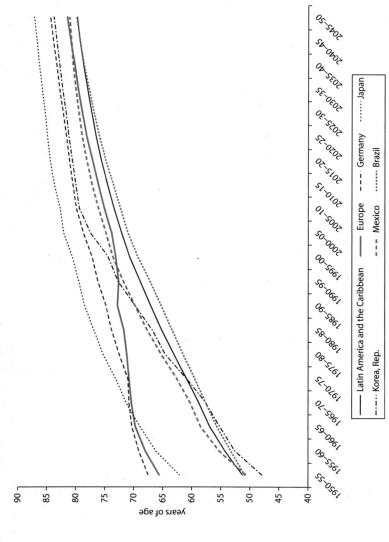

| Latin America and the Caribbean | —— Europe | – – Germany | ⋯⋯ Japan |
| - - Korea, Rep. | – – Mexico | ⋯⋯ Brazil | |

Source: United Nations 2008.

The evolution of mortality has not been uniform across Brazil. Figure 2.3 presents box-plots of life expectancy at birth for the period 1997–2006 for Brazilian states.[2] In 1997 the state with lowest life expectancy, Alagoas, had a life expectancy of 63.0, around 15 percent lower than that of the state in the best situation, Rio Grande do Sul at 73.3. However, the variations in life expectancy at birth for the different states narrow with time. In 2006 the differences were less striking, with Alagoas (still the state in the worst situation) at 68.3, a figure 8 percent below that of the state of Santa Catarina, with a life expectancy of 73.9 years. Similar patterns are observed when considering infant mortality and child mortality rates as indicators of mortality (these statistics are not shown here).

Mortality is heterogeneous not only across geographic areas in the country, but mainly across socioeconomic strata. Figure 2.4 presents child mortality rates for selected points in time for different per capita family income brackets between 1991 and 2006. The huge gaps observed in the early 1990s are reduced to almost zero in the early 2000s. It is interesting to note how child mortality for the wealthier group remained at such a low level for the whole period. The estimated gap is larger than the corresponding gap estimated for life expectancy (not shown here),

Figure 2.3   Life Expectancy at Birth in Brazilian States, 1997–2006

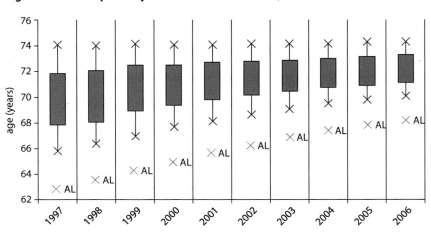

Source: IBGE (2010); PNAD different years (IBGE 2009).
Note: AL = Alagoas state.

Figure 2.4   Brazil: Child Mortality Rates for Boys and Girls by per Capita Family Income

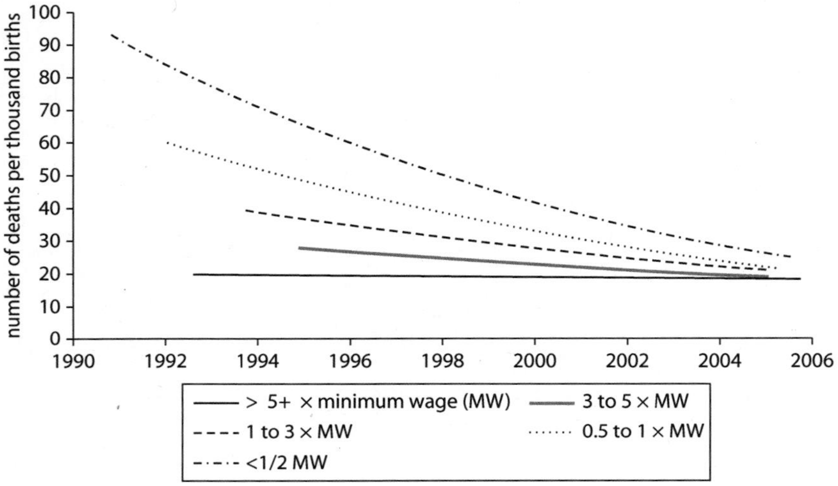

Source: PNAD different years (IGBE 2009).

suggesting that social-strata mortality differentials among children are larger than those among adults.

Fertility

Despite the impressive decline in mortality, the decline in fertility has been the main factor affecting population dynamics in Brazil.[3] Table 2.2 shows fertility trends in Brazil, 1950–2050. Over the last six decades, the total fertility rate dropped from 6.2 children per woman in 1950–55 to 1.8 children per woman in 2005–10. It is expected to keep declining until 2025, at which time it will stabilize at 1.5.

Despite the fact that the TFR started declining in the 1960s, the annual number of births increased from 2.6 million to 4.0 million between 1950–55 and 1985–90 because of the concentration of population in child-bearing ages, and then started decreasing as a consequence of the continuing decline in fertility. The most recent projections are for a steady decrease in the annual number of births.

Figure 2.5 shows trends in total fertility rates for Brazil and a set of comparator countries and regions for 1950–2050. The Brazilian TFR presented a sharp decline from 1960 up to 1991 followed by a deceleration

Table 2.2   Brazil: TFR and Annual Births, 1950–2050

Year	Total fertility rate	Annual births (1000s)	Year	Total fertility rate	Annual births (1000s)
1950–55	6.15	2,572	2005–10	1.80	3,129
1955–60	6.15	2,918	2010–15	1.70	2,828
1960–65	6.15	3 303	2015–20	1.60	2,667
1970–75	5.38	3,330	2020–25	1.52	2,502
1975–80	4.72	3,441	2025–30	1.50	2,365
1980–85	4.31	3,741	2030–35	1.55	2,288
1985–90	3.80	3,974	2035–40	1.60	2,200
1990–95	2.60	3,757	2040–45	1.70	2,183
1995–2000	2.45	3,519	2045–50	1.75	2,114
2000–05	2.25	3,624			

Source: United Nations 2008.

Figure 2.5   TFR in Brazil vs. Selected Countries, Regions, and the World, 1950–2050

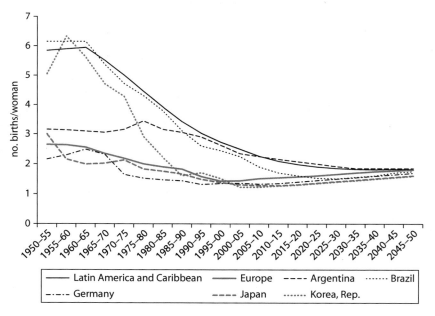

Source: United Nations 2008.

of the decline during the 1990s and a speeding up of the decline from 2000 on.

Opposite to the pattern observed for mortality, fertility decline in Brazil has been very fast, faster than the decline observed in most European, East Asian, and LAC countries. For example, it took only

17.5 years for Brazil to reduce its TFR from 3 to 2 (1988–2006), while it took more than 50 years for the average European country (1924–1977).[4] As with life expectancy, the fastest fertility decline was observed in Republic of Korea, where the TFR decreased from 3 to 2 in less than 8 years (1977–84). The rapidity of fertility change with its consequences on the population age structure is indeed the most important feature of the demographic transition in Brazil.

Table 2.3 presents the age-specific fertility rates estimated for the period 1970–2010. The bottom part shows the relative distribution of the age-specific fertility rates. Fertility decline in Brazil was mainly a result of the elimination of higher order births, or at least of births at older ages. In contrast to other countries, postponement of first birth was not a strategy used by Brazilian women to control their fertility. Increasingly fertility is concentrated around the second fertile age group and a decrease of births in the higher age groups.

As in the case of mortality, fertility in Brazilian states shows a pattern of convergence toward a national average. In 2007, Acre, a state in the northern region, presented the highest TFR among the Brazilian states, 3.0 children per woman. At the other extreme, the lowest TFR (1.7 child per women) was in Rio de Janeiro (see figure 2.6).

Table 2.3   Brazil: TFR and Age-Specific Fertility Rates, 1970–2010

Year	TFR	Age-Specific Fertility Rate						
		15–19	20–24	25–29	30–34	35–39	40–44	45–49
1970	5.83	0.0753	0.2564	0.2971	0.2466	0.1825	0.0856	0.0225
1980	4.06	0.0742	0.1983	0.2104	0.1611	0.1089	0.049	0.0101
1990	2.79	0.0817	0.1569	0.1399	0.0945	0.0551	0.0244	0.0054
2000	2.39	0.0899	0.1401	0.1161	0.0757	0.0407	0.0133	0.0021
2010	1.76	0.0822	0.1271	0.0862	0.0377	0.0141	0.0034	0.0004
Percentage reduction in fertility rate								
1970–2010	69.8	−9.2	50.4	71.0	84.7	92.3	96.0	98.0
Relative distribution of rates by age								
1970	100.0	6.5	22.0	25.5	21.1	15.7	7.3	1.9
1980	100.0	7.6	23.0	25.7	20.6	14.7	6.8	1.6
1990	100.0	9.1	24.4	25.9	19.8	13.4	6.0	1.2
2000	100.0	11.3	27.0	25.2	19.2	11.5	4.9	0.8
2010	100.0	14.6	28.1	25.1	16.9	9.9	4.4	1.0

Sources: United Nations 2008; IBGE 2008.

Figure 2.6   Brazil: TFR in Brazilian States 1950–2007

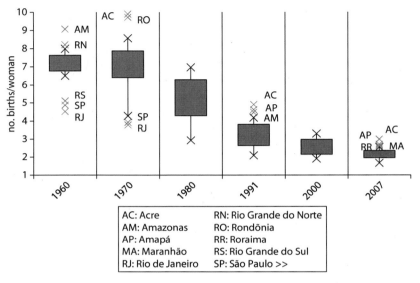

AC: Acre   RN: Rio Grande do Norte
AM: Amazonas   RO: Rondônia
AP: Amapá   RR: Roraima
MA: Maranhão   RS: Rio Grande do Sul
RJ: Rio de Janeiro   SP: São Paulo >>

Source: PNAD different years (IGBE 2009).

The heterogeneity across regions is small when compared with social strata disparities. Figure 2.7 presents the age-specific fertility rates for the same income brackets considered for the mortality analysis: families with income up to half of the minimum wage, income between one-half and one minimum wage, between one and three minimum wages, between three and five, and more than five. The lower stratum presents a much more concentrated and younger pattern. As income increases, the mode shifts to older ages, a pattern similar to that observed in European and other OECD countries. In 2001–06 the TFR was still almost as high as 3.5 children among women in the lowest bracket of income per capita and as low as 1.0 child among women in the highest bracket. However, a clear pattern of convergence is also apparent across socioeconomic groups.

Migration

Brazil has traditionally been a country of in-migration. This was especially true around the turn of the previous century when it received many immigrants from Europe and Asia. The in-migration process continued after World War II.

International migration. It was only with the 1991 census that some evaluation was possible of the out-migration from Brazil to other countries.

Figure 2.7   Brazil: Age-Specific Fertility Rates by Age Group and per Capita Family Income, 2001–06

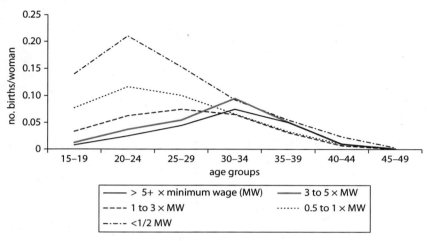

Source: PNAD different years (IGBE 2009).

Carvalho (1996) estimated between 1.0 and 2.5 million individuals above 10 years of age migrated out of Brazil during the 1980s. Oliveira (2008) estimated that around 1.26 million individuals in the 20 to 44 age group out-migrated in the 1980s. Carvalho and Campos (2007) estimated the net migration flow as half a million individuals above 10 years of age leaving the country during the 1990s. Considering the size of the country's population and the incipient international out-migration process, the impact is estimated to be negligible. Presently IBGE (2008) does not take into account in its projection any international migration.

Figure 2.8 presents the natural and total population growth rates for selected regions and countries in 2005–10. Reinforcing the previous analysis, countries like Mexico present a natural growth rate higher than the total growth due to out-migration, while other countries with in-migration (such as the United States) present the opposite pattern. The difference between the natural and total growth rates in Brazil is almost none.

Internal migration. As in the rest of the world, urbanization was a prominent force of industrialization in Brazil, which experienced a sharp spike in population moving to the city in the second half of the 20th century. Unlike the rest of the world, however, urbanization in Brazil has and is still occurring at a much faster rate. The proportion of the population living in urban areas increased from 36.0 percent in 1950 to

Figure 2.8   Natural and Total Population Growth Rates, 2005–10

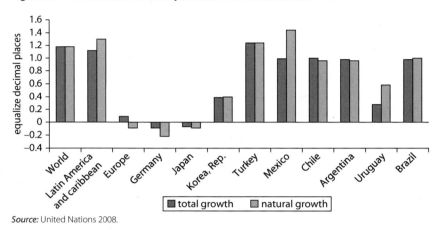

Source: United Nations 2008.

81.2 percent in 2000. The initial spurt of urbanization (in the early 1960s) in Brazil occurred at a rate that was almost double that of the rest of the world. While the rate of growth has gradually declined, it is predicted that over 90 percent of the population of Brazil will be urbanized by 2050, compared to only 70 percent in the rest of the world (see figure 2.9).

Although the proportion of elderly living in urban areas in Brazil, as recorded in censuses, has always been higher than the overall proportion of people living in rural areas, the difference was basically reduced to zero in 2000, which indicates a much more even distribution of people by age in both places of residence (table 2.4).

Changes in Population Size and Age Structure

Population in Brazil has been growing at declining rates for more than half a century (figure 2.10). In 1950, the annual population growth rate was almost 4 percent; it has dropped to 1.0 percent today and is expected to remain positive for the next 30 years, even with fertility already at below-replacement level. The tendency for population to continue to grow beyond the point at which replacement-level fertility is reached is the result of a relatively high concentration of people in the childbearing years and is referred to as "population momentum." This phenomenon results from the large number of young people born during previous eras of high fertility rates. As these youths grow older and move through reproductive ages, the greater number of births tends to exceed the number of deaths

Figure 2.9   Urbanization in Brazil vs. the Rest of the World, 1950–2050

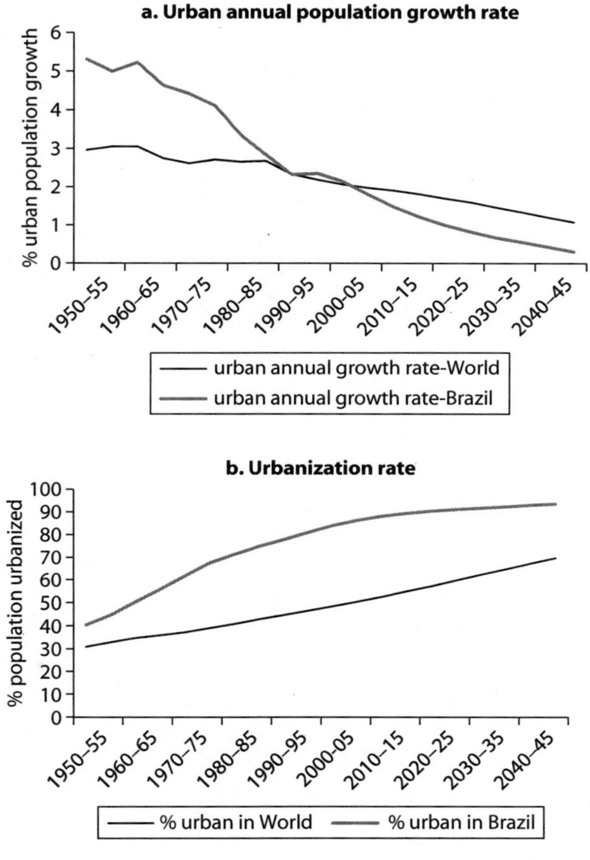

a. Urban annual population growth rate

legend:
— urban annual growth rate-World
— urban annual growth rate-Brazil

b. Urbanization rate

legend:
— % urban in World   — % urban in Brazil

Source: United Nations 2007.

in the older populations for a certain period of time. Not until 2040–50 is the Brazilian population expected to reach a negative growth rate. However, opposing trends are observed in specific age groups: while the adult population (aged 15–59) is growing at declining rates and the young population (aged 0–14) has already started to decline in absolute numbers, the growth rate of the older population (aged 60 and older) is expected to follow an upward trend until 2020–25 and to remain above 2 percent (although with declining values) until 2045–50. After that, the growth rate of elderly might begin to fall, although it will remain well above the growth rates of the other age groups.

Table 2.4 Brazil: Proportion of Population of Major Age Groups by Place of Residence, 1950–2000

percent of population

Age group	1950		1960		1970		1980		1991		2000	
(years)	Urban	Rural	Urban	Rural	Urban	Rural	Urban	Rural	Urban	Rural	Urban	Rural
Total	36.2	63.8	44.9	55.1	52.8	47.2	67.7	32.3	75.6	24.4	81.2	18.8
0–14	30.4	69.6	40.6	59.4	48.9	51.1	62.7	37.3	71.7	28.3	77.8	22.2
15–59	40.0	60.0	47.8	52.2	55.6	44.4	70.9	29.1	77.8	22.2	82.9	17.1
60 +	43.8	56.2	51.5	48.5	57.4	42.6	69.6	30.4	76.7	23.3	81.4	18.6

Source: Brazilian Censuses 1950, 1960, 1970, 1980, 2000.

Figure 2.10   Brazil: Population Growth Rates by Major Age Groups, 1950–2050

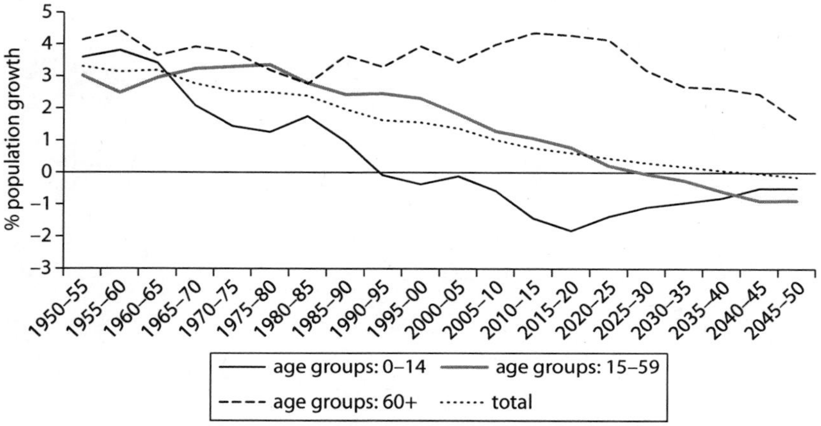

Source: United Nations 2008.

In absolute numbers, the population of Brazil increased 3.5 times over the last half-century—from 54 million in 1950 to 186 million in 2005—and is projected to increase an additional 17 percent over the next 45 years, to reach 218 million in 2050. Again, considerable variation exists among different age groups. While the young population increased 2.3 times between 1950 and 2005 and is expected to decline by around 37.4 percent between 2005 and 2050, the adult population expanded 4.1 times in the first period and is projected to continue increasing over the second period, but only by 2.9 percent. Yet, the most significant change concerns the older population, which increased by 6.3 times between 1950 and 2005, and will increase by almost 300 percent between 2005 and 2050. The magnitude of the older population will match that of the youth population for the first time in history around 2027. By 2050, the older population is expected to be twice as large as the youth population (see figure 2.11 and table 2.5).

As figure 2.12 shows, the youth population has declined since 1990, while the working-age population is expected to expand up to 2025. After that, population growth in Brazil will be entirely caused by increases in the older population.

The demographic transition has important effects not only on the growth of the total population but also on its age structure. The connection between life expectancy and age structure is often misunderstood and erroneously believed to be the cause of population aging. However,

Figure 2.11   Brazil: Population by Age Group, 1950–2050

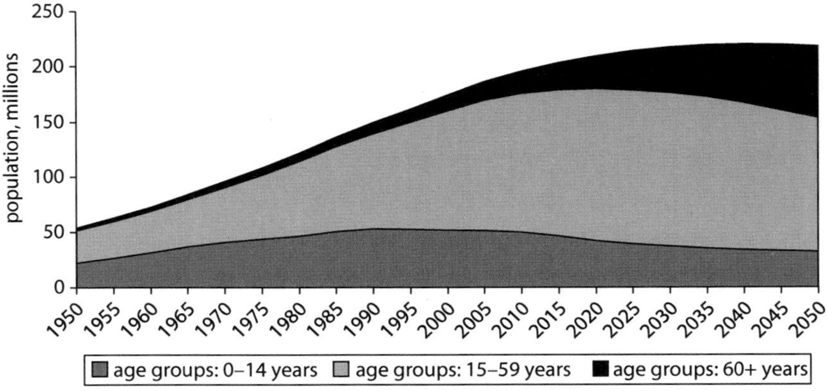

Source: United Nations 2008.

Table 2.5   Brazil: Population by Major Age Group, 1950, 2005, and 2050

Age Group	Population		
	1950	2005	2050
Total	53,974,725	186,109,614	218,512,000
0–14	2,2432,009	51,576,213	32,098,000
15–59	28,915,548	108,477,473	121,389,000
60 and over	2,627,168	14,112,862	64,025,000

Source: United Nations 2008.

over most of the transition in life expectancy, the greatest gains in years lived occur in the 15–64 age group. If we consider, for example, the increase in life expectancy from 40 to 60 years, about 5 of the 20 years gained were at 65 and older, about 2 years were gained in the 0–14 age span, and the remaining 13 years were gained in the 15–64 age span. For those countries with very high life expectancy, however, the greatest gains will be experienced at the end of life. For a life expectancy of 75–80, where most of the developed countries currently fall and Brazil soon will be, the gains at 65+ exceed the gains at 15–64. Population aging due to declining mortality is generally associated with increasing health and improving functional status of the elderly. While such aging puts pressures on pension programs that have rigid retirement ages, that problem is a curable institutional one, not a fundamental societal resource problem,

Figure 2.12   Brazil: Population Distribution by Major Age Group, 1950–2050

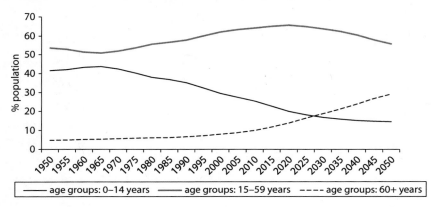

Source: United Nations 2008.

since the ratio of healthy, vigorous years over the life cycle to frail or disabled years has not necessarily changed.

In Brazil, at the moment, it is primarily the decline in birth rates that has produced the main changes in the population age distribution and, more specifically, has led to the increase in the share of the population at older ages. For this reason, population aging due to reduced fertility may well impose important resource costs on the population, regardless of institutional arrangements for old-age support.

The share of the distinct age groups in total population in Brazil has indeed changed considerably over time as they grew at different rates. Although in absolute terms, the youth population will continue to grow until 2020, its proportion has been declining since 1965 and is expected to continue declining. Similarly, the share of the adult population is expected to start declining after 2020, even though its magnitude will continue to expand until 2025–30. Whereas the shares of the youth and adult populations are predicted to decrease, the share of the older population is expected to increase steadily over the entire period under consideration (see figure 2.12).

The process of population aging should speed up considerably in the near future. In fact, between 1950 and 2000, the proportion of population aged 60 and over increased only moderately, from 5.0 percent to 8.1 percent. Over the next 50 years, however, it will rise from 8.1 percent to 29.4 percent, which means, in absolute terms, an increase from around 2.6 million to 64 million in the course of a century (44 million of which will be between 2010 and 2040).

Table 2.6 shows the evolution percentage of the elderly population (60+) in Brazil and selected comparator countries and regions between 1950 and 2050. The figure for Brazil shows an exponential pattern: it doubled between 1950 and 2010 and is expected to triple between 2010 and 2050. It is interesting that although the proportion of elderly was lower than that of what currently are the oldest countries in LAC (that is, Argentina, Chile, and Uruguay) in 1950 and 2010, such proportion is projected to be higher in Brazil in 2050. In 2050 Brazil will have a higher proportion of elderly than did all European countries in 2010. However, the aging process in Brazil will have been much faster because the speed of population aging depends mostly on the speed of fertility decline, which, as noted earlier, was extremely rapid in Brazil. For example, it has taken 60 years (from 1927 to 1987) for Germany to increase its share of elderly population from 10 percent to 20 percent. However, it will take only 27 years for Brazil to experience the same change. Only Republic of Korea will be faster than Brazil.

Because of expected rapid improvements of mortality at old ages in Brazil in the next 40 years, an even steeper increase is expected for the share of the oldest elderly (aged 80+). While in 2010 only 1.5 percent of population in Brazil was aged 80+, that figure is expected to increase to 6.5 percent in 2010, that is, a level higher than currently observed in any population in the world, including Japan.

Table 2.6   Elderly Population (60 and over) as Percentage of Total Population, 1950–2050

Area/Region/ Country	1950	1960	1970	1980	1990	2000	2010	2020	2030	2040	2050
World	8.1	8.0	8.3	8.5	9.1	9.9	11.0	13.4	16.5	19.1	21.9
LAC	5.6	5.9	6.3	6.6	7.3	8.3	10.0	13.1	17.1	21.3	25.5
Europe	12.1	13.1	15.5	16.1	18.2	20.3	22.0	25.6	29.3	32.0	34.2
Argentina	7.0	9.0	11.0	12.1	13.2	13.7	14.7	16.4	18.3	21.7	24.9
Chile	6.9	7.5	7.7	8.2	9.0	10.3	13.2	17.5	22.6	25.5	28.7
Germany	14.6	17.3	19.9	19.3	20.4	23.2	26.0	30.3	36.5	38.1	39.5
Japan	7.7	8.8	10.6	12.8	17.4	23.3	30.5	34.5	37.9	42.5	44.2
Korea, Rep.	5.2	6.0	5.4	6.1	7.7	11.2	15.6	22.8	31.1	37.4	40.8
Mexico	5.4	5.3	5.5	5.5	6.5	7.5	9.4	12.9	17.7	23.9	28.2
Turkey	5.8	6.1	6.8	6.3	6.7	7.8	9.0	11.5	15.5	20.5	24.4
Uruguay	11.8	11.9	12.9	14.7	16.5	17.4	18.4	20.1	22.3	25.1	27.4
Brazil	4.9	5.3	5.7	6.2	6.8	8.1	10.2	14.0	18.9	23.9	29.3

Source: United Nations 2008.

To illustrate the differential growth rate among total population and alternative definitions of elderly population in absolute values, figure 2.13 presents the ratio of the estimated figure for 2050 and the actual count in 1950. The pattern is the same everywhere: total population presents the smallest ratio, followed by population 60+, 65+, and the population 80+ with the highest ratio. Brazil presents the highest ratio for all the alternative definitions of elderly population among countries and regions selected.

Dependency Ratios, the Demographic Bonus, and the Demographic Dividends

The dependency ratio—which relates the number of people in dependent age groups (children under age 15 and persons over age 59, in this study) to that of people in the working-age group (aged 15–59)—is a valuable indicator of the potential effects of demographic changes on socioeconomic development. This section first analyzes changes in the dependency ratio associated with changes in the age structure of the Brazilian population and then discusses what characteristics of a country can make demographic change a positive or negative force for economic growth.

Figure 2.13   Ratio Estimated Total and Elderly Population, 1950–2050

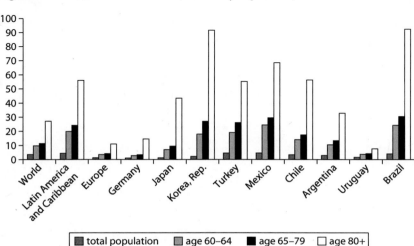

Source: United Nations 2008.

Changes in Dependency Ratios

The dependency ratio can also be disaggregated into a child dependency ratio, which relates the number of children to that of people of working age, and the old-age dependency ratio, which relates the number of older persons to that of people of working age. In general, dependency ratios are expressed in terms of the number of people in dependent age groups for every 100 people of working age. However, the limitations of dependency ratios expressed in terms of age ranges must be understood. First, in most populations, people do not automatically cease to be economically active at a specific age. In addition, not everyone in the working-age group is economically active, particularly among the female population (despite the increasing participation of women in the labor market). Similarly, as professional training gets longer, a growing number of young adults remain in the education system longer and thus outside the labor market longer (thereby extending the period of dependence far beyond adolescence).

Between 1950 and the mid-1960s, the total dependency ratio in Brazil increased due to the relative increase in the child population, until reaching a maximum value of 97 dependents per 100 people of working age. Following the decline in fertility rates in the mid-1960s, the total dependency ratio started a steady decline, which is expected to last until 2020, when the ratio will reach its minimum value of 52 before increasing again, due to the growing proportion of older persons (see figure 2.14).

Figure 2.14   Brazil: Total, Child, and Old Dependency Ratio, 1950–2050

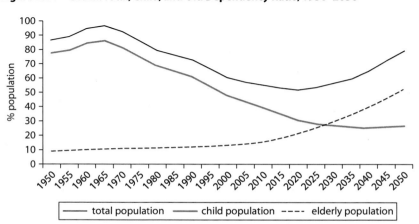

Source: United Nations 2008.

Whereas during the next 10 years the total dependency ratio will decline, it is important to note that its composition will have changed dramatically, indicating a shrinking pool of new workers and an increasing number of elderly. In particular, by the 2020s there will be five people in the age group 15–64 for each person 60 and older. The proportion today was 8 to 1 in 2000; in 2050 it will be less than 2 to 1.

Projections under Low-, Medium-, and High-Fertility Variants

The United Nations revises its official population estimates and projections every two years by incorporating all new and relevant evidence regarding the demographic dynamics in each country or area of the world and formulating detailed assumptions about the future paths of the demographic variables.

However, because future trends cannot be known with certainty, a number of projection variants are produced, most of them differing exclusively in the assumptions made regarding the future path of fertility. For the purpose of this exercise, the medium-fertility variant, usually recommended as the most likely one, is compared with the extreme (and unlikely) cases of the low- and high-fertility variants.[5]

Figure 2.15 and table 2.7 show the dependency ratios for Brazil under the medium, high and low variants. The total dependency ratio is estimated to keep falling modestly until 2020, after which it will start to grow. In the high-fertility variant, the growth would start five years earlier

Figure 2.15   Brazil: Total, Child, and Old Dependency Ratios under Different Population Variants, 1950–2050

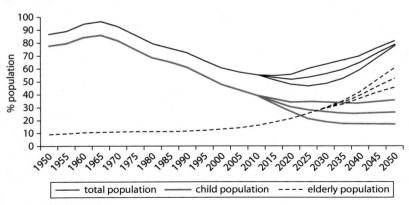

Source: United Nations 2008.

Table 2.7   Brazil: Total, Old, and Child Dependency Ratios under Different Population Variants, 1950–2050

| Dependency Ratio | 1950 | 2005 | Dependents per 100 Persons of Working Age 2050 | | |
			Low	Medium	High
Total dependency	87	57	78	79	82
Child dependency	78	43	17	26	36
Old age dependency	9	14	61	53	46

Source: United Nations 2008.

(2015) and at a slightly higher level (55 instead of 52), and the variation between different assumptions on fertility would be largest between 2025 and 2035. By 2050, however, the differences in total dependency ratio under the three variants are projected to range very little, from 78 to 82 dependents per 100 persons of working age.

The child dependency ratio is estimated to fall under all three variants, dropping from 42 dependents in 2005 to 26 dependents in 2050 under the medium variant. Under the high variant, the drop in child dependency ratio would be more modest, reaching 46 dependents in 2050. Under the low variant, the ratio would reduce by more than half in the period, reaching a value of 17 in 2050. The old-age dependency ratio is estimated to more than triple under all three variants. It is expected to be 53 dependents and to range from 46 under the high variant to 61 under the low variant.

The Demographic Bonus

As noted, during the demographic transition, not only for Brazil but for all countries, there is a period when the proportion of people of potentially productive age grows steadily in relation to potentially inactive ages. In that period, when the dependency ratio drops to record lows, the situation is particularly conducive to development, as there are more possibilities for saving and investment in economic growth, while there is also reduced pressure on education spending. Various terms have been coined to describe this period, including "demographic bonus" or "demographic window of opportunity," which refers to the possibility of increasing rates of economic growth per capita and the levels of well-being of the population during this period.

There is no exact measurement of the beginning and end of the demographic bonus, and its definition in terms of the dependency ratio tends to vary. Following the work of CEPAL (2008) and World Bank (2011), in this study, the period corresponding to the demographic bonus has been subdivided into three phases. In the first phase, the dependency ratio declines but is still fairly high (above two-thirds, that is, two persons in dependent-age groups for every three in working-age groups). In the second phase, the dependency ratio falls below two-thirds and continues to decrease. In the third and final phase, the dependency ratio begins to rise as the proportion of older people increases, but is still below two-thirds. The two-thirds cutoff point was chosen arbitrarily to serve as an illustrative benchmark.

In Brazil the demographic bonus started in 1995 and will last until 2043. However, the most favorable phase of a small and declining dependency ratio will finish in 2020 (figure 2.16). After that the total dependency ratio will be increasing year after year.

The extent and duration of the different phases of the demographic bonus vary significantly across countries (figure 2.17). Generally, countries farther along in the demographic transition have a shorter period of bonus left than countries that are behind in the process. The countries with the fastest fertility decline (Brazil, Rep. of Korea, Mexico, and Turkey) have a longer bonus than countries with a longer (Germany) or smoother (Argentina and Uruguay) fertility decline. In Japan and in Germany and most other European countries, the demographic bonus has already expired.

Labor Market

This section explores the consequences of demographic change on the size and share of the working-age population. As discussed, after that the total dependency ratio will start to increase as the elderly population

Figure 2.16   Brazil: The Demographic Bonus

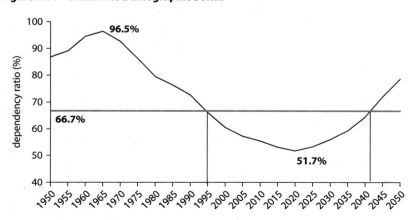

Source: United Nations 2008.

Figure 2.17   Phases of the Demographic Bonus, 1950–2050

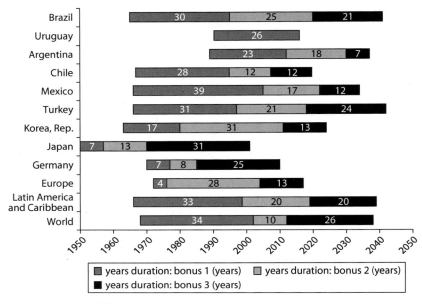

Source: United Nations 2008.

continues to grow faster and faster. A growing working-age population implies more people in economic activity, which, all else being equal, would result in more wealth being generated (first dividend). At the same time, as life expectancy at birth continues increasing, the increasingly older population is expected to live longer, which could result in more savings over the life cycle to finance consumption at old ages (second demographic dividend).

Size of Working-Age Labor Force

Wong and Carvalho (2006) argue that Brazil is currently experiencing the best moment of the demographic bonus. They divide the potential economically active population (ages 15–64) into two groups: the mature working population (25–64), which is expected to continue increasing until 2035, and the junior segment of the economically active population (15–24), which has already started a period of negative growth (see figure 2.18). A fraction of this junior workforce (those aged 15–19) is usually in the qualification phase, and the other (20–24), although economically active, is usually made of people seeking their first job (who usually have smaller economic activity rates). The mature workforce, in

Figure 2.18   Brazil: Population Working-Age Cohorts

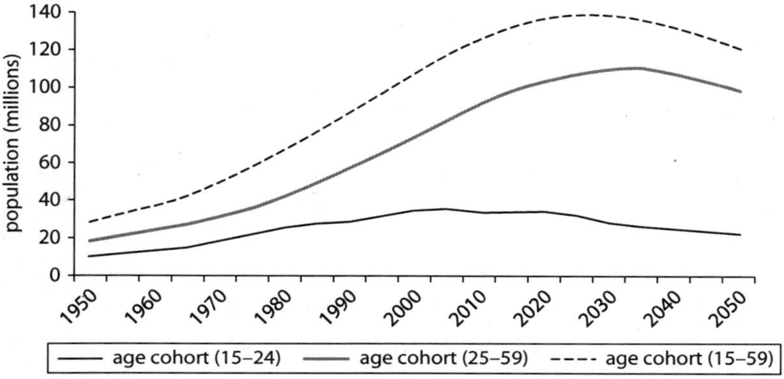

Source: United Nations 2008.

contrast, has higher economic activity rates and usually generates most of countries' wealth and also comprises the most important group of taxpayers.

Frequently, unemployment decreases as the age structure shifts toward older ages. Unemployment rates tend to be higher among younger workers because individuals first entering the labor market tend to spend more time searching for the best match for their skills, they are less costly to release, they tend to have less information about labor markets, and their potential employers tend to have less knowledge about their own comparative advantages and preferences than do older workers (see Behrman, Duryea, and Székely 2001). The junior workforce increased in absolute terms very rapidly until recently in Brazil; thus, demographically speaking, when this cohort entered the labor force, the economy was under pressure to create enough employment to prevent the social and economic instability that would have come from increasing unemployment and displacing older people still at working ages (see Wong and Carvalho 2006). These pressures can be expected to lessen when the period of negative growth of the junior workforce begins, which was observed in Brazil, where unemployment decreased from 10.43 in 1999 to 7.1 in 2008.

An increasing share of the working-age population could boost the prospects for economic growth due to the reduction in the young dependency ratio. And an increasing mature working-age population relative to the junior working-age population, as in Brazil, represents another window of opportunity to accelerate growth, improve saving, increase government revenues and, consequently, increase fiscal capacity to finance public policies. However, as will be shown later in this chapter, a large share of the Brazilian workforce is low-skilled workers, employed in low-quality jobs in the informal sector, earning very low wages and contributing little to economic growth. Moreover, to take advantage of the fact that people will live longer, incentives should be aligned with the goal of strengthening the financial sustainability of the social security system. In other words, workers should be encouraged to stay longer in the labor force and to delay retirement when they are still productive. Having people work longer (in the formal sector) has two benefits: first, they draw a pension for fewer years; second, they keep generating income and contributing to financing the social security system. The next sections discuss these questions.

Labor Force Participation and Retirement Behavior

This section describes the changes in the labor market observed in Brazil in recent years.[6] Pooling data from 25 rounds of the PNAD between 1982 and 2007[7] enables labor market characteristics to be constructed over the life cycle of different cohorts.

There has been very little change in age-specific labor force participation of men across cohorts. Examining labor force participation of men between 10–14 and 75–79 years of age, covering cohorts born between 1928–32 and 1978–82, shows that the age profile is very stable across cohorts (figure 2.19a). Participation starts around 25 percent for children aged 10–14, peaks at around 95 percent for adults aged 30–50, then falls abruptly until it reaches 20 percent for elderly aged 75–79. The subtle changes that can be perceived in this figure correspond to modest reductions in participation for younger cohorts throughout the age distribution. In any case, the changes do not seem to be significant (see Wajnman, Oliveira, and Oliveira 2004 for a period analysis perspective on labor force participation of the elderly).

Women's participation in the labor force, presented in figure 2.19b, shows a radically different picture. As earlier researchers noted (for example, Wajnman and Rios-Neto 1999), there has been a sustained increase in the labor force participation of women in Brazil over the last several decades. In figure 2.19b, this can be clearly seen from the shift in the age-specific profiles across cohorts. Female labor force participation in the 55–59 age group, for example, increased from 29 percent in the cohort born 1928–32, to 43 percent in the cohort born 1948–52. At the same time, in the age group 20–24, it went from 45 percent in the cohort

Figure 2.19   Brazil: Labor Force Participation by Age and Birth Cohort

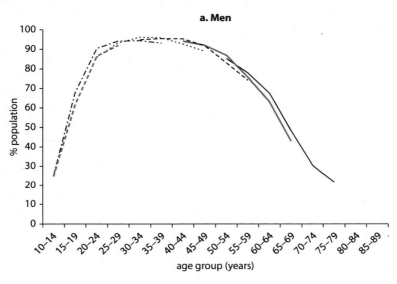

a. Men

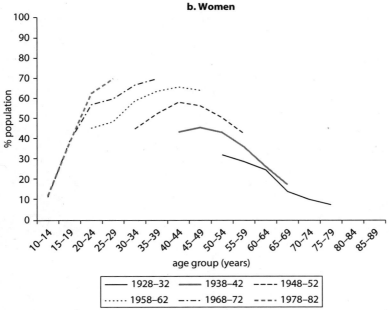

b. Women

| —— 1928–32 | —— 1938–42 | – – – 1948–52 |
| ········ 1958–62 | –·–· 1968–72 | – – – 1978–82 |

Source: Soares (2010).

born 1958–62 to 63 percent in the cohort born 1978–82. The vertical shift is roughly the same order of magnitude across cohorts, apart from the two oldest cohorts in the figure, which are closer together for the older age groups.

Oddly enough, the pattern of change in average hours worked across cohorts (for employed individuals) is almost diametrically opposite for men and women (figure 2.20). For men, there has been a consistent reduction in the average hours across cohorts. In the age group 55–59, average weekly hours for individuals born 1928–32 were 49, in contrast to 45 for the cohort born 1948–32. In the age group 20–24, average weekly hours were 48 in the cohort born in 1958–62, in contrast to 44 for the cohort born in 1978–82. For women, on the other hand, there is no clear pattern and the profile is reasonably stable, apart from some changes at early ages. For prime age women, that is, between 25 and 49 years of age, average weekly hours hover around 38 for different cohorts.

In sum, the patterns of labor force participation and hours per week suggest that men have maintained a roughly constant profile of labor supply on the extensive margin (labor force participation), while reducing it on the intensive margin (hours worked). At the same time, women have maintained a roughly constant labor supply on the intensive margin (hours worked), while increasing it on the extensive margin (increased labor force participation).

The results for retirement rates reveal a different pattern, as shown in figure 2.21. Retirement starts being a relevant phenomenon in the Brazilian labor market as early as age 45–49. By age 55–59, close to 30 percent of all men are already retired. However, male retirement rates are not monotonic through time. In the 45–49 age group, retirement rates increased from 8.6 percent for the cohort born in 1993–37 to 9.8 percent for the cohort born in 1948–52, and then fell back to 4.8 percent for the cohort born in 1958–62. For women, the retirement rate has monotonically increased for recent cohorts, which is intrinsically related to increased eligibility for social security deriving from increased female labor force participation, and also to women's smaller time of contribution, to be discussed later.

The non-monotonic pattern in retirement rates is therefore a pattern to men at relatively young ages, that is, starting with the 45–49 age group, and is related particularly to the issue of early retirement in Brazil (considering early retirement as retirement before 60 years old). The profile across younger age groups suggests a process of increasing retirement rates until the mid-1990s, after which retirement rates started falling.

Figure 2.20   Brazil: Average Hours of Work per Week, by Age and Birth Cohort

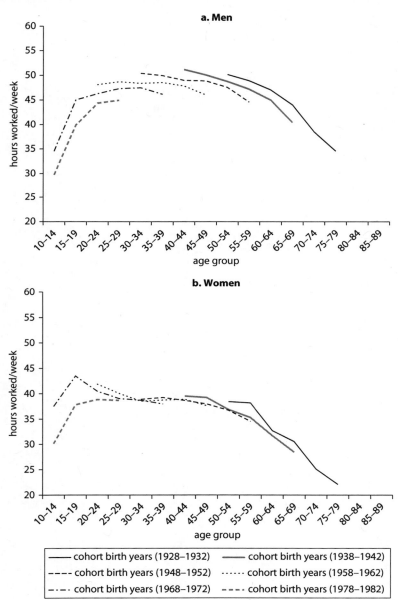

Source: Soares (2010).

Figure 2.21   Brazil: Percentage of Retired by Age and Birth Cohort

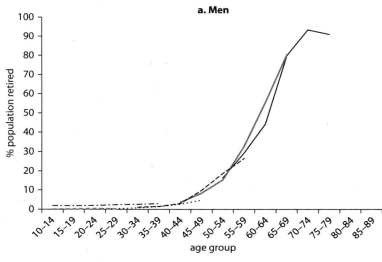

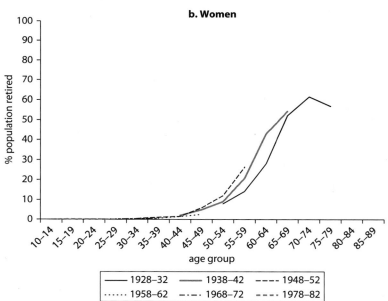

Source: Soares (2010).

Figure 2.22 illustrates the systematic pattern of reduction in the incidence of retirement at earlier ages and increase at later ages for urban men between 1982 and 2007. On the other hand, the retirement rates for people aged 60 and up have increased for men and women as a result of the expansion of pension coverage.

Taken together, the evidence suggests that movements in labor supply across cohorts in Brazil have not been intimately linked to changes in retirement decisions. For women, movements along all margins seem to be driven by the increased labor force participation associated with emancipation of women across various social fronts. For men, even though there has been a reduction in labor supply in the intensive margin (hours), this reduction has been observed throughout the period and across all age groups, even very young ones. Retirement in turn experienced an increase associated with increased access to pensions, but at the same time was slowed down through the reduction in the incidence of early retirement. In the face of these trends, changes in retirement behavior do not seem to be driving the changes observed in the labor market. This may be related to the peculiarity of the Brazilian system, where official retirement bears no implications for withdrawal from the labor force. As Oliveira et al. (2004) note, the absence of retirement

Figure 2.22   Brazil: Percentage Change in the Share of Retired Urban Men, 1982–2007

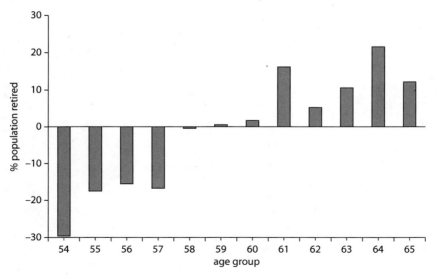

Source: PNAD (IBGE); author's elaboration.

penalties for individuals who continue to work in Brazil weakens the relationship between retirement (and collecting pensions) and labor force participation.

Figure 2.23 presents the age-specific labor force participation of retirees for different cohorts and for men and women separately. Looking at retired men born in 1938–42, labor force participation ranges from 41 percent at age 50–54 to 38 percent at age 65–69. Looking at the numbers for the entire population (used to construct figure 2.19) for this same cohort, male labor force participation is 87 percent at age 50–54 and 43 percent at age 65–69. So retirement seems to be associated with exceptionally low labor force participation only at younger ages associated with early retirement, but not so for later ages. Given that the incidence of retirement is lower at these younger ages, the overall relationship between retirement and labor force participation does not seem to be particularly strong. In addition, if anything, the evidence from figure 2.23a suggests that the labor force participation of retired men in age groups up to 65–69 has been increasing for recent cohorts. So, for example, the labor force participation at age 55–59 was 32 percent for the 1923–27 cohort and 40 percent for the 1948–52, while the labor force participation at age 60–64 was 29 percent for the 1918–22 cohort and 47 percent for the 1943–47 group.

Figure 2.23   Brazil: Labor Force Participation of Retired Men and Women, 1982–2007

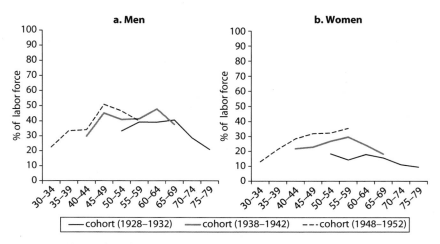

Source: PNAD (IBGE); author's elaboration.

For women (figure 2.23b), there has been a consistent increase in the labor force participation of retirees across cohorts. The figure shows the overall increase in female labor force participation. Compared to overall labor force participation, the differences here are even smaller than those observed for men. Also, the increase in the age-specific labor supply of retirees across cohorts has been much more marked for women than men. In the age group 55–59, for example, the labor force participation of retired women increased from 13 percent in the 1923–27 cohort to 35 percent in the 1948–52 cohort.

However, the majority of retired workers are employed in the informal sector, as can be seen in figure 2.24. Informality is closely linked to age and retirement (see details of informality in Brazil in chapter 5, box 5.1). Mesquita and Neto (2010) argue that as employer contribution rates are high and workers already receive social security benefits, there is a strong incentive to evade social security taxes, with the employer paying part or all wages off the books. Among the self-employed it is even easier to do so.

Mesquita and Neto (2010) suggest that social security rules, together with the increase in eligibility for social security benefits deriving from the increase in the labor force participation, are the factors responsible for the increase in early female retirement (that is, before age 60). Women can retire five years earlier than men, with a contribution period five

Figure 2.24   Brazil: Retirement, Informality, and Labor Force Participation

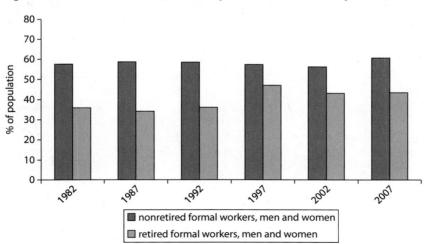

Source: Soares 2010.

years shorter than men's. The argument behind different retirement rules is that women work both outside and inside the household and suffer discrimination. However, many women are single or have domestic helpers in their households, and as more women enter the labor market, discrimination should decrease. Old age retirement should be used as an instrument to compensate for the lack of capacity to work due to old age and it is not an efficient mechanism to compensate for gender discrimination in the workplace or at home. The authors argue that a larger proportion of women in the labor market will result in a lower retirement age, a shorter average contribution period, and longer periods in retirement, because women are entitled to retire younger and have longer life expectancy than men. At the same time, it is important that social policies, including retirement legislation, do allow compensating women for a shorter contribution period, for example, for time spent in childbearing.

The adverse effect of social security rules on labor market behavior becomes clear in a comparison of Brazil to other countries. Although the incidence of early retirement of urban men decreased in Brazil between 1982 and 2007, in comparison to OECD and other LAC countries, Brazilians still retire much earlier. Table 2.8 shows the minimum age of retirement and the expected duration of retirement for Brazil, OECD, and LAC countries. For men, the average minimum age of retirement is 62.1 years in LAC and 63.9 years in OECD countries, while the average age of retirement based on time of contribution in Brazil is 54.4 years. For women the difference is ever greater, as the average age of retirement in Brazil based on time of contribution is 51.3 years, while the average

Table 2.8   Minimum Age and Expected Duration of Retirement, circa 2005

Country or Regional Group	Minimum age of retirement (years)		Expected duration of life after retirement (years)	
	Men	Women	Men	Women
OECD (29 countries)	63.9	62.6	16	20.8
LAC (7 countries)	62.1	60.4	16.7	20.9
Other (66 countries)	62.3	59.9	15.8	21.1
Brazil				
retirement based on time of contribution (avg. age at retirement)	54.4	51.3	23	29.2
retirement based on age				
rural	60	55	19.1	25.9
urban	65	60	15.9	22.1

Source: Rocha and Caetano 2008.

minimum age in LAC is 60.4 years and in OECD countries 62.6 years. Examining Brazilian urban men retirement data based on age shows that the minimum is 65 years old, not much different from OECD and LAC countries.[8] The expected duration of retirement based on age in Brazil is 15.9 years, against 16.7 years in LAC and 16.0 years in OECD countries. Meanwhile, for women, the expected duration of retirement is slightly higher in Brazil than in the other countries and is still worse for rural workers. But what makes Brazil an outlier is retirement data based on time of contribution. This pattern is explained by the fact that in Brazil there is no minimum age requirement to receive this kind of benefit. For example, on average, a woman in Brazil who retires based on time of contribution receives her pension for 29.2 years, against 20.8 in OECD and 21.1 in LAC countries (Rocha and Caetano 2008).

However, when another measure of labor market behavior is used, that is, the unused labor capacity of older workers, Brazil is not that different than OECD countries. The measure proposed by Gruber and Wise (1999) is calculated by summing up the proportions of individuals out of the labor force aged 50–69 and dividing it by 19. The measure is interpreted as follows. Assuming the unused capacity measure between ages 50 and 69 in a particular year is 50 percent, it means that a cohort experiencing the labor force participation rates in that year for their whole life would work only 50 percent of their potential lifetime working years.

Table 2.9 shows that the unused labor capacity and the percent of males out of the labor force at age 59 vary substantially across the 11 countries studied by Gruber and Wise (1999). Unused labor capacity

Table 2.9   Unused Labor Capacity and Men not in the Labor Force (LF), circa 2000

Country	Unused LF 55–65 (percent)	Men not in LF at age 59 (percent)
Belgium	67	58
France	60	53
Italy	59	53
Netherlands	58	47
United Kingdom	55	38
Germany	48	34
Spain	47	36
Canada	45	37
United States	37	26
Sweden	35	26
Japan	22	13
Brazil	**40**	**36**

Source: Queiroz and Figoli (2010).

for ages 55–65 ranges from 67 percent to 22 percent, and the percentage of men out of the labor force at age 59 ranges from 58 percent to 13 percent, for Belgium and Japan, respectively. Brazil compares to those countries on the lower end of the distribution. The unused labor capacity in Brazil is similar to those observed in the United States and Sweden, 37 percent and 35 percent, respectively. The percentage of males out of the labor force at age 59 in Brazil is higher than that of the United States (26 percent) and very similar to the levels in the United Kingdom (38 percent), Germany (34 percent), Spain (36 percent), and Canada (37 percent).

In summary, the evidence shows that although the Brazilian population has incentives to retire earlier than those in other LAC and OECD countries, labor force participation at older ages in Brazil is comparable to those countries. This happens because most Brazilian workers continue to work after they retire. To better understand the determinants of retirement and labor force participation in Brazil, the next sections look at the profile of health and productivity over the life cycle. The goal is to understand to what extent retirement and labor force participation decisions are driven by a worsening of health at later ages and by reductions in labor market productivity.

Notes

1. As an example, in the period 2005–10, Brazil's mortality rates appear to be similar to those of Bolivia and Haiti, if the gross mortality rate is the measurement used. However, in Brazil, life expectancy (which measures mortality without the effect of the age structure) is actually 73.5 years, whereas life expectancy numbers in Bolivia and Haiti are 60 years and 65 years, respectively.

2. Life expectancy at birth for Brazil and states in Brazil was estimated using the survival children method proposed by Brass (1975), with the Trussel variant and the Brazilian model life-table.

3. Since the age structure of the population is mainly a result of previous levels of fertility, those levels will continue to have an impact even when fertility levels have reached the replacement rate.

4. For countries that started the observation period (1950) with total fertility rate above 3 and ended the projection period (2050) with TFR below 2, dates corresponding to 3 and 2 children of TFR were obtained through linear interpolation. All other cases were obtained through linear extrapolation of the two extreme years.

5. Under the high-fertility variant, fertility is projected to remain 0.5 children above fertility in the medium variant over most of the projection period. By 2045–50, fertility in the high variant is therefore half a child higher than that of the medium variant. Under the low-fertility variant, fertility is projected to remain 0.5 children below the fertility in the medium variant over most of the projection period. By 2045–50, fertility in the low variant is therefore half a child lower than that of the medium variant.

6. This section draws heavily on Soares (2010), which looks at cohorts born within five-year intervals and documents the age-profile of labor force participation, hours of work, and retirement across six different PNADs: 1982, 1987, 1992, 1997, 2002, and 2007. So, for example, it tracks the history of the cohort born 1968–1972, from when it was aged 10–14 in 1982 until it was aged 35–39 in 2007, and similarly for other cohorts. The exercise is conducted for males and females separately.

7. Though the PNAD started in 1976, there were substantial changes in the first years of implementation, so it is difficult to create a consistent series starting in the 1970s.

8. The Brazilian pension system has a unique three-tier arrangement when it comes to eligibility conditions for retirement. There are three regimes: (1) retirement based on a minimum age (53M/48W) and a minimum number of years of contributions (30M/25W); (2) retirement based on a number of years of contributions (35M/30W) and no minimum age; and (3) retirement based on age (65M/60W) and a minimum number of years of contributions (15M/15W) (see Robalino et al. 2009).

References

Behrman, J. R., S. Duryea, and M. Székely. 2001. "Aging and Economic Opportunities: Major World Regions around the Turn of the Century." Proceedings of the IUSSP (International Union for the Scientific Study of Population) General Conference, Salvador, Brazil. August 18–24, 2001.

Beltrão, K. and S. Sugahara. 2010. "Demographic Transition in Brazil." Background paper prepared for the Workshop on Aging in Brazil, World Bank, Brazilia, April 6–7, 2010.

Brass, William. 1975. *Methods for Estimating Fertility and Mortality From Limited and Defective Data.* Chapel Hill, NC: Carolina Population Center, Laboratories for Population Studies.

Carvalho, J. A. M. 1996. "O saldo dos fluxos migratórios internacionais no Brasil na década de 80: uma tentativa de estimação." In *Migrações internacionais* v.2, ed. N. Patarra, 227–238. São Paulo: Oficina Editorial.

Carvalho, J. A. M., and M. B. Campos. 2007. "O saldo migratório internacional no Brasil na década de 1990." Trabalho apresentado no V Encontro Nacional sobre Migrações, Campinas, October 15–17, 2007. http://www.abep.nepo. unicamp.br/docs/anais/outros/5EncNacSobreMigracao/comunic_sec_2_sal _mig_int.pdf.

Comisión Económica para América Latina y el Caribe (CEPAL). 2008. "Transformaciones demográficas y su influencia en el desarrollo en América Latina y el Caribe." CEPAL, Santiago de Chile.

Gruber, Jonathan, and David A. Wise. 2007. *Social Security Programs and Retirement around the World: Fiscal Implications of Reform.* National Bureau of Economic Research (NBER) and University of Chicago Press.

IBGE (Instituto Brasileiro de Geografia e Estatística). 2008. "Características da população de origem japonesa." 2008. In *Resistência & Integração: 100 anos de imigração japonesa no Brasil,* 54–71. Rio de Janeiro: IBGE.

———. 2009. PNAD (Pesquisa Nacional por Amostra de Domicílios) 2008. IBGE, Rio de Janeiro; other years cited in text.

———. 2010. "Síntese de Indicadores Sociais. Uma Análise das Condições de Vida da População Brasileira 2010." Estudos e Pesquisa. Informação Geográfica e Socioeconômica 27. IBGE, Rio de Janeiro.

Merrick, T. W., and D. H. Graham. 1979. *Population and Economic Development in Brazil.* Baltimore, MD: The Johns Hopkins University Press.

Mesquita, R. A., and G. B. Neto. 2010. "Regulatory Shortcomings of the Brazilian Social Security." *Economic Analysis of Law Review* 1 (1): 141–60.

Oliveira, F. A. 1999. "Determinantes e Dinâmica do Gasto Social no Brasil: 1980/1996." Texto para Discussão 649, IPEA (Instituto de Pesquisa Econômica Aplicada), Brasília.

Oliveira, Francisco, Kaizô Beltrão, Sonoe Pinheiro, Fernanda Peyneau, and João Luís Mendonça. 2004. "O idoso e a previdência social." In *Os novos idosos brasileiros—Muito além dos 60?* ed. Ana Camarano, 412–26. IPEA (Instituto de Pesquisa Econômica Aplicada), Brasília.

Oliveira, J. de C. 2008. "Migração internacional, dinâmica demográfica e desafios para o dimensionamento da comunidade brasileira no exterior." Paper presented at the First Conference about Brazilian Communities Abroad. Rio de Janeiro. July 17–18.

Queiroz, B. L., and M. G. Figoli. 2010. "The Social Protection System for the Elderly in Brazil." Background paper prepared for the Workshop on Aging in Brazil, World Bank, Brasilia. April 6–7, 2010.

Robalino, D., E. Zylberstajn, H. Zylberstajn, and L.E. Afonso. 2009. "An Ex-Ante Evaluation of the Impact of Social Insurance Policies on Labor Supply in Brazil: The Case for Explicit over Implicit Redistribution." Social Protection Discussion Paper, World Bank, Washington DC.

Rocha, R. R., and M. A. Caetano. 2008. "O Sistema Previdenciario Brasilero: uma Avaliacao de Desemplenho Comparada." IPEA Texto Para Discussao 1331. IPEA (Instituto de Pesquisa Econômica Aplicada), Brasilia.

Soares, R. R. 2010. "Aging, Retirement, and Labor Market in Brazil." Background paper prepared for the Workshop on Aging in Brazil, World Bank, Brasilia, April 6–7, 2010.

United Nations. 2007. "World Urbanization Prospects: The 2007 Revision Population Database." UN Population Division, New York.

———. 2008. "World Population Prospects: 2008 rev." UN Department of Economic and Social Affairs, Population Division, New York.

Wajnman, Simone, Ana Maria Oliveira, and Elzira Oliveira. 2004. "Os idosos no mercado de trabalho: tendências e consequências." In : Os novos idosos brasileiros – Muito além dos 60? ed. Ana Camarano, 453–79. IPEA (Instituto de Pesquisa Econômica Aplicada), Brasília, 453–79.

Wajnman, Simone, and Eduardo Rios-Neto. 1999. "Women's Participation in the Labor Market in Brazil: Elements for Projecting Levels and Trends." Brazilian Journal of Population Studies 2: 41–54.

Wong, L. L. R., and J.A.M. Carvalho. 2006. "O Rápido Processo de Envelhecimento Populacional do Brasil: Sérios Desafios para as Politicas Públicas." São Paulo: Revista Brasileira de Estudos Populacionais 23 (1): 5–26.

World Bank. 2011. Population Aging: Is Latin America Ready? Directions in Development. Washington, DC: World Bank.

CHAPTER 3

Old Age Social Protection Programs and the Aging Challenge

All pension systems—pay-as-you-go or pre-funded, public or private, compulsory or voluntary—distribute the output of today's workers to today's retirees (Barr 2000). They are a part of a country's social protection system whose objectives are to allow individuals to smooth consumption and to prevent poverty among the elderly by guaranteeing a minimum level of income.

To achieve these objectives, pension systems are designed differently from country to country. In general, pension systems can be characterized by the way in which benefits are calculated and the method by which they are financed. In a "defined benefits system" (DB system) benefits are defined ex ante according to a formula that links the value of the pension to variables such as covered income and number of contributions. Alternatively, in a "defined contributions system" (DC system) the value of the pension is determined at the moment of retirement according to the accumulated assets resulting from contributions accrued during the working period, which are then transformed into a stream of benefits that take into account the life expectancy at that point. In both cases, benefits can be financed either by current contributions, that is "pay-as-you-go" (PAYG), or by savings or reserves accumulated before retirement "funded" accounts.

Beyond introducing a savings mechanism[1] and redistributing income, the various programs for the elderly have rules with implications for the rest of the economy. Indeed, savings decisions vary with people's preferences (that is, their personal discount rate), age, liquidity constraints, type of job, and life expectations, among others. Mandatory savings or social security contributions ensure that part of an individual's earnings is set aside to finance consumption by the elderly. Benefit formulas affect a person's willingness to participate in the system or to save privately for retirement. Workers' decisions in terms of sector of choice (formal or informal), as well as specific retirement decisions, are also affected by these rules, with consequences for workers' productivity and overall economic output. Non-contributory pensions are an instrument to prevent poverty in old age, but eligibility requirements and benefits levels may also affect workers' decisions.

Brazil's very generous public pension system has contributed to reducing poverty. The system extends benefit coverage to most of the elderly population and provides protection to poorer segments of society. Indeed, as shown in chapter 1, Brazil has almost completely eradicated poverty among the elderly. Public transfers, including pensions, have played a key role in achieving this.

These achievements of the old age social protection system come at a high cost: expenditure is very high compared to other middle-income countries or countries with similar age structure (figure 3.1). Expenditures

Figure 3.1   Demographic Dependency Ratio and Social Security Expenditure as Percentage of GDP

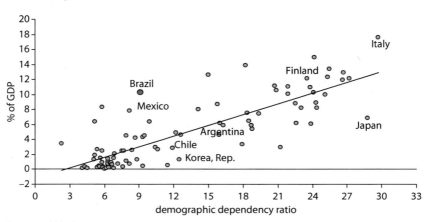

Source: World Bank 2006.

have increased significantly since 1988 when Brazil was spending 2 percent of GDP on pensions. Indeed, as for all components of the Brazilian welfare system, the 1988 Federal Constitution has been a defining moment for the pension system because it established a set of measures that expanded social security coverage, included previously excluded workers, and changed the determination of social security and assistance thresholds, in addition to introducing the indexing of these benefits to the minimum wage.

Over the next 40 years, Brazil's working population will have to support an increasing number of elderly who will represent an ever higher proportion of the population. The life cycle model described in chapter 1 identifies three phases in an individual's lifetime. During the first and the last, they are net consumers, whereas in the second they are net producers of output. Thus, the overall consumption in an economy relies crucially on the number and productivity of individuals in the second phase. The smaller the share of working-age population, the higher the burden, because it means more people in the economy are dependent on their production. Moreover, for a given share of working-age population, countries face very different prospects depending on the relative share of children and elderly. As shown in chapter 2, while the dependency ratio[2] in 2050 is predicted to be equal to the level in 1980, its composition will be very different. In 2050, about 30 percent of the population will be aged 60 and over, compared to less than 10 percent in 1980. This has very important implications for the economy as the lower birthrate will result in a smaller future labor force, and hence, all other things being equal, in a lower aggregate output in the future. This is bound to put more pressure on old age income support and to present some critical trade-offs in public policy.

Population aging poses important challenges to the pension system irrespective of how it is financed. In a public PAYG system, contributors receive promises from the government that future earmarked taxes (compulsory contributions) will provide them with goods and services in their old age. When tax revenue fails to meet pension promises, pensions have to be financed by debt and may become unsustainable. Contributors to a pre-funded pension system also obtain a claim on future output, but in a different way: they accumulate financial assets (bonds and equity) that are later sold to younger workers. If the supply of financial assets in the market increases because large numbers of retirees want to sell, all other things being equal, their price can fall, thus lowering the market value of the pension fund and of the assets accumulated by old people.[3]

While Brazil can currently afford the generosity of the system, demographic changes are bound to make the old age social protection system increasingly more expensive. The current system deficit is about 3 percent of GDP, a third of which comes from the non-contributory rural program. However, as chapter 6 will show, a scenario without further reforms predicts pension expenditures would reach more than 22 percent of GDP by 2050. This implies either a growing deficit and an inevitable crowding out of other types of expenditures or an increase in debt.

A reform of the system is unavoidable. In particular, the analysis in this study suggests that Brazil should move toward a more integrated social protection system, avoiding the dualism between informal workers being attended by social assistance and formal workers having access to social insurance. To be successful, a reform should (1) ensure a smoother and more proportional relationship between contribution and benefits, (2) ensure horizontal equity and transparency, (3) increase the participation in social insurance programs, and (4) promote savings.

While chapter 6 will present the public finance implications of the increasingly larger share of Brazil's old age population, this chapter describes how Brazil's social protection system for the elderly is organized to achieve its goals and how it affects individuals' economic behavior, and then details the main shortcomings of the system that should be addressed to increase its effectiveness and efficiency in light of the upcoming rapid aging of the population.

Structure of Brazil's Social Protection System for the Elderly[4]

In a 1994 book, the World Bank argued that the best way for most countries to meet the challenges of an aging world is through a multi-pillar taxonomy of old age security comprising: (0) a mandatory tax-financed public program designed to alleviate poverty; (2) a mandatory funded, privately managed program (based on personal savings accounts or occupational plans) for savings; and (3) a supplementary voluntary option (through personal saving or occupational plans) for people who want more protection (see table 3.1) (World Bank 1994; Holzman and Hinz 2005). In this multi-pillar taxonomy, the Brazilian pension system would be defined as a system with sizable zero and first pillars, no second pillar, and a third pillar of moderate size (see table 3.2).

The main objectives of the zero pillar are redistribution and poverty alleviation. It comprises the minimum pension provided to formal contributors, the rural pension program, and the social assistance benefits to

Table 3.1   Pillars of Old Age Income Security

Pillar	Objective	Financing	Program features
0	Poverty alleviation and redistribution	Government	Mandatory, public managed, means tested, minimum benefits
1	Income replacement and some redistribution	Contribution—PAYG or partially funded	Mandatory, publicly managed, defined benefits or notional defined contribution, earning-related benefits
2	Income smoothing through savings	Tax-preferred private savings or insurance; fully funded	Mandatory, privately managed, defined contribution, benefits equal contributions plus returns of investment
3	Income smoothing through enhanced savings	Tax-preferred private savings; fully funded	Voluntary, privately managed, defined benefits or contribution, benefits equal contributions plus returns of investment

Source: World Bank 2006.

the poor elderly. These programs cover large numbers of workers who move in and out of informality during their working lives, and they entail a significant degree of redistribution. The rate of subsidization differs according to the program: the social assistance program is totally subsidized, the rural program strongly subsidized (revenues cover about 10 percent of expenditures), and the minimum pensions for urban workers partially subsidized (workers need to contribute for 12 years to be entitled to the minimum pension).

The first pillar comprises the mainstream programs of the General Regime of Social Security (RGPS) and the Social Security Own Regimes (RPPS). These are contributory programs with mandatory participation, managed by the public sector, and operating on a defined benefit basis. The RGPS comprises all private-sector workers who participate in formal social security (self-employed workers, domestic workers, rural workers) and those participating on an elective basis. It is administered by the National Institute of Social Security (INSS) and is compulsory for formal sector workers.

The RPPS comprises government employees at the federal, state, and municipal levels. These programs are administered by the respective governments and are compulsory for civil and military government workers. The Brazilian pension system does not include a second pillar—a mandatory, fully funded, privately managed scheme. However, it does include a voluntary third pillar of moderate size involving closed and open[5] pension plans that work under a capitalization system.

Table 3.2   Structure of the Brazilian Pension System (World Bank Classification)

Zero pillar	First pillar	Second pillar	Third pillar
Regime for Private Sector Workers (RGPS = 7% GDP) Contributory PAYG Scheme for Urban Workers			
Zero pillar	*First pillar*		
• Minimum pension	• Old age pension based on length of contribution (LOC) rule (35/30) • Old age pension based on age rule (65/60) • Survivor pension • Disability-related pension		
Special Scheme for Rural Workers (Partially Funded by Earmarked Rural Taxes)			
Zero pillar	*First pillar*		
• Old age pension based on age rule (60/55) • Survivor pension • Disability-related pension			Closed occupational pension plans managed by single and multi-em-ployer pen-sion funds
Regime for Public Sector Workers (RPPS = 2% of GDP) Scheme for Public Sector Workers at Federal, State, and Municipal Levels of Government		None	
Zero pillar	*First pillar*		
• Minimum pension	• Old age pension based on length of contribution (35/30) and age rule (65/60) • Survivor pension • Disability-related pension		
Social Assistance (= 0.4 % of GDP) Non-Contributory Benefits to the Poor (RMV, BPC)			
Zero pillar	*First pillar*		
• Old age pension based on means test and age rule (65) • Disability pension based on means test			Open pension plans man-aged by in-surance com-panies

Source: World Bank 2006.

Achieving the Pension System Objectives

As mentioned earlier, pension systems have a dual objective: to prevent poverty among the elderly and to allow consumption smoothing. This section presents the different programs within the Brazilian systems that contribute the achieving these objectives.

Poverty Reduction, Redistribution (Zero Pillar)

As shown in chapter 1, poverty among Brazil's elderly has been almost eradicated, and social spending has played a significant role in reducing poverty and inequality over the last 10 years. The main programs for poverty prevention in old age are: (1) a means-tested benefit targeted to the elderly poor population, (2) a rural program, and (3) a minimum pension guarantee and benefit top-up to workers who have contributed for a specified number of years. These benefits go primarily to low-income workers, both rural and urban, who move in and out of informality during their working lives.

Means tested benefit. The benefit targeted to the elderly poor is the *Benefício de Prestação Continuada* (LOAS-BPC or BPC). It was established by law in 1993 and implemented in January 1996 in substitution for a previous problem targeted to the elderly, the *Renda Mansal Vitalicia* (RMV).[6] It is a temporary social benefit for the disabled and the elderly over age 65 with per capita family income of less than 25 percent of the minimum wage. After qualifying for the program, an individual is entitled to receive a monthly transfer equal to the minimum wage for as long as she/he qualifies for it. Legislation requires a revision of eligibility every two years.

LOAS-BPC is a well-targeted program that has grown since 2003 and now covers about 7 percent of the elderly population. The value of the benefit for LOAS-BPS recipients has increased faster than the average value of benefits for retirement and survivors' pension: 93 percent compared to 49 percent between 2003 and 2009 (table 3.3). This faster increase results from linking the benefit to the minimum wage, which experienced substantial growth over the last decade.

Since 1996 expenditure on LOAS-BPS increased faster than the number of beneficiaries. The number of elderly beneficiaries rose from about 0.5 million in 1996 to more than 1.5 million in 2009, while expenditure increased five times faster, from 56 million to 750 million over the same period. The reasons for these increases are: (1) the reduction in the

Table 3.3   Brazil Pension System: Percent of Elderly Benefiting and Value Received, 2003–09

% of elderly (60+) and average value of benefits

% Elderly population[a]	2003	2004	2005	2006	2007	2008	2009
Retirement	72.57	71.52	71.75	70.48	69.55	68.70	69.23
Survivor Pension	32.70	32.09	31.79	31.03	30.52	29.82	29.90
LOAS and RMV							
(Elderly)	5.22	6.31	6.72	6.92	3.07	3.25	3.03
Average value (monthly R$)							
Retirement	462.37	498.80	520.26	559.76	588.10	634.67	683.89
	(1.00)	(1.08)	(1.13)	(1.21)	(1.27)	(1.37)	(1.49)
Survivor Pension	366.59	401.25	422.42	464.18	492.32	536.67	582.13
	(1.00)	(1.09)	(1.15)	(1.27)	(1.34)	(1.46)	(1.59)
LOAS and RMV	240.99	260.99	301.14	351.05	381.12	414.63	465.71
(Elderly)	(1.00)	(1.08)	(1.25)	(1.46)	(1.58)	(1.72)	(1.93)

Source: *Statistical Yearbook of the Social Security, Historical Volume* (AEPS); PNAD (IBGE, various years 2003–10).
a. The fact that the aggregated percentage exceeds 100 percent is due to the possibility of benefits accumulation provided by legislation.

Figure 3.2   Beneficiaries and Expenditure for LOAS-BPC Elderly, 1994–2010
(December of each year)

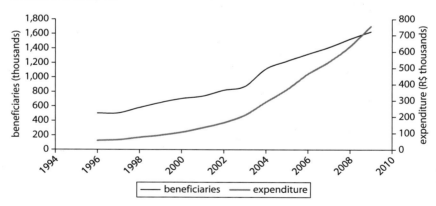

Source: Giambiagi and Tafner 2010.

minimum age requirement from 70 to 65,[7] (2) the exclusion of BPC benefits received by other family members in the calculation of familial per capita income, and (3) the increase in the minimum wage (see figure 3.2). However, the total expenditure for BPC is still rather small compared to the rest of the pension system: about 1 percent of GDP if considering both elderly and disabled beneficiaries, or about 0.6 percent for elderly only.

Rural pension program. The 1988 federal constitution established guidelines for social security reform that reduced the existing differences in the treatment of rural workers. It decreased the minimum retirement age for both men and women, increased the benefit floor to minimum wage, and extended access to the length of service (now length of contribution) benefits. These changes resulted in a substantial inflow of rural retirees in the system and an increase in spending. From 1990 to 1993 the number of rural pension beneficiaries almost doubled, mainly due to the lower eligibility requirement (see figure 3.3). This program has contributed substantially to extending coverage to a large segment of the population and to poverty reduction. Though formally a social security benefit, the old age pension to rural workers is really a social assistance program since rural workers are basically exempt from having to make contributions (Mesquita and Neto 2010). It is partly financed by taxes on agriculture sales but it is also strongly subsidized (revenues cover about 10 percent of expenditures). The cost of the rural program is about 1 percent of GDP.

Minimum pension. The Brazilian system also includes a minimum pension guarantee equal to the minimum wage that is provided to members

Figure 3.3   Rural Pension Beneficiaries, 1980–2008

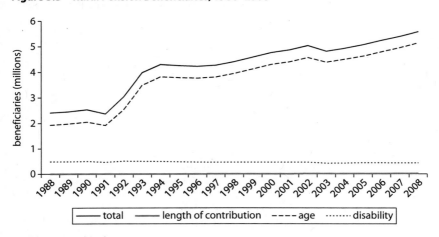

Source: Queiroz and Figoli 2010.

of the RGPS and RPPS. The rate of subsidization varies. For rural workers it is almost completely subsidized, while for urban workers it is
partially subsidized, since workers need to contribute for 12 years to
be entitled to it. This minimum benefit is indexed to the minimum
wage, while benefits above the minimum are indexed to consumer
prices. A large share of beneficiaries receives exactly a minimum wage
(almost two-thirds of retirement and survivor's pension are equal
exactly to the minimum wage) (see table 3.3). Indeed, more than half
of all individuals whose income is equal to the minimum wage are not
in the labor force (figure 3.4).

Establishment of the minimum pension has certainly contributed to
lifting elderly out of poverty, especially in rural areas. The nominal
values increased more than seven-fold between 1994 and 2010, and
the real value increased three times during the same period (table
3.4). The real value of pensions above the minimum wage increased
by 25 percent between 1995 and 2010 (Giambiagi and Tafner 2010),
while the minimum wage increased by 120 percent. Inevitably, it has
also contributed to increasing pension expenditures. Since the minimum wage has increased substantially over the last 15 years and at a
faster rate than inflation, it has contributed to reducing inequality
among the elderly because the higher levels of benefits have not seen
the same increases.

The expenditure on transfers equal to the minimum wage has more
than doubled over the past 10 years (figure 3.5). LOAS-BPC, which since

Figure 3.4   Distribution of Minimum Wage Earners as Percentage of Total Population

Source: Giambiagi and Tafner 2010.

Table 3.4   Nominal and Real Minimum Wage, 1994–2010
correlated with retirement and survivor pension benefits of value equal to one minimum wage as % of total

Year	Nominal value	Minimum wage deflated by INPC	Accumulated real variation[a]	Quantity (%)	Value (%)
1994	70	70.00			
1995	100	81.54	22.63		
1996	112	96.40	16.18		
1997	120	104.30	15.05		
1998	130	108.61	19.69		
1999	136	112.83	20.54		
2000	151	118.86	27.04	63.0	33.0
2001	180	126.30	42.52	63.9	35.4
2002	200	138.58	44.33	63.0	34.9
2003	240	164.27	46.10	62.3	34.4
2004	260	175.87	47.84	61.9	34.2
2005	300	187.50	60.00	62.9	36.3
2006	350	193.52	80.86	63.9	39.0
2007	380	199.90	90.09	64.3	40.1
2008	415	209.84	97.77	64.3	40.7
2009	465	222.26	109.22	64.5	41.1
2010[b]	510	229.93	121.81	64.8	41.3

Sources: Ipeadata; IBGE; *Statistical Yearbook of the Social Security* (AEPS 2009). For 2009, *Social Security Statistical Bulletin* (BEPS) (MPAS 2009).
Notes: a. Compares the adjustment noted with the accumulated INPC (*Índice Nacional de Preços ao Consumidor*, national consumer price index) variation between the preceding adjustment and the previous month.
b. For 2010 the January–March average was employed.

2004 includes RMV, grew from 0.08 percent in 1997 to 0.6 percent in 2009. INSS expenditures, which include the rural pensions and the minimum pension to urban workers, more than doubled during this period, from 1.17 percent to 2.74 percent of GDP.

The consensus among researchers is that pension transfers, especially the rural pension program, have been a key factor explaining the substantial decline in poverty rates in Brazil. They also help to explain why Brazil has one of the lowest old age poverty ratios in Latin America. At the same time, researchers also agree that Brazil's redistributive pension programs are not as cost-effective as they could be, and that poverty would decline further if resources were reallocated to better targeted programs. The proportion of old people in poor families is small, which implies that non-contributory pensions may not be the best way to reduce general poverty, since most of these pension benefits are not shared within families (World Bank 2010).

Figure 3.5   Expenditure in Benefits Equal to the Minimum Wage, 1997–2009

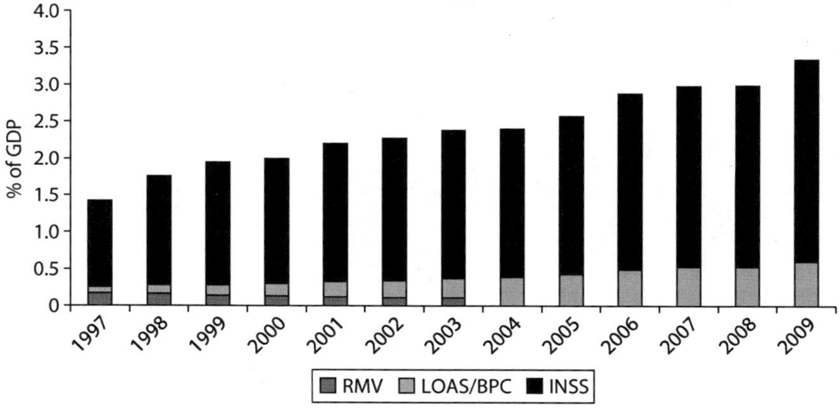

Source: Giambiagi and Tafner 2010.

Consumption Smoothing (First Pillar)

The two mandatory regimes, RGPS and the RPPS, offer the full range of pension benefits, including old age, survivor, and disability pensions, as well as short-term sickness benefits. RGPS, administered by the INSS, is the central component of Brazil's pension system. It has more than 40 million contributors: private-sector workers, self-employed workers, domestic workers, rural workers, and those participating on an elective basis. The RPPS comprises government employees at the federal, state, and municipal levels. It is administered by the respective governments and is compulsory for government workers (civil and military). It has about 5 million contributors. The total contribution rate charged on participating workers is 31 percent of gross wages, of which 11 percent is paid by the employee and 20 percent by the employer. There are also elective regimes aimed at those who want benefits to complement the government programs. The complementary pension system still plays a modest role, covering only about 5 percent of the labor force and providing additional benefits primarily to higher income workers.

RGPS has eight times as many beneficiaries as RPPS but its expenditures are only 3.5 times higher (7.2 vs. 2.0 percent of GDP). However, RPPS expenditures doubled between 1992 and 1994, but have remained roughly constant ever since, while RGPS expenditures increased from 2.5 percent of GDP in 1988 to 7.2 in 2009 (figure 3.6).

Figure 3.6   Expenditures for RGPS and RPPS, 1991–2009

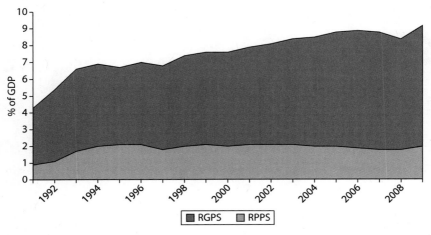

Source: Giambiagi and Tafner (2010).

The deficits of the two systems were very similar in 2009: RPPS showed a deficit of –1.7 percent of GDP, and RGPS (which is managed by the Instituto Nacional do Seguro Social, INSS), –1.4 percent. The total deficit was –3.1 percent (figure 3.7). Hence the government transfers to the two systems were of similar dollar amounts, even though per capita the RPPS was much higher. However, the trend is changing: the RPPS expenditure has remained roughly constant since the mid-1990s, while the RGPS deficit has gone from 0 in 1997 (expenditure and revenues from contributions were both equal to 5 percent of GDP) to the current –1.4 percent. Union transfers have increased substantially to finance the increase in expenditures.

Pension system coverage. Coverage has to be considered from two perspectives: the contribution phase, as individuals work, and the benefit phase, as they retire. The census data[8] from 1960 to 2000 show a substantial increase in the percentage of individuals contributing to social security in 1980, but no substantial change after that (figure 3.8). In 2000 more than half the working-age population was not contributing to social security.

In the benefit phase, Brazil has achieved almost universal coverage of the old age population.[9] The number of beneficiaries has increased dramatically since 1960. While only about 20 percent of individuals 65 and

Figure 3.7   Expenditure and Revenues: RGPS and RPPS, 2009

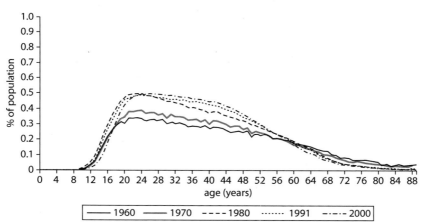

Source: Giambiagi and Tafner 2010.

Figure 3.8   Percentage of Individuals Contributing to Social Security, 1960–2000

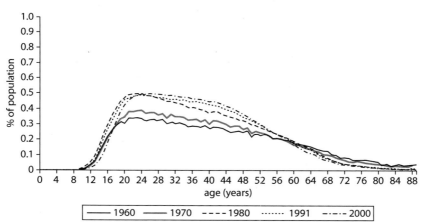

Source: Queiroz and Figoli 2010.

older were receiving some type of public pension in 1960, this percentage was more than 85 percent in 2000. Big jumps in number of recipients were observed after the centralization of the program under the supervision of the federal government (1970s) and following the changes in the constitution of 1988 (figure 3.9).

Compared to the average for the rest of LAC, Brazil presents a higher coverage in both benefit and contribution phases[10] (tables 3.5 and 3.6):

Figure 3.9   Percentage of Individuals Receiving Any Type of Public Pension, 1960–2000

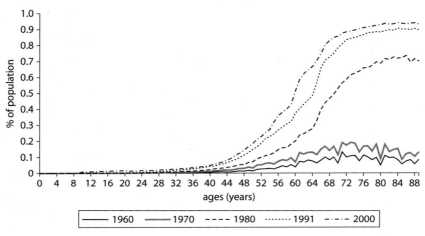

Source: Queiroz and Figoli 2010.

Table 3.5   Coverage in the Contribution Phase: Brazil and Rest of LAC

Countries	Contributors as % of labor force				
	Total (%)	*Men (%)*	*Women (%)*	*Urban (%)*	*Rural (%)*
Latin America[a]	30.1	30.9	28.9	34.4	16.7
Brazil	**44.7**	**46.3**	**42.4**	**49.9**	**17.3**

	Quintile (%)				
	1	*2*	*3*	*4*	*5*
Latin America[a]	12.5	21.1	29.4	38.1	49.2
Brazil	**17.0**	**35.7**	**46.1**	**57.2**	**67.2**

Source: Rofman and Lucchetti 2006.
Note: a. The average for Latin America excludes Brazil.

44.7 percent of the labor force contributes to social security, compared to an average of 30.1 in the rest of LAC. This percentage is higher for men than women, in urban than in rural areas, and for the richer quintiles.

In the benefit case, the differences are much larger. In Brazil 86.7 percent of the population over 65 receives benefits, compared to an average of 34.9 percent in the rest of LAC (table 3.6). Indeed, while the rest of LAC has similar levels of coverage in the two phases, Brazil is different because coverage is twice as high in the benefit phase as in the contribution phase.

Table 3.6   Coverage in the Benefit Phase
beneficiaries/population 65 +

Countries	Beneficiaries as % elderly population (65 +)				
	Total (%)	Men (%)	Women (%)	Urban (%)	Rural (%)
Latin America[a]	34.9	40.7	29.9	40.4	18.1
Brazil	**86.7**	**89.9**	**84.2**	**85.6**	**92.1**
	Quintile (%)				
	1	2	3	4	5
Latin America[a]	14.4	22.7	31.4	39.6	50.1
Brazil	**78.8**	**90.5**	**90.9**	**86.7**	**86.5**

Source: Rofman and Lucchetti 2006.
Note: a. The average for Latin America excludes Brazil.

The actual imbalance in coverage in the phases can be seen in the so-called system dependency ratio (beneficiaries to contributors) and the old age dependency ratios (old age population to the working-age population). The latter is frequently used as a benchmark that mature pension systems should try to achieve.

Indeed, the ratios of beneficiaries to contributors for both RGPS and RPPS are high. Mature pension systems in the OECD have system dependency ratios that are twice as high as their old age dependency ratio (table 3.7). The situation in Latin America and Central Europe looks worse, with a system dependency ratio almost three times higher than the benchmark. However, these differences are even larger in Brazil, except for the urban RGPS. The low level of the old age dependency ratio and the very large difference between the system and the old age dependency ratios are consistent with the high coverage rate in the benefits phase and the low rate in the contribution phase.

The last available figures from the Brazilian Social Security Administration (2008) show that on average about 40 million workers contribute to the system and 23 million are beneficiaries (Queiroz and Figoli 2010).

Challenges to the Pension System of a Rapidly Aging Population

A well-designed pension system attempts to strike a balance between the level of protection it provides, the ability of the system to provide those benefits (sustainability), and the incentives that its rules imply for productive work and retirement decisions.[11] Given the great variety of pension arrangements available, the World Bank has devised a conceptual framework for the analysis of pension systems and pension reforms

Table 3.7   System and Old Age Dependency Ratios Across Country Groups

	System Dependency Ratio (% pensioners/ contributors)	Old Age Dependency Ratio (% pop. 65+/ pop. 15–64)	Difference between the Two Indicators (%)
OECD (10)	50.3	24.6	204
Latin America (9)	30.2	11.0	275
Central Europe (8)	62.0	21.3	291
Overall Average (27)	47.1	19.1	246
Brazil	**53.8**	**8.1**	**664**
RGPS	53.4	8.1	659
Urban RGPS	38.0	8.1	469
RPPS	57.0	8.1	704
Brazil excluding social assis.	48.4	8.1	598

Source: World Bank 2006.

(box 3.1). This conceptual framework facilitates assessment of the ability of any pension system to meet its objectives. Applied to Brazil, given the system characteristics discussed in the previous section, this framework showed that Brazil provides adequate benefits in the form of generous social insurance for an expanding formal sector and social assistance for the informal sector. These benefits are also predictable, since they are clearly defined in the regulation and even in the constitution. However, the generosity of benefits implies that the system is not likely to be affordable in the long run (especially in the context of the population's rapid aging process), which raises issues of sustainability and the robustness of the system to face shocks. In addition, given that the contributory system needs public subsidies to pay for the benefits it promises, the redistribution of public spending is not as progressive as it would be if all public subsidies were targeted to the poor or covered portions of the population otherwise not covered.

While the social insurance system is well integrated (World Bank 2010), Brazil's programs for the elderly were designed with little consideration of the impact that the elderly programs might have on the performance of others. For example, as will be shown later in more detail, the social insurance program rules are likely contributing to the growth in informality, and thus to the potential population eligible for social assistance. In the same vein, the rules of the non-contributory programs may exacerbate this problem, for example when they pay high benefits. As in many other countries, there is little coordination in the design of different

Box 3.1

World Bank Pension Conceptual Framework

The World Bank has developed over the years a conceptual framework based on its experience with analytical and operational work in pension reform. The Bank's experience suggests there are no universal solutions or a single model that can be applied to all settings, which is one of the reasons why it was useful to develop principles to guide this analysis. When considering potential modalities for pension systems, applying the conceptual framework starts with an assessment of the initial conditions, then applies the multi-pillar typology (see tables 3.1 and 3.2). The design of the system is then evaluated against primary and secondary evaluation criteria that allow responding to country-specific conditions, needs, and objectives. The primary evaluation criteria proposed in the framework are the following:

- **Adequacy:** Capacity of the system to provide benefits sufficient to prevent old age poverty for the elderly and consistent with a consumption smoothing objective for the vast majority of the population.
- **Affordability:** A system that is within the financial capacity of the society, does not unduly displace other necessities or result in untenable fiscal consequences.
- **Sustainability:** A system that is financially sound and can be maintained over a foreseeable horizon.
- **Equitability:** A system that provides progressive income redistribution consistent with social preferences and similar entitlements to participants across generations and income groups.
- **Predictability:** A system that provides benefits that are not subject to the discretion of policymakers or administrators and protects the retiree from inflation and as much as possible from longevity risks.
- **Robustness:** A system that has the capacity to withstand major economic, demographic, or political shocks.

The conceptual framework also prompts policy makers to consider the trade-offs among these criteria needed to achieve a balanced approach to pension analysis. Given that all pension systems are effectively claims against future economic output, it is important that the system design is as consistent with economic growth as possible. Thus, the conceptual framework has the following as secondary evaluation criteria: (1) minimization of labor market distortions, (2) contribution to savings mobilization, and (3) contribution to financial market development.

Source: World Bank 2008.

types of social insurance programs and among social insurance and social assistance programs. As the aging population puts pressure on the systems, it becomes ever more urgent to clarify the design of redistribution arrangements within the social insurance system and to ensure the compatibility with the design of social assistance programs. The existing rules of social insurance and social assistance programs in Brazil are likely to distort households' labor supply and saving decisions. They provide incentives to employees to reduce labor supply, avoid formal work, and reduce saving (World Bank 2010).

The social protection system for the elderly is characterized by a high level of subsidization. Many programs pay benefits with no proportionality to contributions. While the system has one non-contributory means-targeted program, LOAS-BPC, which is managed by the Ministry of Social Development but paid out by the INSS, many of the benefits paid under RGPS and RPPS are in fact highly subsidized. Indeed, many of the active benefits do not keep any proportionality to past contributions. For example, the old age pension to rural workers, though formally a social security benefit, is highly subsidized.[12] The constitutional provision that the minimum wage is the lowest value for any retirement or survivor benefits clearly implies a high level of subsidization.[13] Moreover, the fact that the benefit received by participants of the non-contributory program is also equal to the minimum wage can create disincentives to participation in the formal system.

The next sections discuss in greater detail three issues that should be addressed in order to improve the efficiency, coverage, equity, and affordability of the old age social protection system, which will put increasing pressure on the aging population. To be discussed are early retirement and its implications with an aging population, the effects of informality, and, finally, the level of benefits and their implications in terms of cost and incentives.

Early Retirement

Pension systems can affect labor supply by influencing retirement decisions.[14] Various factors ultimately influence retirement decisions, including minimum and mandatory retirement ages and vesting periods. However, benefit formulas play an important role as well by affecting the value of the pension at different retirement ages (see Bodor, Robalino, and Rutkowski 2008). For example, minimum pension guarantees that are large relative to earnings can encourage early retirement or reduce contribution densities (see Robalino et al. 2008). Delaying retirement imposes both costs and benefits, public and private. The private costs mainly consist of delaying "leisure." The private benefits include maintaining higher earnings while working as well as providing the potential for a larger pension eventually. Hence, depending on how their pensions grow as a result of their additional contributions, individuals have more or less of an incentive to delay retirement (World Bank 2010). There are also public benefits to delaying retirement that have to do with the sustainability of the system: workers contribute longer to the pension system as well as to the labor force, and consequently they will benefit for a shorter period of time, reducing the wedge between benefits and contributions.

Brazilian workers retire as soon as possible, once they reach the vesting period for contributions or the minimum retirement age.[15] The median retirement age[16] for males has declined from 69 years in 1960 to 63 years in 2000 (Querioz and Figoli 2010), which corresponds to an average decline of 1.5 years per decade (table 3.8). As discussed in chapter 2, the trend toward early retirement is a common feature of the labor market in developed nations, with OECD showing a steady decline in average retirement age from 1950 to 1995 (Sveinbjorn and Scarpetta 1999).

Chapter 2 demonstrated that the large deviations from international patterns happen in the LOC program, as there is no requirement of minimum age for retirement. Indeed, while the expected duration of retirement in the urban old age program is roughly in line with international averages, Brazil is one of the few countries in the world that maintains a large retirement program based entirely on years of contribution, and that has resulted in excessively long periods of retirement. Among retirees by LOC a large percentage of both men and women (73.1 and 78.2 percent respectively) did so with the minimum number of years of contributions necessary, 35 for men and 30 for women (tables 3.9 and 3.10). This results in very low average age for retirement by LOC, 54 for men and 51 for women and results in long expected duration of retirement (23 years for men and 29 years for women). This implies that on average

Table 3.8   Median Retirement Age, Males 1960–2000

Year	Brazil	USA	Italy	Germany	Japan	Netherlands
1960	69	66	65	65	67	66
1970	65	65	63	65	68	64
1980	65	64	62	62	67	61
1990	65	63	61	60	67	59
2000	63	63	61	61	67	59

Source: Queiroz and Figoli 2010.

Table 3.9   Frequency of Contribution for Retirees by LOC, Men, 2008

Time of contribution (years)	Percentage	Accumulated %
Up to 35	73.1	73.1
36	11.0	84.1
37	6.3	90.4
38	3.9	94.3
39	2.3	96.6
40 or more	3.4	100.0

Source: Giambiagi and Tafner 2010.

Table 3.10   Frequency of Contribution for Retirees by LOC, Women, 2008

Time of contribution (years)	Percentage	Accumulated %
Up to 30	78.2	78.2
31	8.5	86.7
32	4.8	91.5
33	2.9	94.3
34	1.7	96.0
35 or more	4.0	100.0

Source: Giambiagi and Tafner 2010.

women who retire under LOC contribute for almost as many years as they benefit.

Indeed, concerned with early retirement and with the need to control spending, the government initiated a pension reform in 1998–99 (box 3.2). The 1999 reform was centered on a new benefit formula, called the *fator previdenciário*[17] that links benefits more closely with contributions and the expected duration of the payout phase. The *fator* is a factor that adjusts the value of the benefits and depends on the contribution period and life expectancy at retirement. All else being equal, the higher the life expectancy, the lower the value of the benefit. The formula implies a 40 percent decline in replacement ratios for workers who do not increase the period of contribution, while rewarding workers who delay retirement and continue contributing. It is a way to encourage workers who reach eligibility to remain in the labor force. While the formula has some desirable properties, the link between contributions and benefits is obscured by suppressing the value of contributions paid early in the career and overvaluing those made just prior to retirement.

The formula also introduces substantial redistribution by favoring teachers, women, and older retirees with longer contribution histories. Despite creating an automatic actuarial adjustment, the design of the

Box 3.2

Pension Reforms

The increase in pension expenditures and deficits in the 1990s contributed to an overall increase in fiscal deficits and the public debt, leading to a crisis at the end of the decade. The crisis prompted the government to initiate a program of fiscal reforms, including pension reforms. The first important step was taken in December 1998 through Constitutional Amendment No. 20, which removed the generous benefit formula from the constitutional text and opened the way for further reforms. It also introduced a benefit ceiling in the RGPS, eliminated most special regimes, and introduced a minimum age of retirement in the RPPS (60 for men and 55 women) with a period of transition, as well as a minimum vesting period of 10 years in the RPPS. The second important step took place in November 1999 involving a reform to the RGPS. This reform was centered in a new benefit formula called the *fator previdenciário* that links benefits more closely with contributions and the expected duration of the payout phase. The third step was Constitutional Amendment No. 41 in 2003, which reformed the RPPS. This reform was aimed at reducing the growing expenditures in civil service pensions, especially at the level of states and municipalities, and reducing benefit inequalities. The reform harmonized RPPS and RGPS rules and by several measures that included a new benefit formula and indexation rules for new civil servants, stricter retirement conditions for existing workers, a reduction in survivor pensions above the RGPS contribution threshold, and the imposition of a special contribution tax of 11 percent on all pensioners.

Source: World Bank 2006.

fator previdenciário generates a pattern of evolution of social security wealth (SSW) that does not give strong incentives to delayed retirement. Soares (2010) calculates the SSW for a man 53 years of age with 30 years of contributions (not eligible for time of work pension) before and after the introduction of the *fator previdenciário*. As shown in Figure 3.10, before the reform, the SSW increases very timidly up to age 57 and then starts to decrease. After the reform, SSW increases more rapidly up to age 58, and then decreases much more slowly than before the reform. Therefore, incentives to postpone retirement were improved, but it is still the case that postponing retirement beyond age 60 results in diminishing pension wealth.

Figure 3.10   Social Security Wealth for Man Age 53 with 30 Years of Contributions

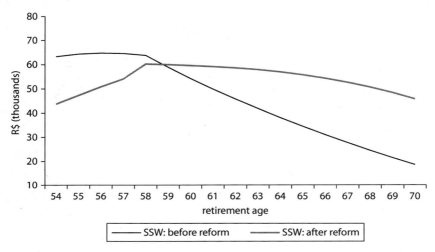

Source: Soares 2010.

Early retirement only becomes a problem when benefits for retirees are not commensurate with contributions. It is particularly undesirable in a country with an aging population, as it worsens the system dependency ratio, and hence the financing of the system. Demographic changes lead to a rising burden of dependency, and as chapter 6 will demonstrate, pose serious problems for public finances through pressure for expenditure on pensions, health, and other social services. Early retirement implies that individuals who could still contribute to the system start receiving benefits at a relatively young age. While we have seen that in Brazil often retirees continue to work, they do so in the informal sector and thus stop contributing to the system anymore. Moreover, the increase in life expectancy will result in longer average duration of retirement. Thus Brazil will have more retirees being so for a longer period of time.

With an aging population and a higher dependency ratio, Brazil will need to improve incentives for workers to work and contribute for longer periods of time. The activity rate of older workers is a key factor. Indeed, many countries are considering or raising the retirement age. This enables a system to both collect contributions over a longer period of time and to pay benefits for a shorter period of time (ISSA 2010).

However, it is important to avoid changes that may worsen the incentives of workers to contribute, such as increasing the vesting period to qualify for LOC. Rather than mandating longer contribution periods, the rules should reward such choices, for example with benefit premiums for years in excess of the minimum.

Clearly, even when benefit formulas are actuarially fair, individuals may still prefer to retire early. This has been demonstrated in several population and affiliate surveys that collected information in countries like Chile, where actuarially fair benefits dominate the pension landscape but early retirement is widespread. In general, other things being equal, early retirement is positively correlated with the likelihood of working after retirement, being formally employed during the worker's active life, and a preference for future versus present consumption. It is negatively correlated with preferences for consumption over leisure and being risk averse. Thus, when aging starts reducing the size of the working-age population, governments should consider subsidizing delayed retirement by increasing the implicit rate of return on contributions (see Robalino et al. 2009; World Bank 2010).

Informality in the Labor Force

While it has been progressing toward a more formalized workforce, a large share of Brazil's labor force is still in the informal sector. In 2009, out of the 84.4 million in the economically active population, only 56.6 million contributed to and were protected by social security. The design of pension systems also affects informality and contribution densities. Recent studies have argued that informality is not always the result of exclusion from the formal sector because some workers, after assessing the expected costs and benefits, deliberately choose informal work (see Perry et al. 2007). In general, by remaining in the informal sector, both employers and low-paid workers gain from not having to pay taxes or contribute to social security, but obviously workers lose access to its benefits. In the case of Brazil, however, some of the costs of choosing informality are reduced by the existence of the non-contributory pension program BPC.

Indeed, the fact that a worker who has never contributed to social security can receive a pension equivalent to one minimum wage, which is also the benefit floor for contributory pensions, is likely to create distortions in the decisions about whether to contribute or not during the years in the labor force. This incentive to avoid contribution is particularly strong for workers whose wage is close to the minimum wage, as their pension is likely to be equal to the minimum wage in any event, and hence contributing implies a cost without a corresponding benefit. Thus unskilled/low-wage earners are less likely to see benefits in formalizing, at least in terms of the benefits in terms of old age pension.

Camargo and Reis (2007) find evidence that the LOAS-BPC has reduced the probability that low-skilled, young, and/or self-employed individuals, who are more likely to be affected by it, will contribute to social security. The authors compare young, low-skilled, self-employed individuals with less education, who are likely to have been in the labor market for a short time and with low expectations of career advancement and salary increases, with higher skilled self-employed individuals who have more education and thus better career expectations, as well as with older self-employed people. They find that more educated workers did not alter their contribution, as they are more likely to participate in the contributory pension available to formal employees. The probability that they will contribute to social security is much lower for the young, less educated, who are more likely to benefit from the non-contributory program, because they will get a pension equal to the minimum wage without contributing. Excluding formal workers (*com carteira*), the percentage of workers contributing to social security has decreased between 1992 and 2004 (see table 3.11).

The ability of low-income individuals to choose between retiring by LOC or by age or using BPC programs, which all have the same minimum benefit, but require 35, 12, or 0 years of contribution, respectively, encourages benefit arbitrage and contribution evasion. The issue is most pronounced in the case of urban men, who would qualify for the same minimum benefit at the age of 65 either without contributing at all by claiming social assistance or with a 12-year contribution by retiring through the Age Rule program. Indeed, the minimum guarantee can also create incentives for workers to participate only until they have complied with vesting requirements and to evade thereafter (Holzman and Hinz 2005).

In the case of Brazil, Carvalho Filho (2008) shows that generous pension transfers can considerably reduce the supply of adult workers. Thus, the 1991 reform of the rural pension—which reduced the minimum eligibility age, increased benefits, and extended the program to non-heads of households—resulted in an increase of 25.4 percentage points in the number of rural workers aged 60–64 receiving pension benefits. In addition, the proportion of rural workers aged 60–64 who "did not work in the week of reference" increased by 12.56 percentage points, more than urban workers of the same age during the period immediately before and after the reform. In addition, "total hours of work in all jobs" for rural

Table 3.11   Workers Contributing to Social Security, 1992–2004
% of population

	1992	1996	1999	2004
Type of work				
Formal (*com carteira*)	98.54	96.59	100.00	99.99
Informal (*sem carteira*)	8.42	9.87	9.16	10.16
Employer	73.28	70.62	64.72	58.44
Self-employed	26.89	24.86	19.95	14.54
Years of Education				
0–3	40.93	36.94	33.91	26.61
4–7	56.13	51.02	47.47	40.45
8–10	66.40	59.90	57.29	51.39
11+	80.46	75.07	75.24	72.65
Age (years)				
18–24	52.24	49.39	49.26	45.71
25–29	62.43	58.04	58.28	55.07
30–39	64.81	60.41	59.50	55.39
40–49	64.57	61.52	59.69	54.80
50+	55.49	51.34	49.64	44.73
Sector of activity				
Industrial	80.29	75.88	74.02	68.77
Services	58.59	55.93	55.84	54.82
Commerce	56.81	53.78	51.96	50.82
Gender				
Men	63.15	58.48	56.51	51.81
Women	56.30	54.49	55.23	51.43
Salary				
<1 × Minimum Wage (MW)	17.47	9.26	6.23	4.31
Equal to 1 × MW	66.73	45.50	49.21	55.65
Btw 1 and 2 × MW	63.92	47.16	49.24	60.17
2 × MW	77.86	64.93	65.53	72.78
Btw 2 and 3 × MW	74.89	61.83	62.94	72.88
3 × MW	84.45	69.77	73.51	77.03
>3 × MW	83.03	72.26	75.37	74.77
Total	60.50	56.88	55.99	51.65

Source: Camargo and Reis 2007.

workers of the "affected age" decreased relative to urban workers by 5.80 hours per week during the period immediately before and after the reform (World Bank 2010).

Increasing the coverage of social insurance in Brazil is a necessary condition for the sustainability and effectiveness of high-quality safety net programs. Indeed, with an aging population it is particularly important to design ways to include informal workers in the contributory social insurance system in order to finance the increased expenditure and avoid increasing the tax wedge on workers already in the formal sector.

In Brazil, as in the other LAC countries, social protection systems need to be effective in an environment where informality is the norm for a large proportion of the workforce. This means, for example, opening up contributory social insurance to the population as a whole (rather than just to workers with formal employment contracts) and ensuring that any subsidies are transparent, equitable, and consistent with promoting work and savings. Such action will open the way to expanding the coverage of contributory social insurance and limiting the proportion of the workforce that needs to be assisted by non-contributory safety net programs (World Bank 2010). The expansion of coverage of contributory social insurance to workers in the informal sector would allow the system to increase its revenues and to boost savings.

Redistribution within and across Generations

Most public pension systems redistribute income, both within and across generations. They redistribute within a generation if the system has progressive contribution or benefit rules, or if there is minimum benefit or taxable income ceiling for contributions. Also, whenever general revenue taxes are used to finance a portion of the benefits, the distributive effect of the system will then depend on the distributive effects of these taxes. Between-generation redistribution, which is more common in PAYG systems, occurs, for example, when new cohorts of plan members receive lower rates of return on their contributions than older cohorts.

The de facto redistribution is as important as the stated consumption smoothing (insurance) function. However, this redistribution is often implicit and nontransparent and can be regressive. Within the insured populations, wide variations exist in the ratio of contributions paid to benefits received. The result is that, depending on earnings levels and on their behavioral responses to the incentives within the system, some plan members systematically receive more than they put in (an implicit subsidy), while others systematically receive less (an implicit tax) (World Bank 2010).

Indeed, there is a large difference in the Net Present Value[18] (NPV) of pension benefits across workers, depending on the type of work and type or retirement (table 3.12). Turra and Rocha (2010) construct an age-time matrix of benefits and taxes for each subgroup in the birth cohort,

Table 3.12   Net Present Value (NPV) by Type of Retiree

	Annual retirement benefit in 2000 (mean value) (R$)	Net present value at birth (R$)	% of all retirees in 1997
Retirement by age (urban)	5,848	5,848	7.0
Retirement by age (rural)	1,780	4,759	18.7
Retirement by LOC	7,854	6,058	14.1
Retirement (public servants, central government)	21,739	32,251	4.4

Source: Turra and Rocha 2010.

including cohort members retired due to age (urban and rural)—which are significantly more prevalent among low-skilled individuals—members retired by LOC, and public sector retirees (federal civil servants). All subgroups experienced positive NPVs, thus all have benefited from positive transfers made by younger generations. However, there are large differentials in life cycle gains, which is equivalent to saying that the relationship between contributions and benefit varies greatly. For example, the NPV for civil servants is about six times larger than that for private workers retired due to age. Moreover, the difference between the two groups is higher in terms of NPV than in terms of the average retirement benefit. This implies that public servants contribute less relative to private workers. On the other hand, the NPV for retirement by LOC is lower that its annual retirement benefit. This means that workers who retire by LOC have been paying larger social security contributions than workers who retire by age.

The value of pension benefits based on time of contribution is substantially higher than those based on other criteria (table 3.13). While the percentage of retirees by time of contribution is 12.8 percent of total retirees, the total values of these benefits is equivalent to 32.3 percent of the total. The value of survivor pensions is higher than those of retirement by age: 28 percent of pension benefits are paid to survivors compared to 34 percent for age. However, the value of the two types of benefits are both equivalent to 25 percent of the total.

A program that obviously entails a high degree of redistribution, and which also provides higher incentives to "game" the system, is the survivor pension. Survivors' benefits in Brazil represent a high share of total pension benefit. In 2009 Brazil spent R$101.6 billion (3.2 percent of GDP) for survivor benefits. This is equivalent to 25 percent of total social security expenditure and is 3.5 times higher than the average expenditure

Table 3.13   Percentage of Retirees by Pension Type

	Quantity		Value (R$ million)	
	Total	% of Retirees	Total	% of Retirees
Total by Retirement Program	**22,736,409**	**100**	**15016.4**	**100**
Retirement	**15,076,295**	**66.3**	**10370.8**	**69.1**
By age	7,856,916	34.6	3764.0	25.1
Disability	2,902,600	12.8	1757.6	11.7
Time of contribution	4,316,779	19.0	4849.3	32.3
Survivor pension	**6,457,846**	**28.4**	**3800.3**	**25.3**
Benefits	**1,130,431**	**5.0**	**815.0**	**5.4**
Sickness	1,078,270	4.7	790.8	5.3
Custodial	**25,516**	**0.1**	**9.7**	**0.1**
Accident	26,645	0.1	14.5	0.1
Maternity	**71,166**	**0.3**	**0.2**	**0.0**
Other	**671**	**0.0**	**0**	**0.0**

Source: Giambiagi and Tafner 2010.

in OECD countries for this type of pension. This program is very expensive compared to those in other countries because the rules fail to adjust benefits to the number and needs of dependents and also fail to prevent abuse of the system.

Indeed, survivor pension expenditures in Brazil are much larger than those in most other countries. As shown in figure 3.11, other countries spend on average 0.8 percent of GDP on survivor pensions, or less than 10 percent of total expenditures. Although the RPPS contributes to this outcome, the RGPS alone spends more on survivor pensions than such programs in other countries.

Survivor benefits are equivalent to the full value of the retirement pension paid or payable to the deceased and can be accumulated with the retirement benefit. For example, if both members of a couple are retired and one dies, the survivor is eligible for a survivor benefit. As suggested by Mesquita and Neto (2010), this produces two inconsistencies. One is that the per capita income of the dependents actually rises with the passing of the retired person. The other is that a benefit intended to support the dependents of the deceased who may not be able to support themselves is often paid to individuals who have other sources of income. Forty-four percent of beneficiaries of the survivor pension also have some other income, through work or their own retirement benefits (figure 3.12).

There is consensus that Brazil's redistributive pension programs are not as cost-effective as they could be and that poverty would decline

Figure 3.11   Survivor Pension Expenditures in Brazil vs. Other Countries
(% of GDP)

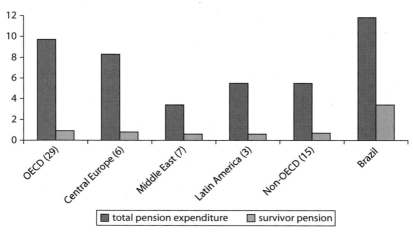

Source: World Bank 2006.
Note: Number of countries in parentheses.

Figure 3.12   Composition of Beneficiaries of Survivor Pensions

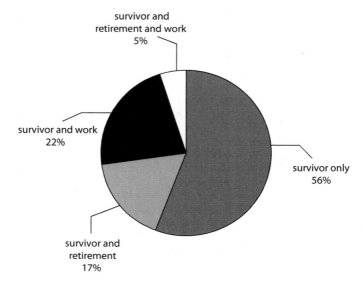

Source: Giambiagi and Tafner 2010 from the *Pesquisa Nacional por Amostra de Domicilio* 2006 (IBGE 2006).

further if resources were reallocated to better targeted programs. The proportion of old people in poor families is small, which implies that non-contributory pensions may not be the best way to reduce general poverty since most of these pension benefits are not shared within families.

The liabilities of a DB system consist of the current benefits paid to the retired population plus all the future benefits promised to partici-pants in the system when they retire. The generosity of the Brazilian pension system (urban, rural, and public sector), coupled with the coun-try's rapid aging, will mean that the cost of these liabilities will continue to increase in the near future. On the other hand, in a PAYG system, the assets that back the liabilities comprise all the contributions paid into the system by participants, current and future. The aging of the population implies that, while the working-age population increases, the value of this asset will also increase, but in due course, more people will exit than enter the workforce and the value of this asset will decrease.

While the generosity of the system is currently affordable for Brazil, given the favorable age structure, the demographic changes will have direct consequences for the old age social protection system. The system needs to address the issue of the relationship between contributions and benefits. Indeed, it should ensure a very smooth one, such that more con-tributions correspond to higher retirement benefits. The current rule that establishes equivalence between the minimum wage, the minimum pen-sion, and the value of the non-contributory program clearly works against such an ideal relationship.

If the value of benefits continues increasing at the pace of the last decade, pension expenditure will increase even faster because there will be an ever increasing number of elderly. While the expansion of coverage and the generous benefits have contributed to reducing poverty and inequality, moving forward the government will have to think about trade-offs. Anchoring the minimum pension to the minimum wage and its evolution may not be the most effective mechanism for poverty reduction. Indeed, as has been shown, poverty has been significantly reduced for the elderly; thus increasing the real value of their benefits can be a regressive policy.

Given the duality of the Brazilian labor market, the old age social pro-tection system is characterized by horizontal inequity. A low-skilled indi-vidual who has been earning a minimum wage in the formal sector throughout his or her career will receive the same pension as a similarly low-skilled individual who has worked in the informal sector. However, the former contributed to the social security during his working life whereas the second did not. This is a characteristic of the system that needs to be addressed, not just for "fairness" reasons but for the perverse incentives that it creates in terms of labor supply and contributions. Brazil can be praised for the existence of a non-contributory pension and a minimum pension that allow protection of individuals from the risk of old age indigence. However, the same system should also reward those workers who contributed to pay for it, for example, by ensuring that the non-contributory benefit is lower than the benefit received by workers who have a positive history of contributions.

The main challenge that affects the pension system in Brazil, given its design, is that the value of the PAYG asset is not aligned with the value of its liabilities. As chapter 6 will demonstrate, pension expenditures are projected to reach 22 percent of GDP by 2050. That the system cannot sustain its benefit level with its own contributions implies that it will increasingly rely on government expenditure to cover this gap. This raises the policy question of whether backing the solvency of the pension system for formal and public-sector employees is a priority for public-sector expenditure in the face of the multiplicity of needs in the country. Furthermore, increasing reliance on government transfers to pay for contributory pensions gives rise to distributive concerns about public spending, since participants in these pension systems are not the neediest segment of the population.

Conclusions

The analysis here shows that Brazil's expected rapid aging process over the next 40 years creates important challenges for the country's pension system. Income protection for the elderly means facing the tasks of improving its sustainability, providing more adequate incentives for longer productive careers, and improving its equity, while maintaining adequate benefits that ensure consumption smoothing and that protect individuals and their families from old age poverty. The good news is that the system has the basic components to achieve these objectives. The multi-pillar design of the system allows it to respond to the needs of different segments of the population. A more balanced reliance on non-contributory schemes and a strengthening of complementary voluntary schemes could provide incentives that are compatible with the aging process, and safeguard the adequacy of the benefits provided by the system. A more equilibrated scheme also would mean effectively sharing the risks that affect the pension system among all stakeholders: government, employers, and individuals. The increasingly aging population makes it more compelling to expand contributory social insurance coverage. Thus, vesting periods should be eliminated or substantially reduced to widen access to benefits.

Brazilian policy makers will need to consider the financial sustainability of non-contributory programs. The expansion of these programs has increased pension coverage and contributed to reducing poverty among the elderly. However, the aging of the population is expected to increase the costs of these programs. Therefore, their long-term financial sustainability will depend on how the level of the transfers and eligibility conditions evolve over time. Decision makers will also need to assess the incentive-compatibility of their rules with the goals of increasing coverage of contributory social insurance.

It is important to improve the management of implicit and explicit subsidies within the contributory system and those outside the contributory system. Because public resources are limited, it makes sense to focus the redistributive power of the pension system on those individuals who need it most. This means ensuring that benefits from the contributory programs are defined on the basis of past contributions, ending any implicit subsidies, and instead using limited public resources to supplement the benefits of workers with limited or no savings capacity. Resources that finance non-contributory pensions carry an opportunity cost because they are reallocated from other expenditures that may have higher social rates of return (such as prenatal care, early childhood development, and basic infrastructure). While assessing this opportunity cost is a difficult and probably elusive task, Brazil needs to take it into account in order to make efficient allocations of resources directed to continuing pursuing the goal of poverty reduction.

Notes

1. In a PAYG system the contribution rate is known as a payroll tax. In a contributory, earnings-related PAYG pension scheme, it is better to think of it as a contribution rather than a tax.

2. The dependency ratio relates the number of people in dependent age groups (children under age 15 and persons over age 59, in this study) to that of people in the working-age group (ages 15–59).

3. In a DC system, this decline translates automatically into a reduced real value of the pension benefit—thus contributors bear the risk. In a DB system, a crisis can erupt, despite pre-funding, when revenue from sales of bonds and equity is less than that required to meet pension promises and, once again, the promised benefits might become unsustainable (Willmore 2003).

4. This section is adapted from the 2006 World Bank Report, "Brazil: Towards a Sustainable and Fair Pension System" (World Bank 1996).

5. "Closed" pension plans are structured and supported by companies and usually restricted to their group of workers and former workers; "open" plans are operated by the private sector and open to any person who has been active in the RGPS.

6. The origin of the Brazilian social assistance pension program dates back to the early 1970s. The military regime had created a social assistance pension program in 1974–75, the *Renda Mensal Vitalícia* (RMV, or Lifelong Monthly Income), which was a basic flat-rate pension owed to those who were invalid or aged 70 and older, who were not able to provide for themselves or be provided for by their family. Individuals were required to document at least 12 months of contribution to social security throughout their working lives, which meant that only those who had previously worked entered the beneficiary group.

7. The minimum age requirement was reduced twice, in 1998 to 67 and in 2004 to 65.

8. Data from the 2010 census are not available at publication time.

9. Taking retirement and survivor pension benefits into account, approximately 96 percent of all persons 70 and over have social security protection. A residual of only 4 percent in this age group has no social protection. Among them, more than 70 percent are not poor and almost 15 percent are still working.

10. Note: These data come from household surveys and hence may differ from census data.

11. This section draws heavily on Mesquita and Neto (2010).

12. Individuals are supposedly required to provide proof of past work in the rural sector for a total period of at least 180 months and should be working as a rural worker at the time the benefit is claimed. However, in many cases it is virtually impossible to verify whether the claimant really worked as a rural worker for the required period or just lived in a rural area (Mesquita and Neto 2010). Thus workers are exempt from contributions, and the revenues from taxation of agricultural production account for less than 10 percent of expenditure.

13. Because more than two-thirds of Brazilian workers earn less than twice the minimum wage per month, in practice they retire with near full or full earnings (Mesquita and Neto 2010).

14. As discussed, in Brazil individuals can retire based on two rules: (1) Length of Contribution (LOC) and (2) Age. Under the LOC rule, pensions are awarded to men with 35 years and women with 30 years of contributions with no retirement age restrictions. Teachers must contribute only 30 years (25 for

women). Under the Age rule, urban contributors can retire at the age of 65 (men) and 60 (women) and rural workers at ages 60 (men) and 55 (women). Contribution vesting is being gradually increased from 12 to 15 years by 2011. For rural workers this contribution requirement is waived with a proof of rural residency, making this a strongly redistributive program (World Bank 2006). Indeed, the majority of workers retire with the Age rule pension rather than completing the vesting period for the LOC (World Bank 2009), despite the fact that the age pension is considerably lower than the LOC pension.

15. There is strong evidence that the rural social pension scheme reduced the labor supply in preretirement ages and induced retirement at early ages. When given the opportunity of earning a benefit that guarantees their subsistence, withdrawal from the labor force is found to be the preferred decision for about 40 percent of benefit recipients, despite the fact that benefits come with no strings attached (there is neither a means test nor a requirement to retire) (Carvalho Filho 2008).

16. The median retirement age is the youngest age at which less than 50 percent of the population is in the labor force (Burtless and Quinn 2001).

17. The formula for the *fator previdenciário* is:

$$Benefit = Fator \times WageBase$$
$$Fator = \frac{0.31PC}{LE}\left(1 + \frac{0.31PC + RA}{100}\right)$$

where *PC* is the period of contribution (women and male teachers get a five-year bonus; bonuses for female teachers add up to 10 years), *LE* is life expectancy at the age of retirement, *RA* is the retirement age, and Wage Base is an average of 80 percent of highest wages since 1994.

18. NPV is the difference between the present discounted sum of all benefits and the present discounted value of all social security taxes paid.

References

AEPS. *Anuário estatístico da previdência social : suplemento histórico (1980 a 2008)* (Statistical Yearbook of the Social Security, Historical Volume). Ministério da Previdência e Assistência Social. Empresa de Tecnologia e Informações da Previdência Social, Imprenta Brasília, DF.

Barr, N.A. 2000 "Reforming Pensions: Myths, Truths, and Policy Choices." IMF Working Paper 00/139, International Monetary Fund, Washington, DC.

Bodor, A., D. A. Robalino, and M. Rutkowski. 2008. "How Mandatory Pensions Affect Labor Supply Decision and Human Capital Accumulation: Options to Bridge the Gap between Policy and Economic Theory." MPRA Paper 12046, University Library of Munich, Germany.

Burtless, G., and J. Quinn. 2001. "Retirement Trends and Policies to Encourage Work Among Older Americans." In *Ensuring Health and Income Security for an Aging Workforce*, ed. P. Budetti, R. Burkhauser, J. Gregory, and A. Hunt, 375–415. Kalamazoo, MI: W. E. Upjohn Institute for Employment Research.

Camargo, J. M., and M. C. Reis. 2007. "Lei Orgânica da Assistência Social: Incentivando a Informalidade." In *Previdência no Brasil: Debates, Dilemas e Escolhas*, ed. Paulo Tafner and Fabio Giambiagi. Rio de Janeiro: Instituto de Pesquisa Economica Aplicada.

Carvalho Filho, I. E. 2008. Old-age Benefits and Retirement Decisions of Rural Elderly in Brazil, *Journal of Development Economics* 86 (1): 129–46.

Giambiagi, F., and P. Tafner. 2010. *Demografia: A ameaça invisível: o dilema previdenciário que o Brasil se recusa a encarar.* Rio de Janeiro: Elsevier.

Holzman, R., and R. Hinz. 2005. *Old-Age Income Support in the 21st Century An International Perspective on Pension Systems and Reform.* Washington, DC: World Bank.

IBGE (Instituto Brasileiro de Geografia e Estatística). 2006. PNAD (Pesquisa Nacional por Amostra de Domicílios). Rio de Janeiro: IBGE, other years cited in text.

ISSA (International Social Security Association). 2010. *Dynamic Social Security for the Americas: Social Cohesion and Institutional Diversity.* Developments and Trends. Geneva: ISSA.

Mesquita, R. A., and G. B. Neto. 2010. "Regulatory Shortcomings of Brazilian Social Security." *Economic Analysis of Law Review* 1 (1): 141–60.

Ministério da Previdência Social (MPAS). 2009. *Social Security Statistical Bulletin* 14 (12) (December 2009). MPAS, Brasilia.

Perry G. E., W. Maloney, O. S. Arias, P. Fajnzylber, A. Mason and J. Saavedra-Chanduvi. 2007. Informality: Exit and Exclusion. The World Bank, Washington, DC.

Queiroz, B., and M. Figoli. 2010. "The Social Protection System for the Elderly in Brazil." Background paper prepared for the Workshop on Aging in Brazil, World Bank, Brasilia, April 6–7, 2010.

Robalino, D., E. Zylberstajn, H. Zylberstajn, and Luis Eduardo Afonso. 2008. "An Ex-Ante Evaluation of the Impact of Social Insurance Policies on Labor Supply in Brazil: The Case for Explicit over Implicit Redistribution." Social Protection Discussion Papers 0929. World Bank, Washington, DC.

Rofman, R., and L. Lucchetti. 2006. "Pension Systems in Latin America: Concepts and Measurements of Coverage." Social Protection Discussion Paper 0616, World Bank, Washington, DC.

Soares 2010. "Aging, Retirement, and the Labor Market in Brazil." Background paper prepared for the Workshop on Aging in Brazil, World Bank, Brasilia, April 6–7, 2010.

Sveinbjorn, B., and S. Scarpetta. 1999. "The Retirement Decision in OECD Countries." OECD Economics Department Working Papers 202, Organisation for Economic Co-operation and Development, Paris, France.

Turra, C. M., and R. Rocha. 2010. "Public Transfers among Dependent Age Groups in Brazil. Background paper prepared for the Workshop on Aging in Brazil, World Bank, Brasilia, April 6–7, 2010.

Willmore, L. 2003. "Universal Pensions in Mauritius: Lessons for the Rest of Us." United Nations DESA Discussion Paper 32. Department of Economic and Social Affairs, United Nations, New York.

World Bank. 1994. *Averting the Old Age Crisis: Policies to Protect the Old and Promote Growth*. World Bank Policy Research Report 13584. New York: Oxford University Press.

———. 2006. "Brazil: Towards a Sustainable and Fair Pension System." unpublished report, World Bank, Washington, DC.

———. 2008. "The World Bank Pension Conceptual Framework." In *World Bank Pension Reform Primer*. Washington, DC: World Bank.

———. 2009. "Social Insurance and Labor Supply: Assessing Incentives and Redistribution." Technical report, World Bank, Washington, DC.

———. 2010. "From Right to Reality: How Latin America and the Caribbean Can Achieve Universal Social Protection by Improving Redistribution and Adapting Programs to Labor Markets." Directions in Development 55547, World Bank, Washington, DC.

CHAPTER 4

Health Care and Long-Term Care

The increases in life expectancy at birth (LEB) in the last few decades in Brazil have been impressive: a child born in 2008 can expect to live 10 years longer than one born in 1980. In the same 28 years, the median age of the Brazilian population increased from 20.2 to 28.8 and is projected to reach 35.8 in 2025 and 46.2 in 2050. This means that by the time a child born in 1980 reaches age 70, the median age of the Brazilian population will have more than doubled, an absolute increase of 26 years.

Recent estimates indicate that in a few years, LEB in Brazil will reach 75 years. By 2050 the LEB will be higher than 81 years, which is above the LEB enjoyed by the majority of the developed (aged) countries today. Furthermore, 2008 figures indicate that the LEB for a female child, 76.7 years, is 7.6 years higher than for a male child, 69.1 years. This is well above the differential that prevails for most of the world and reflects higher male mortality rates at all ages—particularly those for young adults who have high death rates from accidents and violence. If even some of such deaths could be prevented, a significant increase in overall LEB could be achieved.

However substantial the recent increases, Brazil's LEB is still considerably lower than that of other Latin American and Caribbean (LAC) countries, notably Argentina, Chile, Costa Rica, Cuba, and Uruguay, indicating that there is much room for improvement in Brazil (figure 4.1).

Figure 4.1   Life Expectancy, Brazil and Other LAC Countries, 2005–10

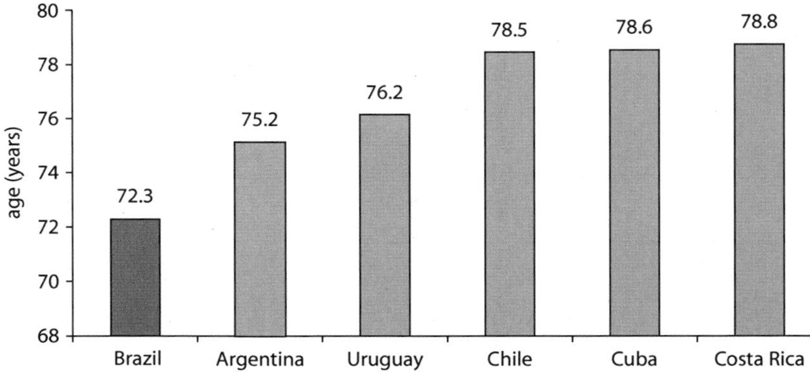

Source: United Nations 2008.

Not only have Brazilians enjoyed substantial LEB increases, but once they reach "old age," they can also expect a greater life expectancy than in the recent past. For instance, life expectancy at age 60 (LE60) in 1980 was 15.4 for men and 17.8 for women; respective figures in 2005 were 19.1 and 22.6. At age 75, life expectancy (LE75) increased in the same 25-year period (1980–2005)—3.4 years for men and 3.0 years for women—that is, an increase of just over one year per decade when considering both sexes together. Interestingly, life expectancies for men at older ages in Brazil compare favorably with those in more developed countries. For instance, in 2005 a Brazilian man at age 75 expected to live 10.9 more years, the same as in Canada. The figures for Denmark, Sweden, and Switzerland were, respectively, 9.8, 10.6, and 11.2. This suggests that older men in developed countries have accumulated more risk factors for non-communicable diseases (NCDs), such as smoking, sedentary lifestyles, excessive alcohol consumption, and over-rich diets, while their Brazilian counterparts belong to cohorts that were spared such excesses. For women, the "protection" conferred by less affluent lifestyles is not as clear. For Brazilian women, LE75 in 2005 was 12.4—for Canada, Denmark, Sweden, and Switzerland the figures were 13.3, 11.8, 12.7, and 13.7, respectively. At the same time, in the decade up to 2008, the very old (80 years and older), experienced a 10 percent increase in life expectancy: LE80 in 1998 was 8.72 (8.31 for men, 9.05 for women); the respective figures in 2008 were 9.51 (8.94 and 9.93, respectively).

Figure 4.2 shows that the only population group that has remained stable in the period 1990–2010 is the youngest one (0–19). All the

Figure 4.2   Brazilian Population Growth, 1990–2007

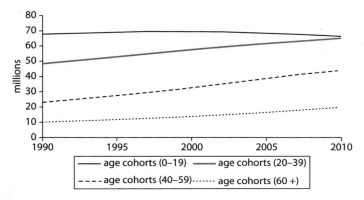

Source: United Nations 2008.

remaining subgroups (20–39, 40–59, and 60+) experienced substantial increases—the fastest one was the oldest (60+). Within that group, the very old (80+) increased faster than the age group 60–79. From 1990 to 2010 the 60+ group almost doubled while the 80+ cohort almost tripled.

The very old, with their disproportionately higher demands on health care and social services, are expected to experience exponential increases in number within the next four decades. Today Brazil has some 1.1 million men and 1.6 million women aged 80 and over, which is expected to increase in 2050 to 5.2 million and 8.6 million, respectively. These figures show that, as is the case for most of the already aged world, the Brazilian population will experience a feminization of aging, which has important health care and long-term care policy implications. Today the longer lives of these very old women are often marked by poor health and frailty. They are particularly prone to nonfatal but debilitating conditions. Added to this is frequent loneliness—as they more often than not outlive male partners—which means they can end their lives not only in widowhood but also commonly in poverty.

This chapter investigates the implications of longer life expectancy and a larger share of the old population on the provision of two important services for the elderly, health care and long-term care.

Health Care and Disease Patterns in Brazil

Brazil is firmly progressing into the epidemiological transition in which a shift in health and disease patterns brings death rates down from previously high levels in which people die young, primarily from communicable diseases, to low levels with death concentrated among the elderly, who die from degenerative diseases. In Brazil, the epidemiological transition has not followed the model experienced by most developed countries: old and new health problems coexist and, despite the predominance of chronic and degenerative diseases, the communicable ones still play an important role. This chapter focuses on noncommunicable diseases—the main cause of mortality and morbidity among the elderly in all countries.

The leading causes of death in Brazil are cardiovascular diseases (CVDs) (30 percent), cancer (15 percent), and "external causes" (accidents, violence) (12 percent). Regional differences reflect disparities in socioeconomic levels. For instance, data from the Brazil Ministry of Health indicate that the population aged 20–74 has experienced a decrease in cardiovascular disease mortality rates of around 1.4 percent a year for the period 1990–2006. These declines, however, have been pronounced in the south and the southeast, while the northeast has seen an increase in these rates. Similar patterns—declines in certain regions while others see increases—in mortality rates for specific CVDs for the oldest age group, 60–79, are shown in table 4.1.[1]

Table 4.1 shows the mortality rates for the age group 60–79 for all CVDs for the country as a whole and desegregated by region. Both men and women experienced a decline in mortality rates for CVDs that was pronounced in both south and southeast regions, while the northeast region showed an increase. Furthermore, CVD mortality rates in 1990 were around 2.5 times higher in the south compared to the northeast, but that relative difference was reduced to only about 20 percent by 2007. This shows that the southern regions share the trend apparent in the developed world since the 1970s of decreasing mortality rates in CVDs

Table 4.1   Adjusted Mortality Rates for Cardiovascular Diseases, 1990–2007
per 100,000 population

Brazil and regions	Women 60–79		Men 60–79	
	1990	*2007*	*1990*	*2007*
Brazil	998.8	730.8	1406.6	1102.3
North	638.8	564.8	796.9	828.8
Northeast	515.3	710.2	689.1	1005.7
Southeast	1242.8	742.4	1825.4	1159.9
South	1224.5	773.1	1763.1	1168.8
Center-West	918.0	741.5	1187.4	1139.4

Source: Ministry of Health 2009.

at all ages, including older age. This is not the case in the northeast—a region still at an earlier stage of the epidemiological transition.

Table 4.2 shows mortality rates for cerebrovascular diseases. An average decrease of around 3.6 percent per year was observed for the country as a whole—however, in the northeast, a small but significant increase was again registered. This decrease of 3.6 percent per year was larger than that shown by ischemic heart disease (IHD) for the same years; it was on the order of 1.9 percent, with once again the northeast region experiencing an increase rather than a decrease of these conditions.

Table 4.3 illustrates mortality rates for ischemic heart disease. Of particular interest is that, while the rates in 1990 for the southeast region were substantially higher than for the northeast, the declines (particular among women) in the former have been rapid while the increases in the latter have been considerable.

Another noncommunicable disease of great importance which shares some of the risk factors for CVDs (namely unhealthy diet and a sedentary

Table 4.2   Adjusted Mortality Rates for Cerebrovascular Disease, 1990–2007
per 100,000 population

	Women 60–79		Men 60–79	
Brazil and regions	*1990*	*2007*	*1990*	*2007*
Brazil	348.2	234.6	481.4	339.7
North	249.1	229.7	291.8	308.1
Northeast	211.7	253.2	264.1	346.3
Southeast	404.1	218.7	587.7	331.9
South	455.9	259.1	648.5	373.2
Center-West	301.9	217.1	418.2	312.1

Source: Ministry of Health 2009.

Table 4.3   Adjusted Mortality Rates for Ischemic Heart Disease, 1990–2007
per 100,000 population

	Women 60–79		Men 60–79	
Brazil and regions	*1990*	*2007*	*1990*	*2007*
Brazil	274.3	216.7	457.2	382.1
North	138.1	140.5	216.2	239.1
Northeast	106.3	199.4	175.4	315.0
Southeast	359.8	225.8	625.3	415.1
South	370.4	244.5	612.7	444.0
Center-West	180.0	200.8	291.0	375.0

Source: Ministry of Health 2009.

lifestyle), and which itself can lead to an increased risk for CVD, is diabetes. Table 4.4 shows the adjusted mortality rates for diabetes for women and men above age 60. As a whole, substantial increases, particularly for men, can be observed.

These four tables show that noncommunicable diseases are still common causes of death for older people in Brazil. However, the declines that have been experienced can be attributed to a variety of factors such as: (1) changes in lifestyle—more recent cohorts of older people have greater concern with health and higher levels of health literacy; (2) early detection and increased access to appropriate treatment for secondary risk factors, such as high cholesterol and hypertension; and (3) effective medical interventions, such as new drugs, pacemakers, and open heart surgery, that were previously unavailable. It is important to restate that it can be misleading to interpret national figures. In a country as vast as Brazil regional differences are substantial. The stages of the demographic/ epidemiological transition can be markedly varied. Thus, while the wealthier southeast and south regions are already showing the same patterns as more affluent societies—decreasing rates of mortality and morbidity for CVDs—the less affluent northeast still presents a trend in the opposite direction.

The cancers (for all ages) with the highest incidence in Brazil (2006) for men in order of prevalence are prostate, lung, stomach, colon, and esophagus; for women the cancers are breast, cervix, colon, lung, and stomach. Mortality rates are on the increase for all except stomach cancer. These trends are opposite of those prevalent for other noncommunicable diseases. They reflect the high prevalence of cigarette smoking among the cohorts now reaching the ages when the disease is manifested (and more recent higher smoking rates among women). Also note that breast cancer

Table 4.4   Adjusted Mortality Rates for Diabetes, 1990–2007
per 100,000 population

Brazil and regions	Women 60–79		Men 60–79	
	1990	*2007*	*1990*	*1990*
Brazil	144.3	221.3	97.6	184.5
North	64.2	200.7	45.4	136.7
Northeast	100.8	280.9	72.0	224.6
Southeast	183.6	198.4	125.7	174.8
South	131.8	206.2	90.3	174.5
Center-West	115.4	205.3	67.3	159.4

Source: Ministry of Health 2009.

rates are expected to increase in a reflection of the reproductive experiences of younger women—such as the postponement of the first full-
term pregnancy and the shorter cumulative breastfeeding experience.
More positively, the rate of stomach cancer is expected to continue to
decline, reflecting improved food hygiene and preservation. Also anticipated are declines for cervical cancer, as Pap smear screening becomes
more widespread and the vaccine for HPV (human papilloma virus) in
young teenagers becomes more widely available. On the other hand, the
recorded incidence of prostate cancer is expected to increase as more
men reach very old age and the disease is more accurately diagnosed.

When considering the age group 60+, mortality rates for all cancers
have experienced a 25 percent increase within the period 1980–2005—
from 484.1 to 606.6 per 100,000. The increase for the most frequently
lethal cancer in men, lung, was from 54.9 to 82.8 per 100,000 (50.7
percent), while for women, breast cancer went from 38.9 to 56.7 per
100,000 (45.8 percent). Regarding the latter, 52 percent of women aged
60+ have never had a mammogram—64 percent if they were users of the
SUS (Unified Health Service) and 23 percent if they were used private
services. In 2003, only 31 percent of SUS users had received mammogra-
phy over the previous two years compared to 67.5 percent of those who
had access to private services (IGBE 2003).

Data obtained from a telephone survey (VIGITEL, Surveillance of
Risk and Protective Factors for Chronic Diseases) in the capitals of all 26
states and the Brasilia federal district show a high prevalence of the risk
factors associated with the main noncommunicable diseases among older
interviewees. While only 8.5 percent were current smokers, 67.5 percent
consumed fresh vegetables and fruits only irregularly; 20.6 percent
reported eating meat with excessive fat; 87.5 percent reported a sedentary lifestyle; and 62.4 percent were overweight. Of those who self-
declared as hypertensive (55.5 percent), the vast majority reported
concomitance of two or more other relative risks for NCDs and 48 percent reported three or more (Kalache 2010).

As noted earlier, deaths from external causes are of enormous significance in Brazil (128,388 deaths in 2006). In contrast to most countries,
homicides lead the ranking, with road accidents second. Rates are much
higher for men than for women in all age groups—an overall relative risk
(RR) of 5.4 in 2006. In young age groups the RR is even larger. There is
almost 16 times the probability of a young man aged 20–24 being murdered as a young woman. With road accidents it is 4.7 times as much. The
rate is four times higher for suicide. These sex differentials persist well

into old age. Among those aged 75+ the risk for a man to be murdered is 5.1 times higher than for a woman of the same age. In 2006 the mortality rate for homicide (all ages) was 26 in 100,000, while for road accidents the rate was 19.4 in 100,000. These disturbing statistics show an urgent need to implement multisectoral interventions. These unacceptably high mortality rates attributable to "external causes" are a major contributing factor to a relatively low life expectancy at birth and at all ages. This is particularly the case for men in Brazil, for instance, compared to other Latin American countries.

Falls are especially significant in older age, both in terms of mortality and as a cause of hospital admission. Out of the total number of admissions (662,652) in 2006, no less than 42.5 percent (281,324) were attributed to a fall—at a huge human and economic cost. Admission rates increased to 15.1 in 10,000 in 2006 from 13.9 in 10,000 in 1998. Rates were considerably higher for women than men, at 20.3 and 10.1 per 10,000, respectively, in 2006. Compared to road accidents, at 2.2. for women and 7.2 for men, the significance of these numbers of falls stands out as a public health concern. Hospital admissions prompted by a fall were three times higher among males aged 10–39 compared to women of same age. In older age (75+), however, the opposite is observed: women are 30 percent more likely to be admitted to a hospital as the result of a fall. This reflects the higher incidence for women of suffering serious consequences from a fall. This is in part related to osteoporosis, but it is also influenced by the fact that older women are more likely to be widowed and living alone. It is more usual for a man of the same age to benefit from a family caregiver at home.

A common feature of the health scenario is that older people often present with multiple pathologies. Typically, an older person presents hypertension in association with diabetes, high cholesterol, osteoporosis, and respiratory conditions, among others. The presentation of these diseases may differ from that at younger ages. The multiple pathologies often provoke simultaneous use of multiple drugs that can produce a host of unanticipated crossover effects. Frequently, older people can get confused, showing symptoms of intoxication from simultaneous drug use.

These problems are best controlled by improved training in old age care for future cohorts of health care professionals. As elsewhere, Brazil has a dramatic shortage of geriatricians. This need for specialists, however, can be mitigated by training *all* medical doctors in old age care. More geriatricians are required—in part because they are the trainers of future doctors—but even more pressing is the need for *all* future doctors to be familiar with old age care. Gastroenterologists, neurologists, cardiologists, and family medicine specialists alike will increasingly be dealing with older people in their practices. Despite Brazil's passage through the advanced stages of the epidemiological transition, its medical schools are still training doctors for the requirements of the 20th century. Students are schooled in child care and reproductive health but are presented with little or nothing about aging-related issues. A doctor graduating in 2010 with an average 40 years of medical practice ahead will witness a three-fold increase in the elderly population—63 million people.

Whatever their specialty, doctors will be confronted with increasing numbers of older patients regardless of their level of preparedness. Curriculum reform reflecting Brazil's rapid aging is critical if the country is to avoid an epidemic of iatrogenic conditions—and the consequent escalating health care costs.

Even though in 2006 the proportion of older people in Brazil was about 10 percent, they incurred some 26 percent of hospital costs. Given Brazil's rapid population aging, it is clear that without vigorous policies to stem hospital admissions by this age group, the cost will escalate dramatically in the coming decades. Figure 4.3 shows the coverage of influenza vaccination for the population aged 60+ in Brazil since the beginning of this campaign in 1999 until 2007. This has been a particularly successful public health intervention, achieving coverage rates ranging from

Figure 4.3   Coverage of Influenza Vaccine for Population 60 and over in Brazil, 1999–2007

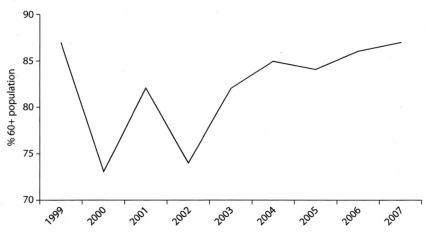

Source: Health Surveillance Department, Ministry of Health 2008.

73 to 87 percent (consistently very close to or well above the 75 percent coverage target). In more recent years (not shown in the figure), the uptake has declined but nevertheless it still remains around the 75 percent mark. This public health intervention is an example of the kind of policy that can result in a prevention of diseases and their complications. Not only can it postpone death and suffering, but it can also lead to substantial savings related to hospital admissions and the treatment of serious respiratory conditions triggered by an episode of older age influenza.

One of the most poignant illustrations that the epidemiological/demographic transition has reached an advanced stage is when an increasing proportion of all deaths occur in older ages. Already, in Brazil, over 60 percent of all deaths occur after the age of 60—only 11 percent happen before the age of 20. Further increases are expected. Studies throughout the world have shown that the bulk of health care costs occur in the last years of life. Brazil must focus greater attention on medical care in older age if for no other reason than because of the savings to be gained. Furthermore, the older an individual is at the time of death, the lower are the costs associated with care in the preceding year. A death at age 40 or 50 costs relatively more than a death from the same cause at age 80 or 90 because more and usually more expensive treatments are available for younger than older patients. Keeping people healthy well into their old age not only extends life and productivity but also helps to contain health care costs.

Equally important is investing in health promotion and disease prevention throughout the entire life course. Better health in older age depends not only on medical interventions targeting older people but also on assisting individuals to grow older in better health, which will be discussed later in this chapter. It is particularly important to focus on the four main risk factors for NCDs: smoking, physical inactivity, excessive alcohol consumption, and unhealthy diet. Current data show a substantial decrease in smoking rates in Brazil—it is now lower even than in more health-concerned countries such as Canada (Iglesias et al. 2007). These decreases were possible due to a combination of multisectoral policies: health education illustrating the harm, fiscal policies that increased taxes on tobacco to discourage smoking, and laws banning smoking from public spaces and prohibiting advertisements and sponsorship of sports and cultural events.

However, more effort is needed to combat the other three major risk factors for NCDs. Some community-based interventions targeting sedentary lifestyles ("Agita Brazil," a national program of the Ministry of

Health to encourage physical activity, for example) have been successful. There have also been public information campaigns from both public and private sectors, but more is required if the high rates of physical inactivity are to be reduced. Typically, the sedentary person is a woman of low socioeconomic/education level, rural or semi-urban, whose physical activity level decreases as she ages. Equally worrying are the trends to unhealthy diets, to a preference for high fat/sugar/carbohydrate and salty foods—the so-called "white" diet. Finally, the social acceptability of the high consumption of alcohol not only manifests itself through diseases but also in violence and road accidents. In broad terms, the affluent, well-educated classes have learned healthier behaviors but the lower socioeconomic classes continue to be burdened with problems related to excess weight, smoking, and sedentary lifestyle.

The Strategy to Address Chronic Health Care in Brazil

Although the epidemiological shift from acute to chronic care has already occurred in Brazil, health care is still focused on acute care. It signals a need for a reorientation toward chronic care, which would require a difficult but unavoidable reorganization of the health care system. Treating hypertension or diabetes requires different equipment and personnel than infections or gastroenteritis. Doctors must be mindful of the patient's treatment outside of the short office visit. In fact, the greater part of the treatment is away from the health premises, which serves to illustrate the crucial importance of home and community care. Additionally, as individuals age, the value of self-care increases. One of the reasons that men die earlier than women is their notorious resistance to such self-care.

The emergence of chronic diseases requires a continuum of care that has to start with health promotion, primordial prevention, and primary/secondary/tertiary prevention. Hypertension is a good example of a condition that can mostly be prevented in the first place. The opportunities to prevent it, however, are often missed. Once it has become established, proper treatment and follow-up can effectively prevent cardiovascular complications. Missed opportunities to deal appropriately with them are then translated into major CVDs for which proper diagnosis and treatment will be required to prevent the onset of a major medical problem such as stroke that would then require prompt acute treatment. These major problems, if untreated, result in disabilities that require rehabilitation, without which the chances of a recovery with no or minimal loss of functional capacity decrease. As the Brazilian population ages, the focus on a continuum of care (particularly from the public sector) must be sharpened considerably.

Despite significant progress, important challenges remain for the Brazilian health system—challenges that are paradigmatic of middle-income countries, in which the rising volume and changing composition of demand for health care will exert considerable upward pressure on both public and household spending. Over the next generation, an aging population and the growth of chronic diseases will steadily increase demand for high-complexity, high-cost health services. At the same time, rising incomes and the proliferation of new drugs and technologies will feed increased expectations for high-quality and responsive care. If it hopes to build human capital at a cost sustainable to the economy, Brazil will need to carefully manage the double burden of coping with these advanced challenges while completing its unfinished agenda of reducing childhood and infectious diseases among the poor.

In 2005, a World Bank Report (Danel, Kurowski, and Saxenian 2005) provided an overview of the changing NCD burden in Brazil and its root causes, as well as the costs and potential effectiveness of alternative policy interventions. According to the study, seven modifiable risk factors accounted for an estimated 53 percent of all deaths and 30 percent of all disability-adjusted life years lost (DALYs) in Brazil. These included high blood pressure, overweight, alcohol use, tobacco use, high cholesterol, low fruit and vegetable intake, and physical inactivity. The upward trend in chronic diseases is a consequence of urbanization, changing lifestyles, globalization, and improvements in health care, and it is preventable, often at low cost. An effective response requires broad educational and community interventions, as well as changes in economic policy, food supply, and transportation policy and urban design.

The World Bank study found that, taken together, the financial and economic costs of chronic diseases—the added costs to the health care bill and the economic costs due to lost productivity—represented about 10 percent of Brazil's GDP. However, most of the public health budget is still allocated to the control of communicable diseases, as many of these diseases persist among the poorest groups of the population. The public health system and budget also focus on treatment of disease rather than on health promotion and disease prevention and on addressing the social determinants of health. On current trends, chronic diseases will overwhelm the health system and cause considerable needless suffering and lost productivity. The cost of treating NCDs already accounts for nearly half the cost of all hospital admissions.

Closing the equity gap while addressing the increased burden of chronic diseases continues to be the principal challenge facing the Brazilian health system. Brazil has made significant progress on adoption of cost-effective and evidence-based interventions to tackle chronic NCDs and injuries since the NCD study was published. The Ministry of Health (MOH), in coordination with State and Municipal Health Secretariats (SES and SMS, respectively), and other ministries (Ministries of Cities, Transport, Education, and others), has led the development of a public health system with a growing focus on health surveillance and promotion, environmental health, and prevention of chronic diseases and injuries, with noticeable results—for example, smoking prevalence decreased in Brazil from 35 percent in 1989 to 16 percent in 2006. According to the results of the TEL Surveillance of Risk and Protective Factors for Chronic Diseases telephone survey conducted in 26 state capitals and the Federal District, 22 percent of nonsmokers were former smokers. Another example is given by Projeto GUIA, an ongoing evaluation of physical activity programs in 286 municipalities, including the program Academia da Cidade, a community-oriented program to promote physical exercise in poor neighborhoods, which has shown preliminary good results. Scientific evaluation in the city of Recife in 2006–07 found that exposure to Academia da Cidade was associated with a two- to eleven-fold increase in leisure-time physical activity (Simoes et al. 2009; Hallal et al. 2010). In particular, Academia da Cidade increased participation in leisure-time physical activity predominantly among older and poorer women in the more than 20 sites of the city of Recife. In some ways yet to be understood, Academia da Cidade broke a barrier for poor and older women regarding leisure-time physical activity.

Through the Secretariat of Surveillance, the MOH has implemented several activities aimed at identifying risk factors for chronic diseases, promoting health and evaluating the program's impact, as follows:

Non-communicable disease, injury and risk factor surveillance. Several routine information systems have been established that provide data on mortality and morbidity by chronic diseases and injuries; risk factors; health knowledge, attitudes, and practices; and environmental health. National databases are generated by DATASUS in cooperation with the National Epidemiology Center (CENEPI), as follows:

- SIM, the Mortality Information System, provides information on cause, date, place, and municipality of occurrence of death, as well as demographic and other information on the deceased. Data are collected from death certificates in all states and municipalities.

- VIGITEL (Surveillance of Risk Factors for Chronic Diseases by Telephone Survey) monitors the frequency and distribution of risk factors for NCDs in the 26 Brazilian state capitals and the Federal District, through telephone interviews conducted in random samples of adults living in households served by fixed phone lines in each city. Surveys covering 54,000 persons were carried out in 2006, 2007, and 2008, and results were published on the Internet.
- In addition to VIGITEL, a Global Adult Tobacco Survey was carried out in 2008 to monitor tobacco use and evaluate efforts to reduce its use.
- VIVA, the Surveillance System of Violence and Accidents, monitors injuries caused by violence and accidents, and functions at the federal, state, and municipal levels in 900 municipalities.
- PENSE, the National Survey of School Health, is a school-based health survey. IBGE carried out a survey of student health in the 26 state capitals and Federal District in 2009. The survey will be carried out every other year for students in grade 9 in all schools in Brazil.
- SIASI, the Indigenous Health Information System, will also include information about chronic diseases among the indigenous population.

Health promotion and disease prevention

- A national plan for NCD risk factor surveillance and prevention is being implemented in states and capital cities since 2005.
- A National Network for Health Promotion has been financing over 500 federal entities.
- A network of 16 municipalities in large urban areas, corresponding to about 19 percent of the population, has been developing surveillance and prevention of injuries and deaths from traffic accidents.
- A network to promote health and prevent violence is equipped with 254 units in 21 SES, 215 SMS, 16 education and research institutions, and two NGOs.
- The School Health Program, cosponsored by the MOH and the Ministry of Education, aims to strengthen student health behavior in 701 priority municipalities.
- Since 2006, SVS has also promoted several media campaigns aiming at adoption of behaviors that lead to healthier lives, such as reduction of smoking, increasing physical activity, improving traffic safety, and preventing and controlling hypertension and diabetes.

- One of the most successful prevention policies for NCDs in Brazil has been the Tobacco Control Program (Iglesias et al. 2007), which developed surveillance and monitoring initiatives, built institutional capacity, and decentralized tobacco control initiatives to states and municipalities.
- Academia da Cidade is a community-oriented program to promote physical exercise in poor neighborhoods, using individually targeted behavior change, environmental change, and policy change methods.

Health Care Utilization and Health Care Cost of an Aging Population

That the rapidly aging population in Brazil will have significantly larger and more expensive health care requirements has become a widespread concern for policy makers, both because diseases affect different age groups in different ways and because treatment costs vary with the type of disease. In consequence, changes in the country's demographic structure change the cost of the health system and therefore public expenditures. This section will examine the empirical relations between demographic change, health care utilization, and health care costs. A more formal modeling of the public finance implications of population aging for the health sector is presented in chapter 6.

Table 4.5 presents hospitalization through SUS by disease according to the age group. The majority of patients hospitalized by infectious, parasitary, and respiratory diseases are children. Young people are also the majority among those hospitalized for external causes (accidents and violence), genitourinary diseases, pregnancy, and mental problems. Neoplasms and diseases of the digestive system affect mainly the middle-aged group. Elderly people are the first to be affected by diseases of the circulatory system.

Table 4.6 also shows that changes related to the number of hospitalizations by disease follow variations in the demographic structure in the course of the period. From 1995 to 2007, the proportion of the young population (up to 14 years old) dropped 18 percent, while the 60+ years old grew by 25.3 percent.

Between 2000 and 2007 there was a proportional increase in more expensive treatments, typical of adults and old people, and a reduction in the percentage of cheaper hospitalizations, characteristic of youths and children. Between 1995 and 2007, the proportion of hospitalizations by infectious and parasitary diseases and by diseases of the respiratory system fell by 8 percent and 15 percent, respectively. There were decreases

Table 4.5   Public Hospitalization by Disease and by Age Group, 2007

% total hospitalizations

Disease groups	<10 years	10–19	20–39	40–59	60+	Total
			Age groups (years of age)			
Infectious and parasitic diseases	37.84	9.83	18.65	16.09	17.59	100
Neoplasms	5.39	5.61	19.90	37.13	31.97	100
Mental and behavioral disorders	0.20	4.71	48.74	40.11	6.24	100
Circulatory system diseases	0.67	1.28	10.42	32.35	55.28	100
Respiratory system diseases	45.06	6.46	10.11	12.60	25.77	100
Digestive system diseases	11.44	7.42	26.79	30.65	23.70	100
Genitourinary system diseases	8.66	9.52	37.24	26.79	17.79	100
Pregnancy, childbirth, and puerperium	0.00	24.69	72.85	2.39	0.06	100
External causes	11.57	15.06	35.88	22.45	15.04	100
Other causes	26.31	7.74	22.37	21.26	22.33	100
Total	15.98	11.23	33.17	19.31	20.31	100

Source: Ministry of Health 2009.

Table 4.6   Demography and Proportion of Hospitalization by Disease Group

% total hospitalizations

Diseases	1995	1997	1999	2001	2003	2005	2007
Infectious and parasitic diseases	8.79	7.96	7.61	8.04	9.17	8.68	8.08
Neoplasms	3.17	2.97	2.98	3.32	4.91	5.26	5.65
Mental and behavioral disorders	3.47	3.57	3.55	3.31	2.94	2.67	2.56
Circulatory system diseases	9.97	9.71	9.21	9.90	10.56	10.34	10.22
Respiratory system diseases	16.09	17.32	16.48	15.61	15.01	13.70	13.68
Digestive system diseases	7.02	7.08	8.35	8.73	8.17	8.53	8.79
Genitourinary system diseases	7.29	6.43	6.79	6.70	6.60	6.57	6.73
Pregnancy, childbirth, and puerperium	25.85	26.42	25.66	23.91	22.71	23.10	21.94

(continued next page)

Table 4.6   *(continued)*

Diseases	1995	1997	1999	2001	2003	2005	2007
External causes	5.82	5.90	5.68	5.93	6.30	6.90	7.35
Other causes	12.53	12.64	13.70	14.55	13.63	14.24	14.99
Total	100.00	100.00	100.00	100.00	100.00	100.00	100.00
Age structure of population (%)							
0–14	32.8	31.5	30.3	29.3	28.4	27.6	26.9
15–59	59.9	60.8	61.7	62.4	63.0	63.5	63.8
60 or +	7.3	7.6	8.0	8.3	8.6	8.9	9.3
Total	100.00	100.00	100.00	100.00	100.00	100.00	100.00

Source: Ministry of Health (2009).

in genitourinary diseases (by 7.7 percent), pregnancies (by 15 percent), and mental health problems (by 26 percent). However, the proportion of neoplasms and diseases of the circulatory and digestive system increased by 78 percent, 2.5 percent, and 25 percent, respectively.

The cost of hospitalization by patient for each type of disease is shown in table 4.7. On average, pediatric and obstetric treatments, which affect mostly children and younger adults, cost about half as much as tuberculosis treatment, which is more characteristic of the middle-aged and the elderly. The long-term treatments needed for circulatory diseases and neoplasms are even more expensive. As noted above, middle-aged and elderly people are affected by these diseases in larger numbers than younger people.

Because the treatment of diseases of older ages is generally more expensive, medical and health costs are likely to rise as population ages in Brazil, although the magnitude will depend crucially on whether longer life spans mean more healthy years or added years of illness and dependency.[2] Indeed, there is increasing evidence that older people already are healthier than their counterparts of a few decades ago and have healthier lifestyles than previous generations, with the result that the threshold for frailty and disability is being pushed to later old age.[3]

Numerous studies, primarily in Western Europe and Japan, document the impact of aging on health and health expenditures and confirm the high level of use of health services in old age, particularly ambulatory services, medication, hospital admissions, and surgery. The general finding in most assessments, however, is that health expenditure per episode is typically higher for the elderly, though use of health services levels off and even declines for the very old. Yet, many studies also show that aging

Table 4.7 Cost per Hospitalization by Treatment Type, 2000–07

Jan. 2010 R$

Medical specialties	2000	2001	2002	2003	2004	2005	2006	2007
Clinical practice	653.74	596.63	541.53	470.62	500.32	503.98	496.98	515.06
Pediatrics	714.64	653.30	602.79	538.65	576.92	595.70	582.38	635.59
Obstetrics	520.26	499.16	446.11	397.15	441.76	444.15	467.24	489.03
Surgical clinic	1414.89	1432.67	1339.81	1206.14	1195.95	1200.60	1179.15	1189.68
Psychiatry	2469.80	2550.37	2879.76	2055.88	2303.74	2062.65	1843.07	2007.86
Psychiatry (hospital/day)	1183.42	1150.90	1138.36	956.98	846.20	777.33	755.78	747.79
Long-term care (chronic)	9023.52	10294.91	15746.16	13922.40	14024.34	10510.38	8538.42	11218.23
Rehabilitation	2033.63	1614.40	1520.80	1303.31	1205.98	1101.54	1102.69	1035.26
Phthisiology (tuberculosis treatment)	1681.36	1520.34	1372.17	1129.27	1081.74	1068.23	1057.95	1054.61

Source: Ministry of Health 2009.

is not a significant factor affecting health expenditures if proximity to death is taken into account, because a large proportion of lifetime expenditures on health take place in the two years preceding death, irrespective of the individual's age at that time. Furthermore, broader economic trends and technological innovation have a greater influence on total health care expenditures over time than does aging.[4]

The Life Course Approach to Aging and Health

The life course perspective on aging recognizes that older people are not one homogeneous group and that individual diversity tends to increase with age. In this respect, there is more variety among older personalities than among the young. They have had more time and opportunity to accumulate and consolidate differences. Central to the life course approach to aging is the notion of functional capacity—that is, that individuals reach the peak of their physical functional capacity early in adulthood and then progressively decline throughout the life course as a natural result of the aging process. Importantly, however, this is not necessarily a problem. If individuals continue to be independent and capable of performing the activities of daily living, say, at age 85, they will remain a resource to their family, their community, their society, and to the economy. Thus, good policies on aging will help individuals to remain above the disability threshold as they age (as shown in figure 4.4).

Figure 4.4   A Life Course Approach to Active Aging

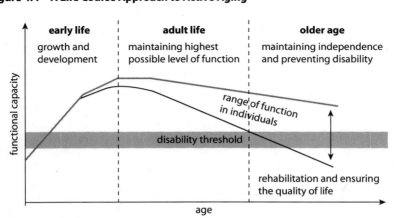

Source: Kalache and Kickbusch (1997).

Throughout the early stages of growth and development, physical capacities, such as cardiac output, muscular strength, and ventilatory capability, gradually increase. They reach a peak early in adulthood and eventually start declining. It should come as no surprise that an individual's functional capacity at age 85 is on the whole lower than it was at age 25. The rate of decline, however, is largely determined by factors related to lifestyle—smoking, alcohol consumption, levels of physical activity, and dietary practices—as well as external and environmental factors (see figure 4.5). Overlaying all of these are socioeconomic factors. It is crucial to recognize that this inevitable decline can be influenced and may even be reversed or retarded at any age through both individual and public policy measures.

An approach to help individuals remain independent as long as possible is to lower the disability threshold—the degree of functional capacity needed to remain independent—by making alterations to the environment in which they live. Good policies in this respect put the emphasis firmly on enablement rather than disability—and that in itself is a positive shift of paradigm in an aging world. It should be noted that redesigning or modifying an urban space with older people in mind benefits the entire community. Interventions aimed at the societal rather than the individual level can have a positive effect and are often cost-effective.[5] A key message to be extracted from the life course perspective is that it is never too late for interventions aimed at maintaining or improving functional capacity, because the results will always be a net gain.

Figure 4.5   Scope for Noncommunicable Disease Prevention: A Life Course Approach

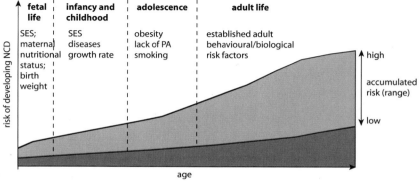

Source: Aboderin et al. 2002.
Note: SES = socioeconomic status; PA = physical activity.

The life course approach to aging is also important in terms of fostering intergenerational solidarity, which benefits both the old and the young. These intergenerational close ties also have important repercussions for health in older age, but they are difficult to measure as they deal with personal, subjective personality attributes by promoting self-esteem, optimism, and self-efficacy, attributes crucial for quality of life at any time but even more so in older age. As empirical evidence shows, they are also related to longevity—probably permeated through a sense of being useful and contributing to society.

The WHO Active Aging Policy Framework

As a response to worldwide aging, in 2002 the World Health Organization (WHO 2002) issued *Active Aging: A Policy Framework*, a document that has greatly influenced policies on aging in both developed and developing countries. "Active aging" is defined as "the process of optimizing opportunities for health, participation and security in order to enhance quality of life as people age." (WHO 2002, 12). The WHO concept of active aging is based on three pillars: (1) *health*, as a universal value, individuals around the world aspire to grow older in good health in order to (2) ensure full *participation* in their societies, and (3) failing that, they need the *security* of being protected. At an international conference on active aging in Seville in 2010 a fourth pillar was added to the definition—the *life-long learning and training* of new skills throughout the life course so that knowledge and abilities do not become obsolete as individuals age (Kalache 2010).

Active aging[6] refers to continuing participation in social, economic, cultural, spiritual, and civic affairs and not only the ability to be physically active or to participate in the labor force. Retired older people, even those who are ill or have disabilities, can remain active contributors to their families, peers, communities, and nations. Active aging aims to extend healthy life expectancy and quality of life for all people as they age, including those who are frail, disabled, and in need of care. Quality of life is a notion of critical importance within the context of aging. It expresses an individual's perception of his or her position in life in the context of the culture and value system in which they live. It is an assessment that relates to their goals, expectations, standards, and concerns. It is a broad-ranging concept incorporating in a complex way a person's physical health, psychological state, independence level, social relationships, personal beliefs, and interaction with salient features in the environment.

An active aging approach to policy and program development has the potential to address many of the challenges of both individual and population aging. When a society's health, labor market, employment, education, recreation, and social policies support active aging, the results will be (1) fewer premature deaths and fewer disabilities associated with NCDs in older age; (2) improved quality of life as individuals grow older; (3) increased active participation of older people in the social, cultural, economic, and political aspects of society, in both paid and unpaid roles and in domestic, family, and community life; and (4) lower costs related to medical treatment and care services. People who remain healthy as they age face fewer impediments to continue working, which is particularly important when considering the association of population aging with an increasing pressure to raise retirement ages—something that can already be witnessed throughout the developed world.

The Age-Friendly Cities Global project. It is ultimately only through policies that are truly intersectoral that the full potential of the active aging paradigm will be realized. This was successfully achieved through WHO's launch of the Age-Friendly Cities Global Network in 2007. Aging and urbanization are indeed the two major demographic trends of the 21st century.[7] The network evolved from the WHO's 2005 launch of the "Age-Friendly Cities" initiative. The starting point was Copacabana, the district in Rio more commonly known for its beach culture, youthfulness, and joy of life. The reality of the area, however, is more complex. Copacabana was urbanized at the beginning of the last century. The process reached its peak in the 1940s through early 1960s when tens of thousands of young people flocked into this relatively small physical area. The survivors of these cohorts are still living there. They have "aged in place." They are loyal to the district in part because of its physical beauty but also because it provides a walking-distance concentration of all the services that in the end make their lives easier—shops, restaurants, banks, pharmacies, and public transport.

Through a process of worldwide consultations in 35 cities—from Moscow, Tokyo, Melbourne, and New Delhi to Nairobi, London, Mexico City, and Rio de Janeiro—eight key features of an age-friendly city were identified and checklists for each of the key areas were developed. A guide with these checklists was prepared to help cities at *all* stages of development examine how they could make their physical plants more age-friendly.

In Brazil, the project has taken particularly deep root in the state of São Paulo. A strategy was devised by the Secretary of Health Aging Unit so that each of the 17 administrative regions of the state would have at least one city leading the process—that is, following the steps required for joining the WHO global network. The project would then cascade to other cities, eventually making São Paulo the first "age-friendly state" worldwide. Due to the size and complexity of São Paulo City, several local districts ("bairros") are involved in the project.

The age-friendly primary health care approach. Increased longevity is unquestionably a success for public health and the result of social and economic development. However, it does bring major challenges to the health sector—particularly when population aging is as rapid as it is in Brazil. Simply copying policies and programs from already aged societies will not work. They aged over many more decades, if not longer, and were by and large wealthy countries by the time they became old. Yet, they are still struggling to adequately respond to their aging.[8]

As discussed earlier in this chapter, with aging comes an increased risk of developing chronic NCDs and loss of functional capacity. Older people with disabilities need help to get through their daily tasks. Such help is most often provided by family members already stretched for time and resources. In order to prepare society for unprecedented numbers of older people, it is of utmost importance that health systems are better prepared to address the consequences of these demographic changes. This requires the adoption of a life course approach, as previously discussed. For instance, hypertension is mostly preventable—yet more than half of the Brazilian elderly population is hypertensive. Once the condition is firmly established, it needs effective treatment, which often is not provided. In the absence of effective treatment, complications emerge, with increased risk of neurological and cardiovascular diseases such as stroke.

Prompt acute care can sharply decrease the risk of serious loss of functional capacity, and rehabilitation should be provided as early as possible in these cases. Primary health care (PHC) plays a fundamental role in this chain that can be referred to as the continuum of care in the community. Every time it fails—consequently leading to institutional care—patients suffer and costs increase.

Most preventive health care and screening for early disease detection and NCD management ideally should take place in PHC settings at the community level. These PHC centers, to which people can self refer, also provide the bulk of ongoing management and care. PHC centers are on the front line of health care and are therefore familiar to older people and their families. They are ideally positioned to provide the regular and extended contacts and ongoing care that older persons need to prevent or delay disabilities resulting from chronic health conditions.

Brazilian health policies have experienced great advances with the implementation of the Unified Health System (SUS, *Sistema Único de Saúde*), which granted universal access to health services as established by the 1988 constitution. In 1994, the MOH launched the Family Health Program (PSF, *Programa Saúde da Família*). This is a new strategy of health assistance, provided by a multiprofessional health staff, offered to a certain number of families in small communities. They are registered at the local health administration and are visited by the program's staff. Residential institutions and nursing homes are also visited. One of the main goals is to contribute to change the health care delivery system from curative care to preventive care.

For the first time, the 2008 PNAD collected information about the households registered in the PSF, representing about 27.1 million or 47.7 percent of the total of Brazilian households. Considering only households with at least one older resident, this proportion is almost the same, 48.8 percent. As expected, and as shown in table 4.8, coverage of the PSF is quite different across the five major regions. The highest coverage is found in the northeast (67.3 percent) and the lowest in the southeast (36.0 percent). When the presence of at least one elderly person with difficulties for the daily life activities (DLAs) is considered, coverage increases to 52.6 percent. Regional differences present a similar pattern.

In 2007–08, the National Institute for Applied Economic Research (IPEA) conducted a census of all Brazilian institutions that provide long-term housing and services for the elderly (IPEA 2007, 2008a, 2008b,

Table 4.8   Proportion of Households Registered in the Family Health Program, 2008

% total Brazil population

	Total	With elderly resident	With frail elderly resident
North	51.7	55.4	53.5
Northeast	64.8	67.3	68.4
Southeast	35.9	36.0	38.9
South	50.3	52.2	58.1
West	49.1	53.9	57.5
Brazil	**47.7**	**48.8**	**52.6**

Source: IBGE 2008.

2008c). Of the 3,549 institutions surveyed, 1,576 were found to receive regular or sporadic visits by PSF staff. This represents 47.8 percent of total Brazilian institutions, indicating the low coverage of the program. The proportion varies according to the institutions' legal status and across Brazilian regions, as can be seen in table 4.9. For instance, even among public institutions, coverage is below 70 percent, and only a quarter of the private institutions receive some visit by the PSF. When regions are considered, the highest coverage is found in the west (69.9 percent), especially among public institutions, and the lowest in the south (38.0 percent), mainly among private institutions.

Long-Term Care

Long-term care (LTC) comprises a variety of services that help meet both medical and non-medical needs of people with chronic illnesses or disability who cannot care for themselves for long periods of time. It is common for LTC to provide custodial and non-skilled care, such as assistance with normal daily tasks like dressing, bathing, and using the bathroom. Increasingly, LTC involves providing a level of medical care that requires the expertise of skilled practitioners to address the often multiple chronic conditions among older populations. LTC can be provided in people's homes, in the community, assisted living facilities, or in nursing homes. Home care may be formal or informal. Formal care is offered by specialized professionals and informal care is provided by family members, friends, and neighbors. Long-term care may be needed by people of any age, even though it is a common need for senior citizens.

The LTC Situation in Brazil

People aged 60 and over who report having difficulties with daily life activities (DLAs) are treated as the demand of long-term care for this

Table 4.9   Institutions Visited by the Family Health Program, 2007–08

Region	Number of institutions				Percent			
	Public	Charity	Private	Total	Public	Charity	Private	Total
North	9	13	0	22	52.9	41.9	0.0	44.9
Northeast	9	150	2	161	50.0	61.2	5.3	53.5
Southeast	41	810	122	973	63.1	59.4	20.2	47.8
South	27	162	59	248	58.7	47.1	21.6	37.4
West	61	108	3	172	84.7	65.9	25.0	69.4
Total	**147**	**1,243**	**186**	**1,576**	**67.4**	**57.9**	**20.0**	**47.8**

Source: IPEA/SEDH (2007, 2008a, 2008b, 2008c)

discussion. These elderly are also referred to as "frail." Figure 4.6 shows that the proportion of the Brazilian population who reported experiencing some difficulties in performing DLAs increases with age and is higher among women than among men. Also, this proportion decreased between 1998 and 2008. Nevertheless, in 2008, 3.2 million persons were still found to be in need of LTC, 2.0 million (63.0 percent) of them women. This represents an increase of 1.0 million individuals in ten years and is in part due to the aging of the Brazilian population.

Moreover, in 2008 among the elderly, 88.0 percent reported experiencing at least one of the 12 chronic diseases investigated by the PNAD. The proportion was 85.5 percent for men and 89.5 percent for women. The most significant disease was high blood pressure, which affected 58.9 percent of men and 66.6 percent of women. High blood pressure, arthritis or rheumatism, back problems, heart disease, and diabetes were also significant (Camarano 2010).

Approximately 85 percent of those with DLA difficulties received at least one old age government benefit[9] in all three years considered in the current analysis (1998, 2003, and 2008). This proportion increases with age and is higher among men (see figure 4.7). At the age of 80+, 93.4 percent of men and 88.0 percent of women received some old age benefit in 2008. Few changes were observed between 1998 and 2008. Most

Figure 4.6   Proportion of Population with Difficulty in DLAs, by Sex and Age, 1998 and 2008

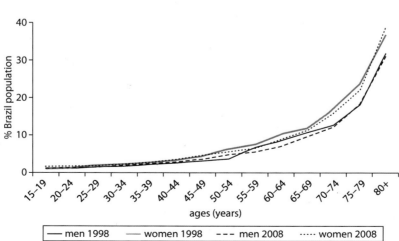

Sources: 1998 and 2008 PNAD (IGBE 1999; 2009).

Figure 4.7   Proportion of Elderly with Difficulty in DLAs Who Received Social Security, 1998, 2003, and 2008

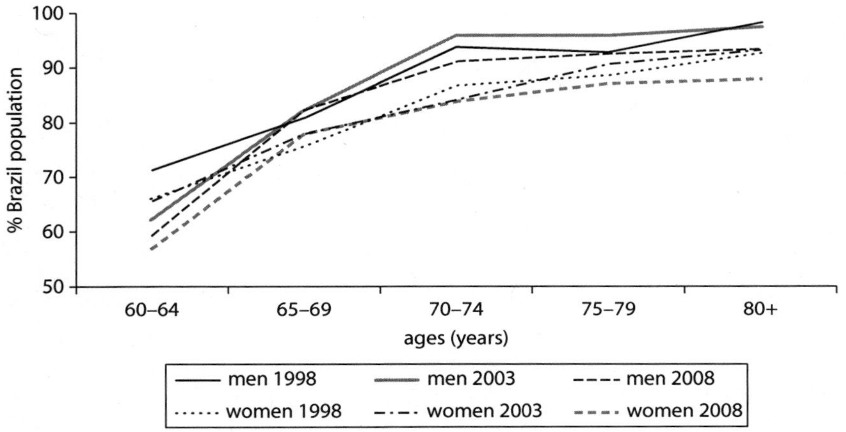

Sources: IGBE 1999; 2004; 2009.

important is the decline in the proportion of people aged 60–64 receiving an old age benefit among both men and women, which suggests some postponement of the retirement age (see chapter 3 for a description of recent changes observed in retirement age in Brazil).

As a consequence, almost 90 percent of these individuals' income came from social security in the three years considered. This proportion is higher among women (89.9 percent in 2008) than among men (75.9 percent in 2008), because of the prevalence of survivor pensions for women and their low proportion of labor income. The contribution of donations from other family members is quite low: it is higher among women and declined from 3.6 percent to 0.9 percent from 2003 to 2008. Individuals who need help with DLAs and receive old-age benefits contribute to their family budget. Receiving a benefit may help them to get support from other family members in a kind of intergenerational cooperation. For example, women with DLA difficulties who lived with relatives in 2003 contributed to about a third of total household income (Camarano 2006).

Informal and Formal Care in the World and in Brazil

The global picture of long-term care is complex and no country can claim to have satisfactorily resolved all the issues as yet. The wealthier world, with a longer period to prepare and greater resources at its disposal, is still struggling to define the best delivery and financing systems for LTC. While developed countries did incorporate LTC into their research and policy agendas (Batista et al. 2008; Pasinato and Kornis 2009; Brodsky, Habib, and Hirschfeld 2003; Howse 2007), and LTC has been absorbed into the social protection system in most of these countries, its scope and financing are still a subject of debate.

Batista et al. (2008) and Pasinato and Kornis (2010) group the developed country experience into three models. Esping-Andersen 2002 and Batista et al. (2008) added a fourth. The models are described as follows:

- **Social Democratic**—As exemplified mostly by Scandinavian countries (Denmark and Sweden) where LTC has been a state obligation since the 1950s, these programs are funded by local taxes and transfers from the national government and represent the largest coverage by publicly funded universal care services. There is no requirement of previous contribution or proof of poverty. Services comprise both formal home care and institutional care.
- **Conservative**—In this model, found in France, Germany, and Japan, the supply of service is reduced and cash benefits (subsidies/social insurance) are prioritized. Care is largely provided by charitable institutions, with funding derived from both private and public sources in varying degrees.
- **Liberal**—This model, represented by the United States, is characterized by a low offer of both public and private social services. The main focus is on poverty reduction, with contributory and non-contributory benefits of low value. LTC for the poor is funded from general taxation with private insurance catering to the non-poor. The general orientation is to retain the elderly in their households.
- **Mediterranean**—Also characterized by a low offer of both public and private social services, this model, found in Italy, Greece, and Portugal, places LTC firmly in the hands of the family, with institutional care of any kind being extremely minimal.

Whether by design or default, it is informal care of the elderly that predominates throughout the world. According to Jacobzone, Cambois, and Robine (2000), it accounts for an estimated 80 percent of the LTC within the OECD countries.

In Brazil, as in most developing countries, the extent of government involvement is low. Elder care receives little importance in policy agendas, and legislation has clearly bestowed the main responsibility on the family

(1988 Federal Constitution; 1994 National Policy for the Elder; 2003 Elders' Bill of Rights). Family care occurs with little support from the state. Public home care programs are scarce. Furthermore, there is strong prejudice against institutional care in Brazil, and government legislation has compounded this bias (Camarano 2008).

The 2003 Elders' Bill of Rights stresses that institutional care is regarded only as an option upon evidence of lack of family or poverty or abandonment (art. 37; par. 1). There is no consensus in Brazil on what defines a residential institution, but the historical view that they are places of exclusion or "elder deposits" persists (Novaes 2003). Sheltering the needy elderly has traditionally been left to Christian philanthropy and it remains a fact that the majority of Brazilian institutions are charities (IPEA/SEDH 2007, 2008a, 2008b, 2008c).

Family Changes and the Provision of Informal Long-Term Care

In Brazil as elsewhere, historical social and family values and practices have determined that care of dependent family members is a female responsibility. Not only do women make up the larger proportion of the older population and are most in need of care, but they are also overwhelmingly the principal caregivers (Lloyd-Sherlock 2004). The availability of women to perform this function is subject to broader social considerations. Factors such as increased female education, a larger role for women in the labor market, changing patterns of marriage/family breakdown, migration, and the reduced pool of children to draw from to begin with, are inevitably creating new paradigms. In addition, a general lack of recognition and outside support for caregivers through sensible public policies further weakens the role. Failure to put in place networks and vocational training programs are missed opportunities for both the caregivers and the society at large.

Table 4.10 suggests that the main potential source of support of older men is the spouse and for women it is the children. In 2008, while the large majority of men, 76.9 percent, live with their spouses, with or without children, the comparable proportion of women is only 43.2 percent. On the other hand, 48.0 percent of the women live with children, whether or not in the presence of spouses. The comparable proportion for men is similar, 45.6 percent. The presence of relatives or domestic servants in households with frail elderly who do not have spouses or children is found in 12.8 percent of households where the frail elder is male and in 27.3 percent in the case of female frail elderly. Summarizing, the data suggest that frail women are less likely than men to get family support.

Table 4.10   Proportion of Elderly with Difficulty in DLAs by Family Composition, 1998, 2003, and 2008

% Elderly population	1998			2003			2008		
	Men	Women	Total	Men	Women	Total	Men	Women	Total
Couples without children	23.7	12.2	16.6	26.5	12.5	17.8	28.2	14.4	19.5
Couples without children and others	7.2	6.7	6.9	7.7	6.2	6.8	7.9	6.5	7.0
Couples with children	23.8	9.0	14.7	20.5	7.4	12.3	20.9	7.0	12.1
Couples with children and others	24.5	19.7	21.5	20.7	18.9	19.6	20.0	15.4	17.1
Women alone	0.0	13.6	8.4	0.0	15.2	9.5	0.0	15.5	9.8
Women alone and others	1.4	12.0	7.9	2.5	11.4	8.0	2.3	11.7	8.2
Mother with children	0.1	11.0	6.8	0.3	10.1	6.4	0.3	11.7	7.5
Mother with children and others	2.1	12.5	8.5	2.7	14.7	10.2	2.9	13.9	9.8
Men alone	8.4	0.0	3.2	10.0	0.0	3.7	10.3	0.0	3.8
Men alone and others	2.4	2.6	2.5	3.0	3.3	3.2	2.5	3.5	3.1
Father with children	3.3	0.1	1.3	3.7	0.0	1.4	2.6	0.0	1.0
Father with children and others	3.2	0.7	1.7	2.4	0.4	1.2	2.1	0.4	1.1
Total	**100**	**100**	**100**	**100**	**100**	**100**	**100**	**100**	**100**

Sources: IBGE 1999; 2004; 2009.

Table 4.10 also shows that the proportion of frail elderly living with spouses or children decreased between 1998 and 2008. This reduction was higher among men if the presence of children is considered and higher among women if the presence of spouses is considered. On the other hand, the proportion of men and women who live on their own increased. As a result, in 2008, 10.3 percent of men and 15.5 percent of women with DLA difficulties declared that they were living alone. An additional 2.5 percent of the frail men and 11.7 percent of the frail women declared they were living alone or with non-family members. This suggests a reduction in female capacity to take care of their family members, which had been found in previous studies by Camarano,

Pasinato, and Lemos (2007) and Camarano (2008). In turn, this puts pressure on the government to offer formal care services, either institutional or home-based.

Figure 4.8 shows the position in the household of elderly who experience DLA difficulties. All indicators vary dramatically by sex. While 72.1 percent of the men headed their households, only 44.4 percent of the women did so, of which 26.0 percent were spouses. On the other hand, while 28.8 percent of the female elderly lived in households of their children, their children's spouses, or other relatives, the comparable proportion for male elderly was 14.3 percent, which indicates a higher dependence on family for elderly women. It is likely that they left their own home to look for support. Fragile elderly who live by themselves or with relatives constitute the group most exposed to family violence and most likely to live in residential institutions or nursing homes (see Branch and Jette 1982; Breeze, Sloggett, and Fletcher 1999; Grundy and Jital 2007; Nihtilä and Martikainen 2008; Wolinsky et al. 1992).

It is important to understand the relationship of the elderly with the younger household members in Brazil since the latter currently experience difficulties in their transition to adulthood, especially in finding employment and independent housing arrangements (for details see Camarano, Mello, and Kanso 2009). For instance, the average number of members in households with frail elderly as household head is 2.8 (see table 4.11). These families therefore comprise elderly and non-elderly;

Figure 4.8   Distribution of Elderly with Difficulty in DLAs by Household Position, 2008

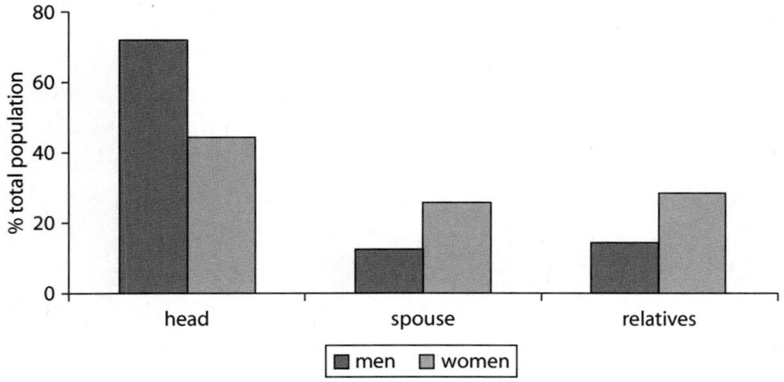

Source: PNAD (IGBE 2008).

Table 4.11   Characteristics of Households with Frail Elderly as Household Heads in Brazil, 2008

Household characteristics	
Average number of members	2.8
% of households with children aged 21+ living in	42.2
% children living in who work	59.7
% children living in who study	7.6
% children living in who not work and do not study	37.6
% of frail elderly contributing to family income	54.6
% of adult children contributing to family income	19.9

Source: PNAD (IBGE 2008).

in fact, 42.2 percent have "adult children" (aged 21 and over) living with elderly parents. Of such adult children, 37.6 percent neither work nor study. They likely count on parental income for their living and provide some help in exchange. As a matter of fact, in these households the contribution of the frail elderly to household income was 54.6 percent in 2008 and the comparable contribution for children was 19.9 percent. This means that frail elderly do need help but also provide help, at least in financial terms, as shown in figure 4.9.

LTC Institutions in Brazil
In Brazil there is no consensus about what residential institutions should provide to the elderly. They are sometimes seen as social assistance institutions and sometimes as health institutions. One of the most important reasons for looking for an institution is poverty and lack of housing. According to Groisman (1999), institutions are not intended to provide health services or therapeutic practices, although residents receive not only housing, food, and clothing, but also health services and medicines. Nevertheless, population aging and the increasing survival of people with reduction of the physical, cognitive, and mental capacities increasingly require that institutions offer something more than just shelter.

There are few LTC institutions in Brazil. They accommodate less than 1 percent (96,969 individuals) of the elderly population in 3,549 sites. Unsurprisingly, given that the bulk of the elderly population resides in that region, they are concentrated in the southeast (34.4 percent in São Paulo) and in the larger cities. Of Brazilian municipalities in this region, 72 percent have no LTC institutions at all, a figure that rises to 90 percent

Figure 4.9   Contribution to Family Income from Elderly with Difficulty in DLAs by Position in Household, 2008

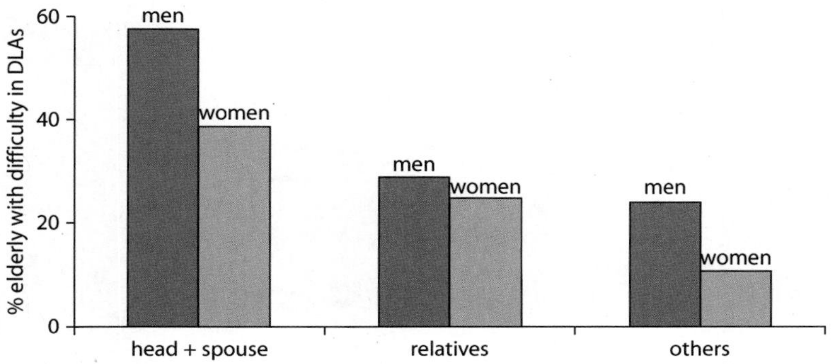

Source: PNAD (IBGE 2008).

in the northern region. The majority of existing LTC facilities are charities (65.2 percent). The private sector accounts for 28.2 percent and the public sector accounts for only 6 percent (IPEA/SEDH 2007, 2008a, 2008b, 2008c).

The age and sex composition of these residents is shown in figure 4.10 and compared to the age and sex distribution of the elderly population in the country. It is noteworthy that the proportion of the elderly population diminishes with age, but that of residents living in residential homes or nursing homes increases. This incidence is more frequent among women, which confirms findings in the literature of frailty at old ages.

The main source of revenue for all the LTC institutions is fees paid by the residents or their relatives. The Elders' Bill of Rights stipulates that up to 70 percent of the older person's social benefits can be paid directly to an institution. Some tax exemptions are available to charitable institutions and there are often additional contributions from government/ university staff as well as volunteers. Public sector institutions, on the other hand, receive government help in the form of medical provision, specialized staff, and medical services. As in most developing countries, Brazil's LTC institutions for the elderly are limited in availability and size of facilities, with little government contribution. The average facility houses only 28.3 people, with 2.2 people per bedroom. Moreover, institutions tend to operate at full capacity, averaging 90 percent bed occupancy (Camarano 2010).

Figure 4.10   Age/Sex Composition of Elderly and Elderly Living in Residential Homes or Nursing Homes, 2007–09

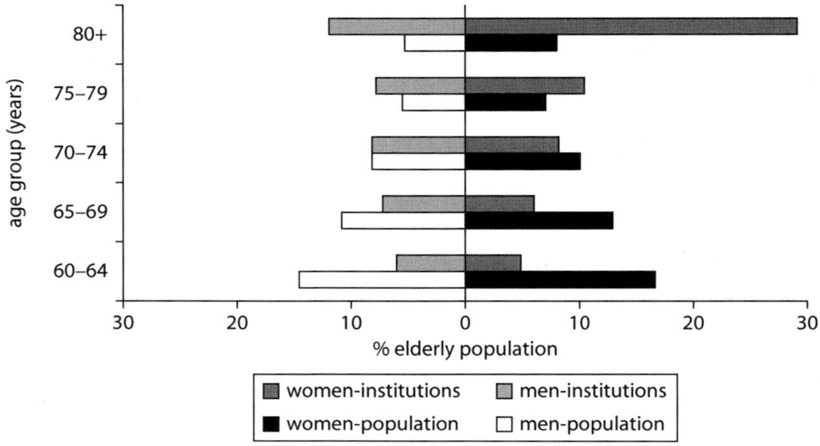

Source: IPEA/SEDH (2007, 2008a, 2008b, 2008c).

Projections of LTC Needs

The demand for formal LTC in Brazil is expected to increase due to the aging of the population and the reduction in the supply of family caregivers. This is the result of fertility reduction, mortality decline at advanced ages, changes in nuptiality and family arrangements, and the steep increase in women's participation in the labor market. Migration of young adults, which weakens intergenerational ties and support mechanisms, is another factor influencing the availability of family care.

Demographic change is not the only factor that explains increase in the demand for LTC and the pressure on public expenditures. According to Jacobzone, Camboias, and Robine (2000), there seems to be no relationship between public expenses for LTC as a share of GDP and the proportion of the very old population. The key variables to understand such a relationship are the health conditions of the elderly population and the arrangements for their care. These authors analyzed OECD countries and found that the potential effects of population aging may be partly offset by a relative improvement in the functional health of the old population, which may even be accompanied by a decrease in the demand for formal LTC. The authors also showed that, although morbidity has increased among the elderly in France and the United States, their general life conditions in those countries have improved.

One of the main policy implications of that study, however, is that it would not be prudent for policy makers to count on future reductions in the prevalence of severe disability among the elderly to offset the increasing demand for LTC originating from population aging. Even though disability prevalence rates have declined to some extent in some countries, population aging usually leads to increasing numbers of people at older ages with some disability that requires long-term care (Lafortune and Balestat 2007).

In other words, the proportion of elderly persons who will demand LTC may decrease as a result of improvements in health prevention, postponement of incapacities, and their better management. Nevertheless, the rapid increase in the numbers of the very old population is likely to produce an increase in the number of those demanding LTC. At the same time, concerns with the reduction of the commitments of the younger generation to older persons may be exaggerated. The decline in the supply of care by close relatives (children, cousins, etc.) may be at least partially compensated for by the supply of grandchildren and higher survival rates of the spouses.

The next sections present two scenarios for long-term care demand and supply each in 2020, 2030, and 2040 in Brazil.[10] In terms of demand, it is certain that the numbers of the very old population in Brazil will dramatically increase in the next 30 years, but there is uncertainty regarding their health and frailty and therefore the numbers of elderly who will need support for DLAs. In terms of supply, there is uncertainty about family arrangements for long-term care, which will be affected by future decisions of family members, especially the female ones, to look for employment outside the household with higher intensity.

LTC Future Demand

Many population projections have already pointed to a sharp increase in numbers and proportion of elderly (for example, IBGE 2008). This section considers the Camarano and Kansos (2009) study, which projects an annual growth rate of 5.5 percent for this age group between 2010 and 2040, resulting in 13.7 million individuals aged 80 and over in 2040, of which 60.5 percent are women. It also means 10.9 million more very old people than in 2010. The entire population aged 60 and above will reach 55.8 million in 2040. Figure 4.11 shows not only the increase in the elderly population but also its changes in age composition.

Figure 4.11   Elderly Population: Absolute Numbers and Growth Rates, 2000–40

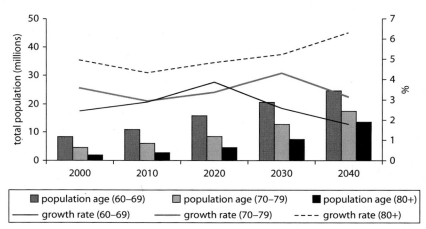

Source: Camarano and Kanso 2009.

Regarding health and frailty conditions, the first scenario (Frail 1) assumes that the proportions of the frail elderly (those with difficulty in performing DLAs) will remain constant at the same level as those observed in 2008, and the second scenario (Frail 2) that such proportions will decline yearly at the same rate as that observed for Great Britain in 1995–2002, which had a decline in the proportion of persons aged 65 and over who reported DLA difficulties of 2.6 percent for men and 1.6 percent for women. For the purpose of projections, these proportions are disaggregated by age and sex to allow analyzing the impact of the demographic factors on the one hand and of functional health on the other. Both scenarios assume that the impact of other exogenous factors remains constant.

Table 4.12 presents the results of the first and second scenarios. If no more improvements in the health conditions of the elderly occur (Frail 1), approximately 4.5 million frail elderly are projected in 2020, which represent 1.3 million more than in 2008. Among them, 62.7 percent would be women. Also in this scenario, in 2040 10.2 million elderly will need long-term care. This figure is 3.4 times higher than that of 2010.

On the other hand, if the proportion of frail old people decreases as a result of various improvements (Frail 2), little more than 3.0 million elderly will need long-term care in 2020, a figure slightly lower than that observed in 2008. Also, women predominate in this group. In the Frail 2

Table 4.12   Scenarios for Elderly Population and Frail Elderly
population thousands

				Scenarios					
				Frail 1: No further frailty improvement			Frail 2: Further frailty improvements		
	Population 60+								
	Men	Women	Total	Men	Female	Total	Men	Female	Total
2010	8,753	10,992	19,745	1,139	1,883	3,021	1,071	1,798	2,870
2020	12,683	16,169	28,852	1,675	2,817	4,492	1,114	2,085	3,199
2030	17,813	23,086	40,899	2,502	4,260	6,762	1,494	2,746	4,240
2040	24,251	31,532	55,783	3,743	6,435	10,178	2,059	3,620	5,679

Source: Camarano 2010.

scenario, improvements in health conditions would compensate for demographic growth till 2020. However, after 2020 those needing LTC will increase in spite of the improvements in health conditions. The figure projected for 2040 will be twice that for 2010. Comparing the results for the two scenarios, improvements in health conditions, as hypothesized, may "save" about 1.3 demanders of LTC in 2020 and about 4.5 million in 2040. These results underscore the importance of greater policy efforts to prevent or postpone as much as possible health and disability problems among the elderly.

Future Supply of Female Caregivers

For the purpose of this analysis, potential caregivers are assumed to be women aged 20–69 who report experiencing no difficulty in DLAs and who do not participate in the labor market. They are spouses, daughters, or other relatives living in the same household as the elderly demanding care. Single individuals are more likely to be caregivers than married ones. It is recognized that there are family caregivers who do not live in the same household as the elderly, but PNAD data do not allow identification of these individuals.

Figure 4.12 shows that the proportion of potential female caregivers decreased for all age groups in 1998, 2003, and 2008. Overall, it decreased from 37.0 percent to 27.4 percent between 1998 and 2008. At the same time, the female activity rate increased from 53.8 percent to 60.5 percent during the same period.

Two scenarios for the projections of future caregivers are presented. The first keeps the proportion of potential caregivers constant at the same level as those observed in 2008 for each age group (Caregiver 1). The second assumes a decrease in such proportion until 2020, taking into

Figure 4.12   Female Activity Rates and Proportion of Potential Female Caregivers, 1998, 2003, and 2008

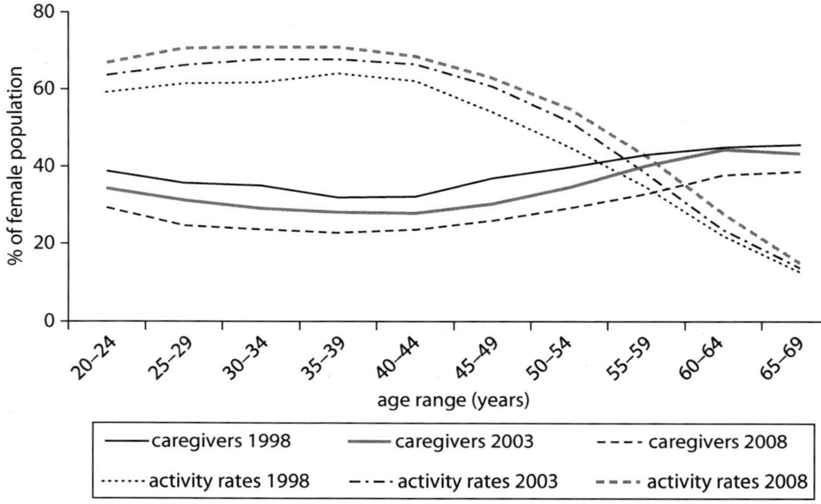

Source: PNAD (IBGE 1998, 2003, 2008).

account the annual variation observed in 1998–2008. For 2020–2040, 50 percent of that variation is assumed (Caregiver 2).

Conclusions for Future of LTC

The combination of the two scenarios of potential demanders and of potential caregivers result in four scenarios for the potential demand and family arrangements for long-term care. Table 4.13 shows the ratios among potential caregivers and potential care demanders projected for 2020 and 2040. The value of this ratio was 5.2 in 2008. In most of the cases, a decrease is expected in the supply of informal care. The only exception is for 2020, when it is assumed that the proportion of frail elderly will diminish and that of caregivers will be kept constant.

The results of the four scenarios in terms of care arrangements for frail elderly are presented in table 4.14. The expected number of frail elderly is disaggregated in two groups: those who can expect to be taken care of by their families and those needing formal care. Considering that in 2008 about 500,000 persons, that is, 16.1 percent of the frail elderly, were not taken care of by a family caregiver because they were living in institutions

Table 4.13   Projections of the Caregiver to Frail Elderly Ratio, 2020 and 2040

| | 2020 | | 2040 | |
Elderly group	Caregiver 1: Proportion of family caregivers remains constant	Caregiver 2: Proportion of family caregivers becomes smaller	Caregiver 1: Proportion of family caregivers remains constant	Caregiver 2: Proportion of family caregivers becomes smaller
Frail 1: No further frailty improvement	4.3	2.5	2.0	0.6
Frail 2: Further frailty improvement	6.0	3.5	3.7	1.0
2008	5.2			

Source: Camarano 2010.

Table 4.14   Expected Number of Frail Elderly by Family Care Arrangements, 2040
thousands of people

| | 2040 | | |
Scenarios	With family	Without family	Total
1. Frail 1 and Caregiver 1	4,016	6,162	10,178
2. Frail 2 and Caregiver 1	4,016	1,663	5,679
3. Frail 1 and Caregiver 2	1,128	9,050	10,178
4. Frail 2 and Caregiver 2	1,128	4,551	5,679
2008	2,741	528	3,269
Residents in institutions 2008		97	
Living alone 2008		431	

Source: Camarano (2010).

or by themselves, three of the four scenarios point to an increase in the demand for non-family care.[11]

Scenario 4 seems to be the most plausible as it assumes a decrease in the proportion of frail old people as a result of improvements in health prevention and postponement and better management of disabilities associated with new medical technology. Even so, an increase in the demand for formal/institutional care can be expected due to family changes and population aging. Brazilian residential institutions would have to increase their capacity eight times by 2040 to meet this increased demand. PNAD data do not provide information on the types of arrangements in place for people living alone. Probably, they rely on support

Table 4.15   Expected Number of Frail Elderly Not Cared for by Families, 2040

thousands of people

	2040		
Scenarios	Living alone	Institutions	Total
1. Frail 1 and Caregiver 1	5,030	1,132	6,162
2. Frail 2 and Caregiver 1	1,358	306	1,663
3. Frail 1 and Caregiver 2	7,387	1,663	9,050
4. Frail 2 and Caregiver 2	3,715	836	4,551
2008	431	97	528

Source: Camarano 2010.

from a domestic helper or a formal caregiver, the demand for which will also increase. Assuming the type of arrangements the elderly had in 2008 remain the same, table 4.15 presents the number of frail elderly not cared by families who will live alone and who will live in institutions in 2040.

These scenarios should not be seen as forecasts, but as an instrument for highlighting the importance of dynamic factors in projecting future social needs. Although population aging is a demographic process, it is also a dynamic process that affects and is affected by public policies. Future developments in the prevalence of severe disability among the elderly are difficult to predict because a number of factors may have either positive or negative effects on old-age disability rates in the future. On the positive side, further improvements in the socioeconomic status of new generations of elderly, including rising levels of education and rising income and better living conditions, can be expected to play a positive role in improving the health and functional status of the elderly. The gradual reduction in some health risk factors such as smoking can also play a positive role. On the negative side, the rising prevalence of certain chronic conditions like arthritis and diabetes and of important risk factors like hypertension and obesity can be expected to reduce functional capacity among the elderly, unless greater efforts are made to address them (Lafortune and Balestat 2007).

Notes

1. The source does not show data for the 80+ age group, which results from the common practice of either total omission or lumping together all individuals over age 60 in one group.

2. A discussion of "expansion" and "compression" of morbidity is presented in the next section of this chapter.

3. Prevention and postponement of disease and disability and maintenance of health, independence, and mobility in an aging population will remain the major health-related challenge of population aging. In addition to these health issues, living longer will also present individual and societal challenges related to quality of life in old age, including independence, social interaction, and community involvement. Some of these questions will be discussed in the sections devoted to long-term care in chapter 6.

4. Howse (2005) concludes that technological innovation and productivity have made a substantially larger contribution to increases in health care spending over the past few decades than has population aging. Johansson (1997) reviews overall expenditure developments in Sweden and shows that cost factors in the general economy play a more important role in the increase of health expenditures than does growth in the number of elderly people. The same conclusion is drawn by Castles (2000), using data for OECD countries for 1965–95. This analysis finds no statistically significant relationship between aging and aggregate health care expenditure and concludes that total health expenditure in a country is almost entirely explained by its level of real GDP per capita. Similarly, Richardson and Robertson (1999) conclude from OECD data for 1975, 1985, and 1995 that health expenditures per capita are not driven mechanistically by demographic factors.

5. For example, the best way to prevent osteoporosis in older age is to focus on nutrition and physical activity of the female child up to late adolescence, by which time the full bone mass will have formed. If such a strategy is put in place at the community level (for example, appropriate/healthy school meals, calcium supplements if indicated, and provision of exercise facilities throughout childhood and adolescence), there will be a larger gain compared to one-to-one interventions.

6. The term "active aging" is meant to convey a more inclusive message than "healthy aging." The semantic change is a recognition of the factors in addition to health care that affect how individuals and populations age. It allows scope for people to realize their potential for social as well as mental and physical well-being—reflecting therefore the WHO definition of "health." In an active aging framework, policies and programs that promote social connections and mental health are as important as those that improve physical health status.

7. See chapter 2 for a brief description of the urbanization process in Brazil, which has been rapid and has increased the proportion of people living in urban areas from 36.2 percent in 1950 to 81.2 percent in 2000.

8. For instance, in 2003, the country's health system, one of the most sophisticated in the world, miserably failed the elderly population in its response to

an unprecedented heat wave. Thousands of older people died of heatstroke, many of them in complete isolation. The alarm was raised by funeral directors puzzled by the high demand, not by health or social care workers. And yet, countries such as France first became rich and then grew old, while developing countries are aging faster before being wealthy. What France and other European countries needed to protect their older citizens in the heat wave was a stronger primary health care sector, which might have provided community-based care to many isolated, frail elderly people and prevented unnecessary deaths.

9. This includes contributory benefits, such as retirement and survival pensions, as well as non-contributory benefits such as BPC.

10. This method has already been used in some OECD projections (for example, Lafortune and Balestat 2007).

11. Almost 40 percent of the institutional residents are non-frail persons who need shelter. This demand is not considered here.

References

Aboderin, I., A. Kalache, Y. Ben-Shlomo, J. W. Lynch, C. S. Yajnik, D. Kuh, and D. Yach. 2002. *Life Course Perspectives on Coronary Heart Disease, Stroke and Diabetes: Key Issues and Implications for Policy and Research*. Geneva: World Health Organization.

Batista, Anália S., Luciana B. Jaccoud, Luseni e El-Moor Aquino, and Patrícia Dario. 2008. "Envelhecimento e Dependência: Desafios para a Organização da Proteção Social." *Coleção Previdência Social, Brasília* v. 28. Ministério da Previdência Social.

Branch, L. G., and A. M. Jette. 1982. "A Prospective Study of Long-Term Care Institutionalization Among the Aged." *American Journal of Public Health* 72 (12): 1373–79.

Breeze, E., A. Sloggett, and A. Fletcher. 1999. "Socioeconomic and Demographic Predictors of Mortality and Institutional Residence among Middle Aged and Older People: Results from the Longitudinal Study." *Journal of Epidemiology and Community Health* 53 (12): 765–74.

Brodsky, J., J. Habib, and M. J. Hirschfeld. 2003. *Key Policy Issues in Long-Term Care*. Geneva: World Health Organization.

Camarano, A. A. 2006. "Mecanismos de proteção social para a população idosa brasileira." Texto para discussão 1179. IPEA (Instituto de Pesquisa Econômica Aplicada), Rio de Janeiro.

Camarano, A. A. 2010. "Options for Long-Term Care in Brazil: Formal or Informal Care?" Background paper prepared for the Workshop on Aging in Brazil, World Bank, Brasilia, April 6–7, 2010.

Camarano, Ana Amélia. 2008. "Cuidados de longa duração para a população idosa." *Sinais Sociais* 3 (7): 10–39.

Camarano, A. A., and S. Kanso. 2009. "Perspectivas de Crescimento para a População Brasileira: Velhos e Novos Resultados." Texto para discussão 1426. IPEA (Instituto de Pesquisa Econômica Aplicada), Rio de Janeiro.

Camarano, A. A., M. T. E. Pasinato, and V. R. Lemos. 2007. "Cuidados de Longa Duração para a população idosa: uma questão de gênero?" In *Qualidade de Vida na Velhice: enfoque multidisciplinar,* ed. A. L. Néri, 127–50. Campinas, Brazil: Alínea Editora.

Castles, F. G. 2000. "Population Ageing and the Public Purse: How Real is the Problem?" Unpublished paper, Australian National University, Canberra.

Danel, I., C. Kurowski, and H. Saxenian. 2005. "Brazil: Addressing the Challenge of Non-Communicable Diseases." World Bank, Washington DC.

Esping-Andersen, G., D. Gallie, A. Hemerijck, and J. Myles. 2002. Why We Need a New Welfare State. New York: Oxford University Press.

Grundy E., and M. Jital. 2007. "Socio-demographic Variations in Moves to Institutional Care 1991–2001: a Record Linkage Study from England and Wales." *Age Ageing* 36 (4): 424–30.

Hallal, P. C., M. C.Tenório, R. M. Tassitano, R. S. Reis, Y. M. Carvalho, D. K. Cruz, W. Damascena, and D. C. Malta. 2010. "Evaluation of the Academia da Cidade Program to Promote Physical Activity in Recife, Pernambuco State, Brazil: Perceptions of Users and Non-users." *Cad Saúde Publica* 26 (1): 70–78.

Howse, K. 2005. "Policies for Healthy Ageing." *Ageing Horizons* 2: 3–15.

Howse, K. 2007. "Long-term Care Policy: The Difficulties of Taking a Global View." *Ageing Horizons* 6 (6): 1–11.

Kalache, A. 2010. "Implications for the Health Sector of the Ageing Process in Brazil." Unpublished paper, World Bank, Brasilia.

IBGE (Instituto Brasileiro de Geografia e Estatística). 2008. "Projeção da População do Brasil por Sexo e Idade, 1980–2050," Revisão 2008. Estudos e Pesquisas: Informação Demográfica e Socioeconômica. IBGE, Rio de Janeiro.

———. 2009. PNAD (Pesquisa Nacional por Amostra de Domicílios) 2008. IBGE, Rio de Janeiro; other years cited in text.

Iglesias, R., P. Jha, M. Pinto, V. L. da Costa e Silva, and J. Godinho. 2007. "Tobacco Control in Brazil." World Bank, Washington DC.

IPEA/SEDH. (Instituto de Pesquisa Econômica Aplicada/Secretaria Especial dos Direitos Humanos). 2007. "Características das Instituições de Longa Permanência para Idosos: Região Norte. Coordenação Geral Ana Amélia Camarano." Brasília: IPEA; Presidência da República.

———. 2008a. "Características das Instituições de Longa Permanência para Idosos: Região Centro Oeste. Coordenação Geral Ana Amélia Camarano." Brasília: IPEA; Presidência da República.

———. 2008b. "Características das Instituições de Longa Permanência para Idosos: Região Sul. Coordenação Geral Ana Amélia Camarano." Brasília: IPEA; Presidência da República.

———. 2008c. "Características das Instituições de Longa Permanência para Idosos: Região Nordeste. Coordenação Geral Ana Amélia Camarano." Brasília: IPEA; Presidência da República.

Jacobzone, S., E. E. Cambois, and J. Robine. 2000/2001. "Is the Health of Older Persons in OECD Countries Improving Fast Enough to Compensate for Population Ageing?" OECD Economic Studies 30. Organisation for Economic Co-operation and Development, Paris.

Johansson P.O. 1997. "Is The Valuation Of a QALY Gained Independent Of Age? Some Empirical Evidence." *Journal of Health Economics* 16 (5): 589–99.

Kalache, A. 2010. "Implications for the Health Sector of the Ageing Process in Brazil." Background paper prepared for the Workshop on Aging in Brazil, World Bank, Brasilia, April 6–7, 2010.

Kalache, A., and I. Kickbusch. 1997. "A Global Strategy for Healthy Ageing." *World Health* 50 (4) (July–August): 4–5.

Lafortune, G., and G. Balestat. 2007. "Trends in Severe Disability Among Elderly People: Assessing the Evidence in 12 OECD Countries and the Future Implications." OECD Health Working Papers 26. Organisation for Economic Co-operation and Development, Paris.

Lloyd-Sherlock, Peter. 2004. "Ageing, Development and Social Protection: Generalizations, Myths and Stereotypes." In *Living Longer: Ageing, Development and Social Protection*, ed. P. Lloyd-Sherlock, 1–21. London/New York: United Nations Research Institute for Social Development/Zed Books.

Ministry of Health (Brazil). 2009. Datasus. www.datasus.gov.br.

Nihtilä, Elina, and Pekka Martikainen. 2008. "Why Older People Living with a Spouse Are Less Likely to be Institutionalized: The Role of Socioeconomic Factors and Health Characteristics." *Scandinavian Journal of Public Health* 36 (1): 35–43.

Novaes, R. H. L. 2003. "Os asilos de idosos no Estado do Rio de Janeiro— Repercussões da (não) integralidade no cuidado e na atenção à saúde dos idosos." Dissertação de Mestrado em Saúde Coletiva, Instituto de Medicina Social, Universidade do Estado do Rio de Janeiro/UERJ, Rio de Janeiro.

Pasinato, Maria Tereza, and George Kornis. 2009. "A inserção dos cuidados de longa duração para idosos no âmbito dos sistemas de seguridade social: experiência internacional." Textos para discussão 1371. National Institute for Applied Economic Research (IPEA), Rio de Janeiro.

Richardson, J., and I. Robertson. 1999. "Ageing and the Cost of Health Services." Conference Proceedings for Productivity Commission and Melbourne

Institute of Applied Economic and Social Research, "Policy Implications of the Ageing of Australia's Population," Australian Government Publishing Services (AGPS), Canberra.

Simoes, E. J., P. Hallal, M. Pratt, L. Ramos, M. Munk, W. Damascena, D. P. Perez, C. M. Hoehner, D. Gilbertz, D. Carvalho Malta, and R. C. Brownson. 2009. "Effects of a Community-Based, Professionally Supervised Intervention on Physical Activity Levels Among Residents of Recife, Brazil." *American Journal of Public Health* 99 (1): 68–75.

United Nations. 2008. "World Population Prospects: 2008 rev." UN Department of Economic and Social Affairs, Population Division, New York.

WHO (World Health Organization). 2002. *Active Aging: A Policy Framework.* A contribution of the World Health Organization to the Second United Nations World Assembly on Ageing, Madrid, Spain, April 8–12, 2002.

Wolinsky, F. D., C. M. Callahan, J. F. Fitzgerald, and R. J. Johnson. 1992. "The Risk of Nursing Home Placement and Subsequent Death among Older Adults. *Journal of Gerontology* 47 (4): S173–82.

CHAPTER 5

Productivity and Education

The overall economic output of a country is determined in major part by its labor force participation and associated productivity. A first positive consequence of the demographic transition, that is, the transformation of countries from having high birth and death rates to low death and birth rates, is that the larger share of working-age population means greater participation rates in the workforce, ultimately accelerating economic growth and increasing public revenues. However, as the demographic transition progresses, the share of the working-age population eventually starts declining, labor force participation rate decreases, and more fiscal pressure is generated mainly to support health and social security expenditures. The larger the old dependency ratio grows, the more labor market behavior at older ages becomes an important factor to determine the overall size of the working population.

Usually, labor force participation is closely related to retirement, that is, the higher the retirement rate the lower the participation rate. Chapter 2, however, showed that these two measures are only weakly related in Brazil. While early retirement[1] is common, individuals continue working long after that, mainly in the informal sector and thus without contributing to the social security system.

This early retirement pattern could in part be a result of older workers tending to have more health problems and becoming less productive than younger ones. If older workers are less productive, firms could replace them with younger workers, providing them the opportunity to retire early, get the pension benefit, and sometimes, rehiring them with an informal contract. In the first study addressing the relationship between productivity and age, Lehman (1953) revealed a creative age curve showing productivity starting to increase in creative occupations such as the sciences, arts, and athletics at around 20, reaching a peak in the period from the late 30s to the mid-40s, and beginning to decline thereafter. Subsequent studies have supported this thesis, although they have also stressed that the effect of aging on productivity depends on the occupation (see Skirbekk 2003 for an overview of these studies). In occupations that are more dependent on cognitive abilities, such as science, the young usually have an advantage. But in managerial occupations, where experience is a more important factor for job performance, older workers tend to perform at least as well as the younger counterparts.

The impact of population aging on productivity at the macro level is not clear. It is known that productivity is enhanced, among other things, by improvements in knowledge, and that it is closely related to innovation, such as developing new working methods and new technologies. Because innovation is intimately related to creativity, and creativity is often higher among the younger members of society, a higher share of older workers would have a negative effect on productivity growth (see UN 2007). However, the human capital theory predicts that demographic changes like those in Brazil tend to result in families investing more in their children's human capital, which could contribute to balancing the negative aggregate impact of an older, less creative population on productivity. Furthermore, a smaller share of younger population would make public investment in education and early training collectively cheaper, which, in turn, would make retraining older workers a more efficient means of improving labor force productivity.

Another possible problem resulting from the demographic transition is the imbalance between labor force productivity and labor force costs. If, for some reason, firms pay seniority wages even with a declining age-productivity profile, major difficulties could result in terms of competitiveness, profitability, investment, and their related variables. Although the neoclassical theory predicts that firms pay the marginal productivity of each worker as a wage (that is, each worker's wage equals the value he/she adds to the firm's production), this chapter will show that there are incentive contract and legislation reasons for this pattern to not be produced.

This chapter presents a discussion of how the labor market productivity in Brazil would change as a result of the demographic transition and how this change in turn would affect economic growth and public finance. It focuses on issues related to the age-productivity profile, opportunities to improve education and training investments, and the wage-productivity gap. In a nutshell, the consequences of population aging are that (1) the working-age population is becoming smaller and (2) the share of the most productive individuals within the labor force is also becoming smaller. Hence, if overall production output is to be maintained, some measures or interventions are needed to increase labor force participation and productivity.

The rest of this chapter will discuss (1) the effect of age on labor force productivity and consequently on productivity growth; (2) how improvements in education and on-the-job training could reverse the trend of declining age-productivity effects, with a description of Brazil's efforts in these areas; (3) how differences between age-productivity and age-wage profiles could damage the firms' competitiveness; and (4) evidence of the effect of the aging labor force on firms' productivity among Brazilian industrial firms.

The Age-Productivity Profile

A large body of evidence supports the idea that cognitive abilities decline after some point in adulthood. On the basis of 91 psychometric studies of how mental abilities develop over the life cycle, Verhaegen and Salthouse (1997) conclude that cognitive abilities (reasoning, processing speed, and episodic memory) decline significantly before 50 years of age and more rapidly thereafter. They found instead that maximum levels are achieved in the 20s and the 30s.

However, not all types of abilities are thought to decline with age. The psychometric studies divide functioning between fluid abilities and crystallized abilities. Fluid abilities concern the performance and speed of solving tasks related to new material, including processing speed and reasoning. These abilities are strongly reduced at older ages. Crystallized abilities, such as apprehending verbal meaning and word fluency, even improve with accumulated knowledge and remain at a high functional level until a late stage in life. Hence, the declining part of the age-productivity profile does not set in equally for all tasks and jobs.

Several empirical studies have supported these ideas. Most research has shown that older workers are at a disadvantage (compared to younger workers) in professions that use a variety of cognitive abilities (such as memory and processing speed), but have an advantage in professions that require verbal abilities, capacity to communicate, or ability to manage. Moreover, older workers seem to be less productive in sectors that are most innovative, as they have more difficulties adjusting in such rapidly changing environments than do younger workers (Daveri and Maliranta 2007).

Furthermore, even if we believe that individual productivity declines with age, it is not a certainty that productivity will decline in aggregate terms. Blanchet (1992) points out that it is one thing to observe productivity problems for aging workers, but this is not sufficient to prove that the plausible changes in the proportion of old workers will turn this individual problem into a significant macroeconomic one. The author's view is that there is a limit to the total effect of the demographic transition on countries' overall productivity, which would not be at all negligible over the short run, but, given that changes are expected to occur over a very long time span, they will be easily overwhelmed by all other potential sources of productivity growth.

The literature analyzing the effect of demographic transition on productivity in aggregate levels is divided by studies that use firm-level data and studies that use macroeconomic data. The first group usually reaches the conclusion that firm productivity declines with the increase in the proportion of older workers (see later section on the "Wage-Productivity Gap"). The second group analyzes this effect based on growth theory and uses cross-country data, resulting in controversial findings. Feyrer (2007) and Tang and MacLeod (2006) find that the share of workforce over 50 years old is negatively correlated with productivity and growth. However, using the same methodology, Lindh and Malmberg (1999) find evidence that a higher share of workers between 50 and 64 is related to higher growth.

Finally, even taking into account the literature that shows a negative effect of aging on productivity, it is important to note that the relative demand for work tasks involving certain cognitive abilities could shift in different ways over time. If the demand for interactive skills, abilities that are relatively stable over the life cycle, increases more than demand for mathematical aptitude, which does decline substantially by age, the value of labor market experience would increase and the effect of aging on productivity could be smaller than expected or even reversed. Also, in many countries, including Brazil, the population has become more educated, which makes training more efficient to avoid human capital depreciation at older ages, as will be discussed in the next section.

Brazil does not have much data on the age-productivity profile. Most studies provide information about the life-cycle–wage profile, but, as the next sections show, this is not always the same as the age-productivity profile. One way to analyze the effects of older workers on the labor market is to present the share of employed workers in the formal sector by age (see figure 5.1). The share of older workers in the formal sector is much smaller than the share of younger workers, with a peak in the 40–44 age group. The section on "Wage-Productivity Gap" will demonstrate that the wage situation is different.

This could be a sign that older workers on average are less productive than younger ones, although more robust evidence will be provided later in this chapter. The informal sector is much less productive than the formal sector, because it has less access to credit markets and less comparative advantage to compete for more skilled workers (see the box 5.1).

Figure 5.1   Percentage of Formal Workers by Age and Birth Cohort
only employed workers

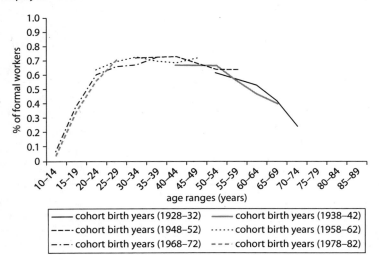

Box 5.1

Labor Market Informality in Brazil

Informality in the labor market is a big problem for the workers, the employers, and the public sector in Brazil. Although the share of informal workers has decreased recently (from 52.1 percent to 48.4 percent between 2002 and 2007), it remains very high. Informal workers do not contribute to the social security system, they receive much lower wages, and they do not have protection against either health problems or unemployment, nor access to old age social security benefits when retired. (Although Brazil has a free universal health system, companies can offer health insurance linked to the social security system, which provides better health assistance in the private sector.)

Brazilian employers are required to withhold 11 percent of the employee's wages for social security contributions and a certain percentage as income tax (according to the applicable tax bracket). The employer is required to contribute an additional 20 percent of the total payroll value to the social security system. Depending on the company's main activity, the employer must also contribute to federally funded insurance and education programs. There is also a required deposit of 8 percent of the employee's wages into a bank account that can be withdrawn only when the employee is fired or under certain other extraordinary circumstances (called a "Security Fund for Duration of Employment"). All these contributions amount to a total tax burden of almost 40 percent of the payroll for the employer and 15 percent of the employee's wages, which is a strong incentive for firms to keep wages off the books, especially because official monitoring of the tax system is weak. High payroll taxes can also provide incentives for informality by reducing the net earnings gap between the formal sector (with its forced withholdings) and informal sectors and self-employment.

The point is that for workers who have the choice between working in the formal sector or in the informal sector or self-employment, other things being equal, the reduced net earnings in the formal sector makes it less attractive.[2] Employees are more likely to collude with employers and avoid registering with the social security system, choose jobs that do not enroll workers, or become self-employed. Low labor productivity in small production units might also "force" evasion if the value of output per worker is below the minimum official cost of labor (minimum wage plus social charges).[3] For example, simulations using matching models suggest that payroll taxes would reduce incentives to create vacancies in the formal sector, thus forcing workers, particularly

(continued next page)

Box 5.1 *(continued)*

middle- and low-productivity workers, into the informal sector (World Bank 2009). Mello and Santos (2009) show that improvement in worker education level explains a huge part of the decrease in informality between 2002 and 2007. As Brazilian workers' average education is expected to continue to increase, the formalization process is expected to continue. However, it is also necessary to improve the institutional and policy framework that determines the level of payroll contributions to reduce incentives for informality and strengthen the enforcement process.

Source: Rocha (2010).

Opportunities to Improve Education and On-the-Job Training

This section will examine the consequences of population aging on the opportunities to improve labor force skills, dividing the analysis in two types of skill formation, formal basic education and on-the-job training.

Formal Basic Education

One of the consequences of population aging is that the share of population of school age will decrease greatly. Blanchet (1992) calculates the optimal adjustment of educational policies as a response to changes in the demographic structure. He finds that the aging of the population resulting from lower population growth makes a relative increase in schooling and on-the-job training a more attractive prospect to improve educational attainment and skills formation. This education increase mainly means staying longer in the educational system before entering the labor market (the age at first entry is higher than with a younger population by about four years, which is not a marginal change). This can be explained by cost considerations. Schooling is more costly from a collective standpoint in an economy where the young are relatively predominant. This collective cost is reduced when population grows more slowly, so that lengthening the initial phase of capital accumulation is possible.

As explained in chapter 2, the young dependency ratio—which relates the number of people in dependent age groups (children under age 15 and persons over age 59, in this study) to that of people in the working-age group (aged 15–59)—has been decreasing in Brazil since 1965 and will continue to do so in the foreseeable future. This will make it possible to increase investment per student without increasing the proportion of resources for education as a share of GDP. Moreover, the size of the junior workforce (age 15–24) has also already started to decrease, which makes it easier to finance policies to better qualify this segment and consequently makes it easier for them to find a first job. Figure 5.2, the unemployment rates in Brazil by age group, shows that unemployment rates at 15–17 and 18–24 are much higher than unemployment rates at ages 24–49 and above 50, which demonstrates the importance of policies that help young workers find their first job and gain experience.

The aging population has an impact on education investment not only from a collective, reduced cost point of view, but also by changing individual education choices. The human capital theory predicts that in societies with higher life expectancy at birth, all other things being equal, families have incentives to invest more in education. This is because as people live longer, they take advantage of the returns to education for a longer period of time. The consequence of investing more in education, given a limited budget, is to have fewer children. At the same time, lower infant mortality usually requires families to have fewer children in order to reach the total number of desired surviving children. This, in turn, also implies fewer and more educated children. The relationship between health, fertility, and education has been well documented by Becker, Murphy, Tamura (1990); Bleakley and Lange (2009); Bobonis, Miguel, and Puri-Sharma (2006); Kalemli-Ozcan (2002); Lleras-Muney and

Figure 5.2   Unemployment Rates by Age Group, 2002–10

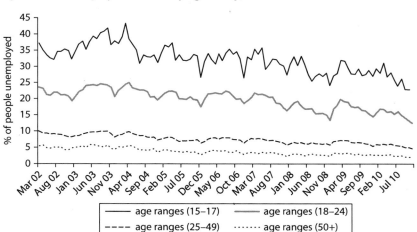

Source: Rocha 2010.

Jayachandran (2009); Lorentzen, McMillan, and Wacziarg (2007); Meltzer (1992); Miguel, and Kremer (2004); and Soares (2005).

As the Brazilian population enjoys an increasingly longer life expectancy at birth, lower infant mortality, and reduced fertility, investments in human capital are expected to increase. Therefore, the next generations should be more educated and productive than the previous ones. However, the real benefit of a population with more years of education can be realized only through a system that provides good-quality education. If the quality of education is low, the additional years if school will not result in a more productive workforce. Therefore Brazilian schools need to provide a better quality education. In 2006, Brazil had one of the worst educational performances in the world in the PISA (Program for International Student Assessment)[4] math score. Brazil was 54th among the 57 countries that participated in the PISA evaluation, with only Krygyz Republic, Qatar, and Tunisia scoring lower. Argentina, Chile, Indonesia, Mexico, Thailand, and Uruguay all scored significantly higher. In other words, Brazil's 2006 math performance defined the bottom of the distribution for countries at its income level (World Bank forthcoming). At the same time, figure 5.3 shows that Brazil has improved its performance in the PISA math score, but it is still much below its counterparts.

A population of children with better educational attainment and young working-age population would also make it easier to retrain these

Figure 5.3   PISA Math Performance, 2000–09

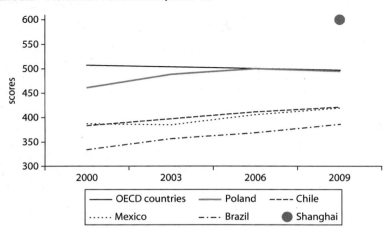

Source: OECD 2010.

generations as they get older and pass their age of peak productivity (Heckman et al. 2005). Of course, an older population would require more resources to finance retraining of a larger share of older workers (who are likely to use their increased political position to ask for it). Under these conditions, it is even more important that those workers who will be retrained have been properly educated when they were younger.

Vocational Education

As noted earlier, the productivity decline at older ages seems to be particularly strong for work tasks where problem-solving, learning, and speed are needed; however, in jobs where experience and verbal abilities are important, older individuals maintain a relatively high productivity level. The ongoing economic changes in the world—which have spurred technological and organization innovation and the economic shift from manufacturing to services—are causing job requirements to change. On one hand, older workers might be better off because physical abilities are becoming less important. On the other hand, continuously changing types of work can mean that an ability to absorb new information is becoming increasingly important relative to long experience (World Bank, 2007b).

How well training practices are adapted to help older workers realize their potential will be critical. A number of studies suggest that older workers may need training to be at a slower pace, more closely tied to the work context, and involve self-directed learning rather than formal classroom training (OECD 2006). The limited evidence available suggests that older workers who have adequate educational attainment and a history of participation in on-the-job training are good training prospects. Targeted training programs seem effective in softening or halting any age-related decline in the ability to learn new skills. Research has demonstrated that such programs can stabilize or even reverse age-specific declines in inductive reasoning and spatial orientation. Furthermore, exercising speed, reasoning, and memory abilities can enhance the functional level of those who undergo training relative to those who do not. As the labor supply ages, firms and workers will need to adapt to the new reality. Evidence to date indicates that access to training decreases substantially through the working life (see figure 5.4) (World Bank 2007b). In the future, firms will have no choice but to expand their training programs to invest more in older employees and to reorient the programs to meet the needs of those workers.

Historically, Brazilian vocational education gained importance in the industrial development of the 1950s with the expansion of the Industrial

Figure 5.4   Share of Population That Took a Vocational Course, 2007

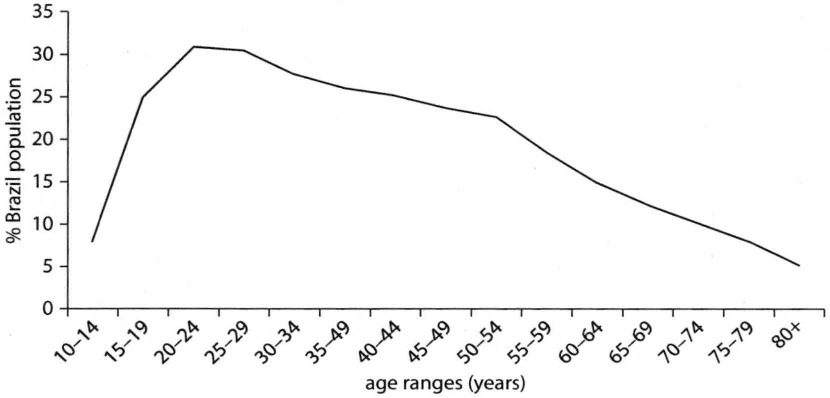

Source: PNAD (IBGE 2007).

Learning National Service (SENAI, Serviço Nacional de Aprendizagem Industrial) and the Commercial Learning National Service (SENAC, Serviço Nacional de Aprendizagem Comercial). These two private vocational training institutions are part of a public system (the "S" system) that collects payroll levies and uses them to fund programs in small enterprises willing to invest in on-the-job-training.

The institutions train workers for diverse jobs in agriculture, commerce, industry, cooperatives, and transport. Moreover, by 1990s vocational training also began in public and private institutions not linked to what is conventionally called the S System (*Sistema S*), that is the set of 12 institutions that receive funds from the Federal Government to provide professional training. The Brazilian National Household Survey (PNAD) shows that in 2007, 22.4 percent of the Brazilian population older than 10 years had taken some type of vocational course, of which 0.7 percent took a tertiary vocational course, 18.5 percent took a secondary course level, and 81.7 percent took professional qualification training without formal education degree. In addition, among those vocational courses, 20.6 percent were in an institute linked to the S System, 22.4 percent in a public institution, and 53.1 percent in a private institution.

The majority of training courses offered in Brazil have few entrance requirements (45.1 percent of the students took a course with no entrance requirements and only 28 percent took a course in which the minimum requirement was primary education completion), which means that vocational courses are used to compensate for the low level of schooling in the population. In addition, among those students, 44 percent never worked in a job in the area of the course taken (the reasons for which were 31.1 percent because the area had no vacancies, 5.1 percent because the course didn't prepare them for the jobs in that area, and 10.8 percent because the majority of the jobs in that area required either experience or advanced formal education). This means that Brazilian training programs need to find out what the private sector employment needs are and adjust their programs to train workers with the needed skills. And they need to improve course quality and raise entrance requirements to match worker qualifications to job needs.

The age distribution of those who have taken vocational courses is presented in figure 5.4. The highest share age groups are 20–29 years old. After that, the percentage of people acquiring training monotonically decreases. It seems that workers at ages with higher unemployment rate (younger ages) are acquiring more training. But, workers at older ages, exactly the ones for who productivity is supposed to decline, are not acquiring sufficient training to keep them at a necessary level of productivity to compete for good jobs. Although there is less unemployment at older ages, as the previous section showed, employment in this age group tends to change from formal to informal and occur in less productive sectors. Thus, there is a room for improvement in vocational training targeted to those over 40 years old.

Studies have documented Brazil's effort to improve active labor market policies (see Rios-Neto and Oliveira 2000). The vocational training in Brazil that started with the S System during the 1950s was well ranked in international comparison for a long period (World Bank 1991) because of its long-duration courses and professional job placements, especially in the manufacturing sector. However, Amadeo (1992) shows many limits of the effectiveness of the S System. The level of schooling of those trained was above the Brazilian average, the system was targeted at employed people, and most of the trained workers were hired in big companies rather than small and medium enterprises. Those who were unemployed had difficulty finding employment after receiving training. Then the federal government decided to expand vocational training by seeking to provide professional qualification of workers. The first attempt was the Professional Recycling Governmental Program (PRP), whose aim was to provide unemployed workers, particularly unemployment insurance beneficiaries, the basic and specific knowledge they needed to reenter the labor market. The program did not work very well, but many aspects were incorporated in the PLANFOR Program, a very ambitious government initiative designed to train 15 million employees between 1996 and 1999. Ultimately a more modest 5 million people received training in the program (Cardoso, Façanha, and Marinho 2002).

The importance of worker training for improving productivity and wages is currently a hot topic among Brazilian social protection authorities. The federal and some local governments have initiated training programs targeted at poor people eligible to receive the federal conditional cash transfer program Bolsa Família, as a part of government strategy of productive inclusion of beneficiaries of cash transfers. The idea is to improve the job skills of a population that would otherwise not receive any training, because they have already left school and depend on the transfer to survive, which reveals how little skilled they are. A study by Soares and Leichsenring (2010) shows that the Bolsa Família beneficiaries have a high turnover rate when employed in the formal sector. Around 50 percent of beneficiaries leave their job after one year and 30 percent stay in the same formal job only six months. The low level of education is usually cited as one of the main reasons for the high turnover. Thus, an increase in investments in training Bolsa beneficiaries and linking the training to the needs of the private sector could improve the productivity of Brazilian society and provide the inclusion of many poor families in the productive sector.

Wage–Productivity Gap

The neoclassical theory of firms assigns workers' wage differentials to differentials in their marginal productivity. The demographic profile of wages follows, therefore, the demographic profile of human capital accumulation, increasing in the early stages of the career and decreasing jointly with the human capital depreciation (Mincer 1974). This hypothesis is based on psychometric studies by medical scientists (Skirbekk 2003), discussed earlier, showing that cognitive abilities deteriorate with age.

However, there have been many hypotheses as to why the age-productivity profile is not always similar to the age-wage profile. One of the most convincing is the deferred compensation hypothesis according to which firms could pay workers whose performance is hard to monitor less than their productivity when they are young and more than their productivity when they are old, as a mechanism to incentivize effort (Lazear 1981). Another explanation uses the sorting and matching models, according to which labor market search, by raising the chance of

finding a good job-worker match, may also imply upward-sloping experience earnings profiles in parallel with flat or declining productivity effects
(see Manning 2000). In other words, employers may use wage as a signal
to attract good workers by offering a wage-experience premium.

Many studies have calculated the effects of workforce characteristics
on productivity and wages using employee-employer firm-level or plant-
level data (in many cases the employee datasets are demographic surveys
linked to the firm- or plant-level data). The work of Hellerstein and
Neumark (1995) and Hellertein, Neumark, and Troske (1999) is particularly important. The first study, using Israeli firm data, shows that the
earning and productivity age profiles are fairly similar. The second study
shows very similar results using U.S. data. These studies conclude that
wages are roughly based on productivity and that the wage profile by age
is consistent with the human capital hypothesis. However, using another
U.S. dataset, they find that the wage profile by age is steeper than the
productivity profile, which can be interpreted as evidence supporting the
deferred compensation hypothesis.

Many other investigations restate the latter conclusion. Crépon,
Deniau, and Pérez-Duarte (2002), using French data, conclude that the
relationship of productivity and age follows an inverted U-shape, but
wages increase with age. Using Finnish data, Ilmakunnas and Maliranta
(2007) conclude that firms profit from laying off older workers (more
than 49 years) in all sectors and hiring younger ones (less than 30 years)
in the industry sector. Daveri and Maliranta (2007) separate age and
seniority effects on productivity. They argue that a person who spends all
his life in the same job would acquire only the specific learning associated
with that job. Then, the seniority (the time a worker spent in the same
job) effect would be a specific human capital accumulation effect. The
age effect, in turn, would be a general human capital accumulation effect,
as workers would have worked in many firms, therefore acquiring general
learning. Their hypothesis is that only seniority has a negative effect on
productivity in sectors characterized by rapid technological innovation.
Indeed, they find that seniority, as a proxy for specific experience, has a
negative effect on Total Factor Productivity in the electronic sector (that
is, a highly important technological sector in Finland during 1990s) and a
positive effect on wages. At the same time, age, as a proxy for general
experience, does not have a negative effect on productivity.

Dostie (2006) uses Canadian data and his results show inverted
U-shaped age-wage and age-productivity profiles. Wage-productivity comparisons show that the productivity of workers aged 55 and older with

at least an undergraduate degree is lower than their wages. Vandenberghe and Waltenberg (2010) use Belgian data and their results indicate a negative productivity differential for older workers ranging from 20 percent to 40 percent, when compared with prime-age workers. These productivity differentials are not compensated for by lower relative labor costs.

Blanchet (1993) states that although it is not clear that the aging labor force affects aggregate productivity, if it is assumed that productivity remains stable while wages increase with seniority, this still may be a source of major difficulties in terms of competitiveness, profitability, investment, and related variables. He also shows that the necessary adjustment to avoid a growing imbalance between productivity and labor costs is not very high. However, Brazil has regulatory legislation forbidding this kind of adjustment, and the result of the imbalance could be a deal between the firm and worker to accept mandatory early retirement, which then results in problems in the publicly financed social security system, as explained in chapter 2.

The age-wage profile for Brazil shows that wages for employed workers in their main occupation do not decline before 65 years, but seem to remain stable between 45 and 65. Figure 5.5 shows the monthly wages in major occupations by age using data from PNAD 2008. Although a small decrease is observed when all workers are considered, the same thing is not observed when only formal employees are kept in the sample. For formal workers, the wages remain stable between 45 and 65.

Figure 5.5   Average Monthly Wages by Sector, Main Occupation, 2008

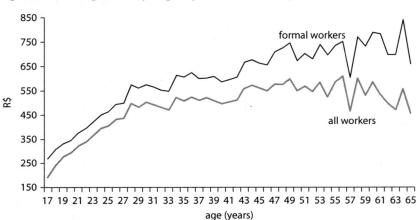

Source: Rocha 2010.

Figure 5.6 shows the current pattern considering hourly wages in the main occupation. For both all workers and formal employees, wages remain stable between 45 and 65, although they are volatile during the older age interval. Therefore, it appears that in Brazil wages do not follow the human capital hypothesis, at least before age 65; this means that the human capital depreciation is not followed by a decrease in wages between ages 45 and 65.

It is important to note that when all workers are considered, monthly wages show a different pattern than hourly wages. Figure 5.7 presents the age distribution of hours worked for all workers and formal employees only. The decline in hours worked is much more prominent for all workers than for formal employees. Clearly, Brazilian legislation makes rules of hours worked more rigid in the formal sector.

The evidence in the patterns described above, together with the evidence shown in the earlier section on the age-productivity profile, suggests that although many older workers drop out of the formal sector and start to receive smaller monthly wages, it seems to be an effect only of fewer hours worked in the informal sector, because the same declining effect is not observed when hourly wages are considered, even for the all workers sample.

The next section presents more robust evidence of the pattern discussed above from Brazil's industrial firms with more than 30 employees. The effects of age and seniority on productivity and wages are analyzed

Figure 5.6   Average Hourly Wages in Main Occupation by Sector, 2008

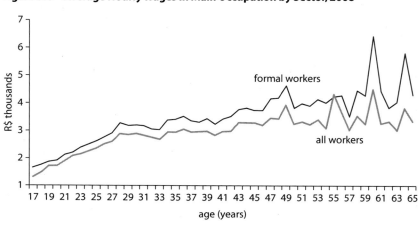

Source: Rocha 2010.

Figure 5.7   Average Hours Worked in Main Occupation by Sector, 2008

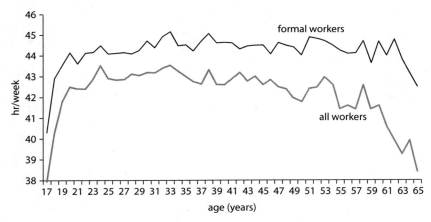

Source: Rocha 2010.

by estimating the difference between the age-productivity profile and the age-wage profile and between the seniority-productivity profile and the seniority-wage profile.

Age, Productivity, and Wages: New Evidence from Brazilian Firms

If productivity declines with age, the aging of the nation's population could negatively affect growth if a higher share of workers are now past their age of peak productivity, that is the age at which workers' productivity is highest.[5] At the same time, if firms pay a wage premium for age or seniority or both, as is expected by the deferred compensation hypothesis, firms might collude with the workers to get them to retire early, which could also affect savings and growth.

To identify the effect of age and seniority on wages and productivity, Rocha (2010) uses regressions at the firm level for industrial firms with more than 30 formal employees, from the Annual Industrial Surveys (PIA) between 1996 and 2007. These datasets have information about firms' revenues, investment, and number of workers, among other factors. The study merges these data with data on workers from the Annual Relation of Social Information Survey (RAIS), which has information on all formal-sector workers including gender, age, and tenure, among others. The methodology for this study is explained in box 5.2.

Box 5.2

Workforce Characteristics, Productivity, and Wages

To calculate the impact of an aging workforce on productivity and wages, Rocha (2010) follows the methodology of Hellerstein, Neumark, and Troske (1999), in which they emphasize the importance of labor quality to calculate production functions. The production function is an econometric version of Cobb-Douglas production function:

$$\log Y_{it} = \alpha \log L^A_{it} + \beta \log K_{it} + \gamma F + u_{it} \tag{1}$$

where Y is the value added by firm i at time t, L^A is an aggregate function of different types of workers, K is the capital stock, F is a matrix of a firm's characteristics that are chosen in order to make the specification in (1) as comparable as possible to the specification for wage equation, and u is the error term. The key variable of the estimation of this production function is the aggregated quality of labor. Let L_{itk} be the number of workers of type k in firm i at time t, and λ_k be their productivity. It is assumed that different types of workers are perfect substitutes, but may have different marginal productivities. The function can be specified as:

$$L^A_{it} = \sum_{k=0}^{K} \lambda_k L_{itk} = \lambda_{i0} L_{it} + \sum_{k=1}^{K} (\lambda_{it} - \lambda_{i0}) L_{itk} \tag{2}$$

where L_{it} is the total number of workers in the firm, and λ_0 the productivity of the reference category of workers and λ_k the productivity of worker type k. Using gender as an example, taking the group of male workers as the reference case, and scaling its productivity equal to 1, the relative productivity of the group of female workers is measured by parameter φ_F. The increase in productivity when it goes from the reference group to the female group is therefore $\varphi_F - 1$. In the general case of k type of workers, it is possible to rewrite equation (2) as:

$$\log L^A_{it} = \log \lambda_0 + \log L_{it} + \log \left(1 + \sum_{k=1}^{K} \left(\frac{\lambda_k}{\lambda_0} - 1 \right) P_{ikt} \right) \tag{3}$$

where P_{ikt} is the ratio of the number of workers of type k over the total number of employees and $\lambda_k/\lambda_0 = \phi_k$. To reduce the dimensionality problem, two restrictions on the form of L^A written above are imposed. The first restriction is that the relative marginal products of the two types of workers within one demographic group are equal to the relative marginal products of those same two types of workers within another demographic group. For example, the relative productivity of senior women to senior men is restricted to equal the relative marginal productivity of

(continued next page)

Box 5.2 *(continued)*

junior women to junior men. Similarly, the seniority difference in marginal productivity is restricted to be the same across sexes. The second restriction is that
the proportion of workers in an establishment defined by a demographic group
is constant across all other groups; for example, females are restricted to be equally
represented within all education levels, seniority groups, age groups, and so on.
To simplify estimation, an approximation of equation (3) can be used and the
result is the function below of the quality of the labor aggregate:

$$\log L_{it}^A \approx \log \lambda_0 + \log L_{it} + \sum_{k>0} (\phi_k - 1)P_{ikt} \tag{4}$$

If we substitute equation (4) in equation (2), the production function can be
written as:

$$\log Y_{it} = \alpha \log \lambda_0 + \alpha \log L_{it} + \alpha \sum_{k=1}^{K} (\phi_k - 1)P_{ikt} + \beta \log K_{it} + \gamma F_{it} + u_{it} \tag{5}$$

Rocha (2010) follows Ilmakunnas and Maliranta (2005) and divides the worker
characteristics into education, years of schooling (0–8, Primary Education; 9–11,
Secondary Education; 12 or more, University Education); age (15–24, Age 1; 25–34,
Age 2; 35–44, Age 3; and 45–64, Age 4); seniority (less than 10 years in the firm,
Young; more than 10 years in the firm, Senior); and gender (Men and Women)
characteristics. The idea is that seniority is an indicator of specific human capital
accumulation and age by itself is an indicator of general capital accumulation. So
the effect of each kind of human capital accumulation on labor productivity and
wages can be measured. The wage equation is estimated in a similar way:

$$Ln(w) = a' + \ln L_{it} + \sum_{k=1}^{K} \left(\frac{\pi_k}{\pi_0} - 1 \right) P_{ikt} \tag{6}$$

where π_k/π_0 is the yearly labor cost differential between the worker type k and the
worker type o. Thus, jointly estimating equations (4) and (5) by a Seemingly Unre-
lated Regression (SUR), it is possible then to test whether wage differentials across
workers in different demographic groups reflect differentials of productivity
between these demographic groups.

The first econometric problem in this kind of estimation is that there is unobserved heterogeneity across firms. It is possible that the firm has unobserved,
time-invariant characteristics that are correlated with the independent variables
and that drive the productivity outcomes in certain way. To solve this problem,

(continued next page)

Box 5.2 *(continued)*

firms, fixed effects are added as controls in the production function (and also in the wages equation).

The second econometric problem is the endogeneity bias. Firms could make adjustments in response to productivity shocks that are correlated with the age structure and other demographic characteristics of workers (see Griliches and Mairesse 1998). For example, a firm could adjust its workforce in response to an innovation shock (whether technological or managerial) by hiring more workers in that specific activity. Therefore, if the shock is a technological innovation, firms tend to increase the share of younger workers, and a positive productivity shock will be correlated with the share of younger workers, only because in that type of activity they have a comparative advantage. At the same time, if the shock is a management shock, such as one that depends on capacity to communicate, firms may prefer to increase the share of older workers, and then older workers will be positively correlated with productivity, only because of their comparative advantage in that kind of activity. However, the direction of the causality here is not clear. Firms may decide to change the age structure of their workforce because of technological or management change. But is not possible to say that they are becoming more productive because of that change in the age structure.

Econometric procedures can be undertaken to avoid this kind of endogeneity. The most prevalent strategy is to use the Generalized Method of Moments as proposed by Blundell and Bond (1999). This strategy uses lagged demographic characteristics to account for this short-term simultaneity. This idea was used by Aubert and Crépon (2003) who find that taking into account unobserved productivity shocks completely reverses the OLS conclusion of Crépon, Deniau, and Pérez-Duarte (2003) that the relationship of productivity and age follows an inverted U-shape However, Gorodnichenko (2006) shows that the Blundell and Bond estimator is in general weakly identified. The problem is that the results depend largely on the specification choices, such as the number of lags the authors use, and also that the instruments are too weak to explain the endogenous variables (see Vandenberghe and Waltenberg 2010).

Another method first used by Hellerstein, Neumark, and Troske (1999) and formalized by Levinsohn and Petrin (2003) will be used. The idea is that firms first adjust intermediate inputs in response to a productivity shock, before adjusting the other inputs. Therefore it is possible to invert the demand for capital and materials to infer a value for the unobserved productivity shock. The estimated productivity shock is then used as a regressor in the production function. The

(continued next page)

Box 5.2 *(continued)*

method assumes that the inversion function is non-stochastic. Alternative, but similar, estimation procedures were proposed by Ackerberg, Caves, and Frazer (2003) and Olley and Pakes (1996), and they are carried out with the same assumption. If this assumption is violated, the estimation will be biased (see Bond and Soderborn 2005; Ackerberg, Caves, and Frazer 2003; and Petrin and Levinsohn 2000). However, Gorodnichenko (2006) provides a Monte Carlo test showing that the LP estimator is less biased than OLS estimates, at least in the case of return to scale estimation.

Finally, the variance-covariance matrix of Huber-White is calculated in order to account to heteroscedastic errors.

Source: Rocha 2010.

The first set of results of Rocha's calculations is shown in table 5.1. The four columns under Productivity present the effect of each variable on productivity. Clearly, firms' productivity declines with age and seniority. The four columns under Wages show the effect of each variable on wages. Wages closely increase with seniority, although they remain stable with age. This result is consistent with the compensation hypothesis. It shows that firms in Brazil apparently pay less than the marginal productivity to younger workers, but compensate them with higher salaries later on, particularly if they stay in the same firm (that is, they have higher seniority).

In order to interpret these findings and to more closely examine the effect of aging labor force on productivity, Rocha (2010) conducts a simple exercise, assuming that the demographic profile in Brazil changes in the same way as the population projections made by IBGE (2008) and that everything else remains constant. Using the estimated coefficients above and considering a productivity index equal to 100 in 2005, the results are shown in figure 5.8. The productivity of Brazilian industrial firms would decrease 16 percent because of the demographics between 2005 and 2050, everything else remaining constant.

The estimates in table 5.1 show that productivity would increase with education. The average number of schooling years in Brazil has increased rapidly during the past two decades (World Bank forthcoming). Taking as a benchmark the educational distribution of average OECD countries, supposing Brazil would reach this same educational distribution in 2050

Table 5.1   Effect of Age and Seniority on Productivity and Wages

| | Productivity | | | | Wages | | | |
Parameter	Estimate	Approx Std Err	t Value	Approx Pr > |t|	Estimate	Approx Std Err	t Value	Approx Pr > |t|
Size of labor force	0.52	0.00	104.75	<0.0001				
Secondary education	0.17	0.01	17.31	<0.0001	0.02	0.00	4.42	<0.0001
University education	0.45	0.02	18.09	<0.0001	0.49	0.01	35.33	<0.0001
15–24	0.54	0.02	25.18	<0.0001	−0.27	0.02	−13.46	<0.0001
25–34	0.43	0.02	19.74	<0.0001	0.01	0.02	0.29	0.77
45–64	−0.35	0.03	−12.65	<0.0001	0.02	0.03	0.63	0.53
Senior	−0.48	0.02	−22.59	<0.0001	0.12	0.01	7.94	<0.0001
Male	0.23	0.02	10.86	<0.0001	0.11	0.01	15.15	<0.0001

Source: Rocha 2010.
Notes: Size of labor force: number of workers in the firm.
Secondary education: equals 1 if worker has secondary education; equals 0 otherwise.
Tertiary education: equals 1 if worker has tertiary education; equals 0 otherwise.
15–24: equals 1 if worker's age is between 15 and 24 years; equals 0 otherwise.
25–34: equals 1 if worker's age is between 25 and 34 years; equals 0 otherwise.
45–64: equals 1 if worker's age is between 45 and 64 years; equals 0 otherwise.
Senior: equals 1 if worker has been at least 10 years in the firm; equals 0 otherwise.
Male: equals 1 if worker is male; equals 0 otherwise.

Figure 5.8   Productivity of Brazilian Industrial Firms, 2005–50

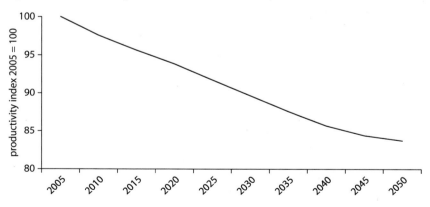

Source: Rocha 2010.

and using the coefficients in table 5.1, Rocha (2010) concludes that the
productivity of Brazilian industrial firms would increase 9 percent
between 2005 and 2050 strictly because of the change in education structure, which would partially offset the effects of demographic changes.

In addition, the coefficient of the older worker age group could change with changes in relative demand for jobs involving interactive skills, as discussed earlier, and, more importantly, it could change because the population has become more educated, which makes training more efficient to prevent human capital depreciation at older ages. Then, the effect of demographics on productivity depends on the level of early stages education, which makes it even more important to provide basic education of good quality for everyone.

In summary, the evidence shows that in the Brazilian industrial sector, wages increase or remain stable with age, and productivity declines with age. An aging workforce would then be a burden to firms, at least in the short run. In addition to the deferred compensation hypothesis, another possible explanation for these results is that legislation restricts the possibility of reducing wages for those workers who have been with the same firm for long periods and forces firms to pay high taxes to lay off workers. In these circumstances, laying off workers when they become less productive is very expensive.

These findings are consistent with findings for European countries, as shown in the previous section. Most of the evidence confirms the conclusion that aging of the workforce could be a burden to firms, because they must pay more than the marginal productivity for older workers. As discussed earlier, this can create incentives for the employer and the employee to agree to early retirement. The more advanced the population aging, the stronger this incentive will be, as firms will have a higher share of older workers. Although contracts are dynamic and firms may change the way they design their payment schemes, evidence in developed countries shows that firms continue to pay the seniority-based wage, even after the share of older population is high (see Lazear 1990; Lee, Mason, and Lee 2004). A possible solution for firms to decrease the burden of an older workforce could be to adopt mandatory retirement rules. Many older workers could be forced to retire and firms could rehire them in an informal status only, with a smaller wage and without the obligation of contributing to the social security system. This evidence is supported by the pattern of early retirement observed in Brazil and described in chapter 2.

As workers continue to age in many middle- and high-income countries, the age profile of the workforce will have less of a share of workers at their peak productivity. Such a scenario suggests that these economies will need to boost their labor productivity growth, which would require a substantial increase in broad capital investments, that is to say, human capital, intangible capital (research and development), and physical capital (see United Nations 2007). The section on improving education in this chapter showed how an aging workforce can improve human capital investments and at least partly offset the effect of the declining labor productivity associated with a higher share of the workforce being past their peak productivity.

In less developed countries, however, most policies still target industry sectors with particular strategic importance to growth. Meanwhile, it is also necessary to improve the productivity of the traditional low-skilled informal sector, a highly important issue for developing and emerging economies, including Brazil. In this context, investments in human capital and infrastructure in Brazil are very important to improving productivity as a whole. Moreover, improved access to technology and the creation of forward and backward linkages in the supply chain between the formal and informal sectors can enhance worker skills and ultimately lead to higher overall productivity growth (ILO 2004).

In conclusion, this chapter demonstrates that negative effects of population aging on productivity at the firm's industrial level can be expected. This may have a negative impact on aggregate economic output (although evidence in this regard is mixed), because a higher share of the workforce would be past its peak productivity. To offset these negative effects, instituting traditional policies of skills promotion and upgrading through training programs are recommended. The demographic changes under way in Brazil should drive more investment in human capital, and consequently, result in improvements of labor productivity. However, better quality of education at younger ages, together with effective investments in retraining older workers, may help Brazil to continue to raise its productivity, even when the age structure of its population continues shifting toward older ages.

Notes

1. Retirement here is defined as receiving a pension; early retirement refers to retirement before age 60.
2. Of course, this also depends on calculations of the benefits they would receive for being in the formal sector.
3. This is an issue that is being analyzed in the case of Brazil. There is evidence for other countries, however, showing that a sizable share of firms in the manufacturing sector have productivity levels below the official cost of labor (see World Bank 2007a; 2009).

4. The Program for International Student Assessment (PISA) is a system of international assessments that focus on 15-year-olds' capabilities in reading, mathematics, and science.

5. This section draws heavily from Rocha (2010).

References

Ackerberg, D., K. Caves, and G. Frazer. 2003. "Structural Identification of Production Functions." Working Paper, University of Arizona, University of California at Los Angeles, and University of Toronto (Canada).

Amadeo, E. J. 1992. "Vocational Education in Brazil: An Evaluation of Senai." Unpublished report, Pontifical Catholic University, Rio de Janeiro.

Aubert, P., and B. Crépon. 2003. "Âge, salaire et productivité : La productivité des salariés décline-t-elle en fin de carrière?" *Économie et Statistique* 368: 95–119.

Becker, Gary S., Kevin M. Murphy, and Robert Tamura. 1990. "Human Capital, Fertility and Economic Growth." Part 2: The Problem of Development: A Conference of the Institute for the Study of Free Enterprise Systems. *The Journal of Political Economy* 98 (5) (Oct.): S12–S37.

Blanchet, D. 1992. "Does an Ageing Labour Force Call for Large Adjustments in Training or Wage Policies?" In *Labor Markets in an Ageing Europe*, ed. P. Johnson and K. F. Zimmermann, 126–50. Cambridge, UK: Cambridge University Press.

Bleakley, H., and F. Lange. 2009. "Chronic Disease Burden and the Interaction of Education, Fertility, and Growth." *Review of Economics and Statistics* 91 (1): 52–65.

Blundell, R., and S. Bond. 1999. "GMM Estimation With Persistent Panel Data: An Application to Production Functions." IFS Working Papers W99/04, Institute for Fiscal Studies, London.

Bobonis, G. J., E. Miguel, and C. Puri-Sharma. 2006. "Anemia and School Participation." *Journal of Human Resources* 41 (4): 692–721.

Bond, S., and M. Soderborn. 2005. "Adjustment Costs and the Identification of Cobb-Douglas Production Functions." Working Paper 05/04, Institute for Fiscal Studies, London.

Cardoso, Larry C., Luís O. Façanha, and Alexandre Marinho. 2002. "Avaliação de programas sociais (PNAE, PLANFOR, PROGER): eficiência relativa e esquemas de incentivo." Texto para Discussão 859, IPEA (National Institute for Applied Economic Research), Rio de Janeiro.

Crépon, B., N. Deniau, and S. Pérez-Duarte. 2003. "Wages, Productivity, and Worker Characteristics: A French Perspective." *Serie des Documents de Travail du CREST*. Institut National de la Statistique et des Etudes Économiques, Paris.

Daveri, F., and M. Maliranta. 2007. "Age, Seniority and Labor Costs." *Economic Policy* 22 (1): 117–75.

Dostie, B. 2006. "Wages, Productivity and Aging." IZA Discussion Paper 2496, Institute for the Study of Labor, Bonn, Germany.

Feyrer, J. 2007. "Demographics and Productivity." *The Review of Economics and Statistics* 89 (1): 100–09.

Gorodnichenko, Y. 2006. "Using Firm Optimization to Evaluate and Estimate Returns to Scale." Working paper, University of Michigan, Ann Arbor.

Griliches, Z., and J. Mairesse. 1998. "Production Functions: The Search for Identification." In *Econometrics and Economic Theory in Twentieth Century: The Ragnar Frisch Centennial Symposium*, ed. S. Strom, 169–203. Cambridge, UK: Cambridge University Press.

Heckman, J. J., F. Cunha, L. Lochner, and D. V. Masterov. 2005. "Interpreting the Evidence on Life Cycle Skill Formation." NBER Working Paper 11331, National Bureau of Economic Research, Cambridge, MA.

Hellerstein, J. K., and D. Neumark. 1995. "Are Earnings Profiles Steeper than Productivity Profiles?" *Journal of Human Resources* 30 (1): 89–112.

Hellerstein, J. K., D. Neumark, and K. R. Troske. 1999. "Wages, Productivity and Worker Characteristics: Evidence from Plant-Level Production Functions and Wage Equations." *Journal of Labor Economics* 17 (3): 409–46.

Ilmakunnas, P., and M. Maliranta. 2007. "Aging, Labor Turnover, and Firm Performance." HEER Discussion Paper 164. Helsinki Center for Economic Research, Helsinki, Finland.

ILO (International Labour Organization). 2004. "World Employment Report 2004-05: Employment, Productivity and Poverty Reduction." ILO, Geneva.

Kalemli-Ozcan, S. 2002. "Does Mortality Decline Promote Economic Growth?" *Journal of Economic Growth* 7: 411–39.

Lazear, E. P. 1981. "Agency, Earnings Profiles, Productivity and Hours Restrictions." *American Economic Review* 71 (4): 606–20.

Lazear, Edward P. 1990. "Adjusting to an Aging Labor Force." In *Issues in the Economics of Aging*, 287–316. Cambridge, MA: National Bureau of Economic Research.

Lee, R., A. Mason, and Sang-Hyop Lee. 2004. "Individual Earnings and Consumption Profiles: What do we Know?" Paper presented at the Symposium on Population Aging and Economic Productivity, Vienna Institute of Demography, December 2–4 2004, Vienna, Austria.

Lehman, H. C. 1953. *Age and Achievement*. Princeton, NJ: Princeton University Press.

Levinsohn, J., and A. Petrin. 2003. "Estimating Production Function Using Inputs to Control for Unobservables." *Review of Economic Studies* 70 (2): 317–42.

Lindh, T., and B. Malmberg. 1999. "Age Structure Effects and Growth in the OECD, 1950–90." *Journal of Population Economics* 12 (3): 431–49.

Lleras-Muney, A., and S. Jayachandran. 2009. "Longevity and Human Capital Investments: Evidence from Maternal Mortality Declines in Sri Lanka." *Quarterly Journal of Economics* 124 (1): 349–397.

Lorentzen, P., J. McMillan, and R. Wacziarg. 2007. "Death and Development." *Journal of Economic Growth* 13 (2): 81–124.

Manning A. 2000. "Moving On Up: Interpreting the Earning-Experience Profile." *Bulletin of Economic Research* 52 (4): 261–95.

Mello F. M., and D. D. Santos. 2009. Aceleração educacional e a queda recente da informalidade. *Boletim Mercado de Trabalho* 39 (May): 27–33.

Meltzer, D. 1992. "Mortality Decline, the Demographic Transition and Economic Growth." Ph.D. dissertation, Department of Economics, University of Chicago.

Miguel, E., and M. Kremer. 2004. "Worms: Identifying Impacts on Education and Health in the Presence of Externalities." *Econometrica* 72 (1): 159–217.

Mincer, J. 1974. *Schooling, Experience, and Earnings*. New York: Columbia University Press.

Olley, G., and A. Pakes. 1996. "The Dynamics of Productivity in the Telecommunications Equipment Industry." *Econometrica* 64 (6): 1263–97.

OECD (Organisation for Economic Co-Operation and Development). 2006. "Live Longer, Work Longer: A Synthesis Report of the Ageing and Employment Policies Project." OECD, Paris.

———. 2010. "Education at a Glance 2010: OECD Indicators." OECD, Paris.

Petrin, A., and J. Levinsohn. 2000. "Estimating Production Function Using Inputs to Control for Unobservables." Working Paper 7819, National Bureau of Economic Research (NBER), Cambridge, MA.

Rios-Neto, E., and A. Oliveira. 2000. "Políticas voltadas para a pobreza: o caso da formação profissional." In *Desigualdade e pobreza no Brasil*, ed. R. Henriques, 589–613. Rio de Janeiro: IPEA (National Institute for Applied Economic Research).

Rocha, R. C. B. 2010. "Aging Labor Force, Productivity and Wages." Background paper prepared for the Workshop on Aging in Brazil, World Bank, Brasilia, April 6–7.

Skirbekk, V. 2003. "Age and Individual Productivity: A Literature Survey." MPIDR Working Paper 2003-028, Max Planck Institute for Demographic Research, Rostock, Germany.

Soares, R. R. 2005. "Mortality Reductions, Educational Attainment, and Fertility Choice." *American Economic Review* 95 (3): 580–601.

————. 2010. "Aging, Retirement, and Labor Market in Brazil." Background paper prepared for the Workshop on Aging in Brazil, World Bank, Brasilia, April 6–7, 2010.

Soares, S., and A. Leichsenring. 2010. "Precariedad laboral, volatilidad de ingresos y cobertura del Programa Bolsa Familia." Working Paper 12, Iniciativa América Latina e Caribe sem Fome, Organização das Nações Unidas para a Agricultura e a Fome, Brasilia, Brazil.

Tang, J., and C. MacLeod. 2006. "Labor Force Ageing and Productivity Performance in Canada." *Canadian Journal of Economics* 39 (2): 582–602.

United Nations. 2007. *Development in an Ageing World.* World Economic and Social Survey 2007. E/2007/50/Rev.1, ST/ESA/314. New York: United Nations.

Vandenberghe, V., and Waltenberg, F. 2010. *Ageing Workforce, Productivity and Labour Costs of Belgian Firms.* CEDE Discussion Paper 19, Center for Studies on Inequality and Development, Niterói, Brazil.

Verhaegen, P., and T. A. Salthouse. 1997. "Meta-Analyses of Age-Cognition Relations in Adulthood: Estimates of Linear and Nonlinear Age Effects and Structural Models." *Psychological Bulletin* 122 (3): 231–49.

World Bank. 1991. "Vocational and Technical Education and Training." World Bank, Washington, DC.

————. 2007a. "Brazil: Towards a Sustainable and Fair Pension System." World Bank, Washington, DC.

————. 2007b. "From Red to Gray: The Third Transition of Aging Populations in Eastern Europe and the Former Soviet Union." World Bank, Washington, DC.

————. 2009. "Social Insurance and Labor Supply: Assessing Incentives and Redistribution." Draft Technical Report. Human Department Latin America and the Caribbean Region, World Bank, Washington, DC.

————. Forthcoming. "Achieving World Class Education in Brazil: The Next Agenda." Latin America and the Caribbean Region, World Bank, Washington, DC.

CHAPTER 6

Public Finance Implications of Population Aging: 2005–50

As shown in chapter 2, the age distribution of the Brazilian population will change dramatically over the coming decades. The number of children in Brazil reached a peak of nearly 70 million around 1999 and has been steadily declining since. Meanwhile, the number of elderly has doubled over the last 20 years and is projected to double again in the next 20. This chapter explores the public finance implications of these shifts in the population age structure, focusing on three key areas of public spending: education, pensions, and health care.

The basic institutional framework for social policies in Brazil, including related expenditures and sources of revenue, was laid down in the 1988 Constitution of the Federative Republic of Brazil. Its main determinants—to a large extent, a reaction to the patterns that prevailed over the authoritarian period—were to extend social rights and social protection to groups hitherto uncovered or unprotected, to promote decentralization in the provision of services, and to ensure funding through earmarking of tax revenues. The outcome of the new framework was a significant increase in social expenditures and a more rigid budget associated with wider earmarking and mandatory expenditures (see figure 6.1).[1]

Figure 6.1   Public Spending on Education, Health, and Social Security as Share of GDP, 1980–2008

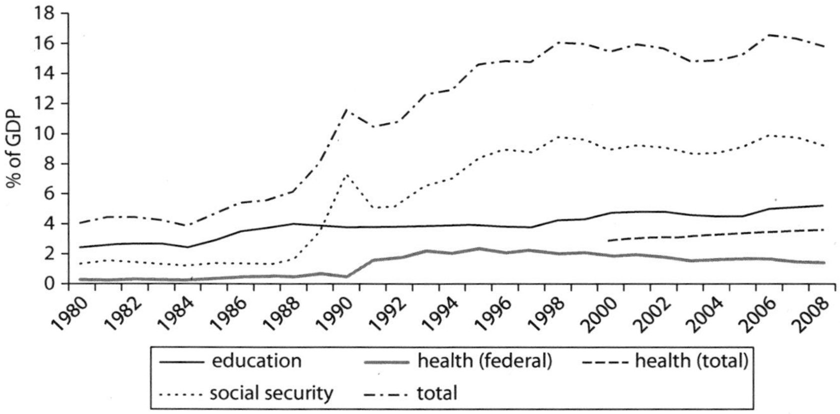

Sources: Tafner 2010; Ministry of Health 2009.

Expenditures on Education, Health, and Social Protection in Brazil

Table 6.1 presents data on total spending on education, health, and social security for 29 countries. The data refer to 2006, in which Brazilian spending had already reached current levels. Comparing Chile to Brazil is interesting because it is also a Latin American country and its GDP per capita is closer to the Brazil's than any other in the sample. Expenditures on education, health, and social security as a proportion of GDP in Chile are consistently lower than corresponding expenditures in Brazil. The result is that even though Chilean social spending (12.1 percent of GDP) is nearly half of Brazil's (23.18 percent of GDP), Chile has average schooling higher than Brazil's and a life expectancy at least four years longer.

Figure 6.2 (a through c) presents spending for each type of expenditure as a proportion of GDP and GDP per capita (in 2009 PPP) of each of the countries in the sample. The last chart (d) shows total social spending. All graphs also show the OLS regression line. Brazilian expenditures are consistently above the regression line, indicating that Brazil has higher spending than the average country in the sample when income levels are controlled for.

This chapter will explain how to measure the size of the challenge for public finance and how public finance will be affected by population

Table 6.1   Expenditures on Education, Social Security, and Health as Proportion of GDP, 2006[a]

Country	Public expenditure on education as % of GDP	Total expenditure on health as % of GDP	Total expenditure on social security as % of GDP	Total social expenditure as % of GDP	GDP per capita (PPP)
Italy	4.7	9.0	17.6	31.3	31,909
France	5.6	11.0	13.4	30.0	34,689
Switzerland	5.5	10.8	13.4	29.7	43,104
United States	5.7	15.5	7.5	28.7	46,436
Belgium	6.0	9.5	12.9	28.4	36,048
Sweden	6.9	9.1	11.1	27.1	37,905
Germany	4.4	10.5	12.1	27.0	36,449
Finland	6.1	8.3	12.1	26.5	34,652
Denmark	7.9	9.6	8.8	26.3	36,763
Poland	5.7	6.2	13.9	25.8	19,059
Netherlands	5.5	8.9	11.1	25.5	40,715
Greece[b]	4.0	9.5	11.9	25.4	29,664
Portugal	5.3	9.9	10.0	25.2	24,021
Hungary	5.4	8.1	11.0	24.5	19,765
United Kingdom	5.6	8.5	10.3	24.4	36,496
Brazil	**5.0**	**8.5**	**10.3**	**23.8**	**10,427**
Spain	4.3	8.4	10.9	23.6	32,545
Norway	6.5	8.6	8.2	23.3	55,672
New Zealand	6.2	9.3	6.5	22.0	28,722
Slovakia	3.8	7.3	10.1	21.2	22,357
Canada[b]	4.9	10.0	5.4	20.3	37,945
Czech Republic	4.6	7.0	8.5	20.1	25,232
Iceland	7.6	9.1	2.0	18.7	37,602
Japan	3.5	8.1	6.9	18.5	32,443
Mexico	4.8	5.7	7.8	18.3	14,337
Ireland	4.8	7.1	4.6	16.5	41,282
Turkey	2.9	4.8	7.1	14.8	13,904
Chile	3.2	6.0	2.9	12.1	14,331
Korea, Rep.	4.2	6.0	1.3	11.5	27,169
General average	5.19	8.63	9.3	23.1	31,091

Source: Education: UNESCO 2009. Health: WHO 2009. Social security: Rocha and Caetano 2008. Per capita PPP: World Bank 2009.

a. Social expenditures are the sum of education, health, and social security.

b. For these countries data on education is referred to 2005.

PPP = purchasing power parity.

Figure 6.2   Expenditures on Education, Health, Social Security, and Total Expenditures as Percentage of GDP, 2006

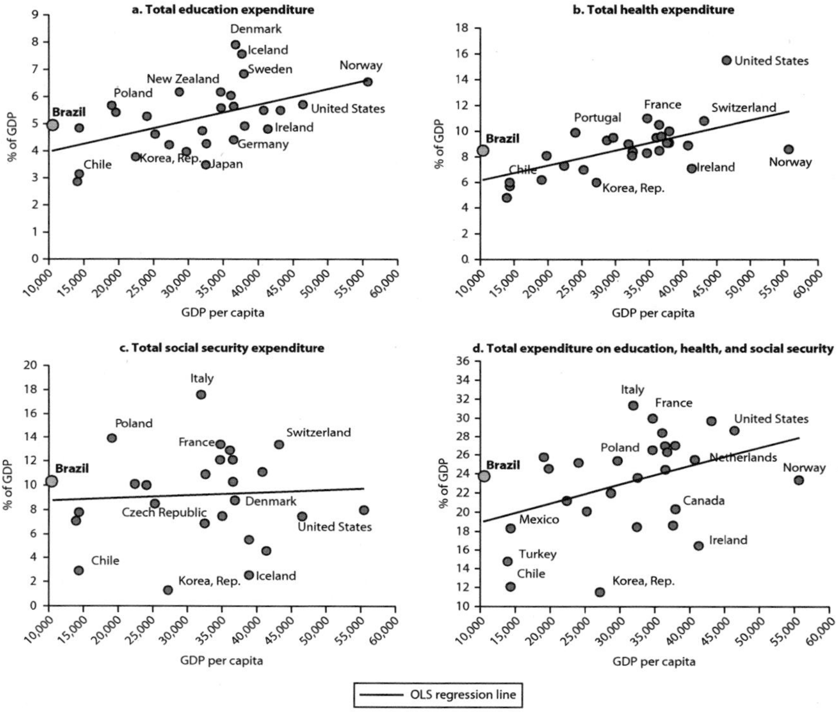

Sources: Education: UNESCO 2009; health, WHO 2009; social security, Rocha and Caetano 2008; per capita PPP, World Bank 2009.

aging. The projections here are based on a simple model by Miller and Castanheira (2010) in which aggregate public expenditures are driven by changes in the age structure of the population, as well as by changes in the average public benefits received by age. The likely increases in public spending over the coming decades are estimated, contrasting the divergent trends in public spending on education, pensions, and health care. The magnitude of these changes is assessed in terms of growth in spending relative to GDP annually over the next 40 years and estimates of the present value of this increased spending relative to current GDP.

Demographic change is one of the most important forces shaping the outcome of social policy, but it cannot be observed in the short term. Its impact is readily apparent in the long-term projections such as those presented in this chapter. The gradual changes in age structure unfolding in the coming decades will present different challenges and opportunities to education, health, and pension programs. Projecting all three expenditure paths with a comparable methodology will provide insight into the interconnections and trade-offs available to national policy makers. Too often, policy reforms of pension, health care, and education systems are debated, analyzed, and implemented in isolation from each other without considering the fiscal links among these systems.

The validity of long-run forecasts, such as those offered here, is subject to discussion. There is considerable uncertainty about the future course of the economy and future policy decisions. In addition, there is considerable demographic uncertainty about how quickly and to what level fertility will decline and about how quickly mortality rates will continue to decline. Mortality may fall more or less rapidly than anticipated—but there is no doubt that the elderly population in Brazil will soar over the coming decades. However, there is much more certainty about forecasting population age structures because they change slowly over time in very predictable ways. All the individuals who will comprise the population of retirees in the year 2050 have already been born—which makes predictions about their future considerably more certain than predicting economic growth rates in the year 2050.

Mindful of the impact of population aging, a number of governments have begun to issue official long-term budget projections: the European Union (European Commission Directorate General for Economic and Financial Affairs, 2006), the United States (U.S. Congressional Budget Office, 2009), Australia (Australia, The Treasury, 2007), and New Zealand (New Zealand, The Treasury, 2006). This chapter presents long-run expenditure forecasts for Brazil, an important first step toward long-run fiscal forecasts.

The Public Sector: Age Structure and the Generosity of Public Benefits

Projecting the future public finance impacts of population aging begins with an assessment of public spending in Brazil today. Spending on education, pensions, and health care is the product of the average generosity of the benefits received by each individual and the age structure of the population. The share of economic output directed toward education, health care, and pensions through the public sector can be decomposed into two multiplicative components. Equation 1 shows the example of public spending on education.

$$B(t)/\text{GDP}(t) = bgr(t)*P(6\text{–}21,t)/P(20\text{–}64,t) \qquad (1)$$

$B(t)$ is aggregate educational expenditures in year t; GDP (t) is GDP in year t; $bgr(t)$ is the average benefit per school-age person relative to economic output per working-age adult equaling $B(t)/P(6\text{–}21,t)/\text{GDP}(t)/P(20\text{–}64,t)$; $P(6\text{–}21,t)$ is school-age population (ages 6–21) in year t; and P(20–64) is working-age population in year t.

Assume that all public education benefits are targeted to individuals aged 6–21 and further that these benefits do not vary by age. In this case, the aggregate public expenditures on education as a share of GDP are simply the product of two scalar factors: one demographic and the other economic. The first scalar quantity, $bgr(t)$, is the "Education Benefit Generosity Ratio," which measures the generosity of average educational benefits relative to GDP per working-age adult. Standardizing by economic output per working-age adult is useful for making international comparisons of benefits as well as for projecting future expenditures, as will be discussed later.

In most countries, the wage bill is about two-thirds of GDP and the labor force is usually about two-thirds of the working-age population. Therefore, the ratio of GDP per working-age adult is roughly equivalent to the wage bill divided by the labor force or the average annual wage per worker. As a rough approximation, the benefit generosity ratios used here could be considered as measuring public benefits received relative to the average worker salary in the economy.

The second scalar quantity, $P(6\text{–}21,t)/P(20\text{–}64,t)$, is the "Education Dependency Ratio," which measures the size of the school-age population relative to the working-age population.[2] By definition, the product of these two terms yields aggregate educational spending as a share of GDP. The results are shown in figure 6.3.

In Burkina Faso, there is nearly one school-age child for every working-age person in the population. The average public investment per school-age child is approximately 4.5 percent of the average annual salary. Hence, public investment in education is approximately 4.5 percent of GDP. The average lifetime educational investment per youth by the public sector is less than a year's wages. This low level of investment is a reflection of both low participation rates and low investment per student in Burkina Faso. Italy lies at the other extreme as shown in figure 6.3. As in Burkina Faso, public investment in education is approximately 4.5 percent of GDP, but with vastly more public investment per youth. The more favorable age structure in Italy allows for much higher investment in youth at the same levels of aggregate spending: There are

Figure 6.3   School-Age Population and Public Education Spending per Youth in Three Countries, 2005–06

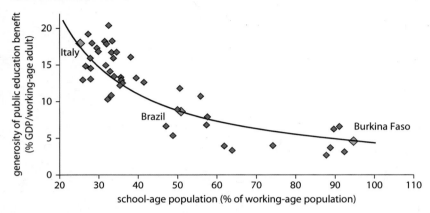

Source: Miller and Castanheira 2010, based on population data from CEPAL 2008 and expenditure data from UNESCO 2009.

nearly four working-age persons for every school-age child. Public investments per youth are 18 percent of the average annual salary in Italy—more than triple the investment in Burkina Faso.

Brazil, which like Burkina Faso and Italy also devotes approximately 4.5 percent of GDP to public investment in education, falls between those two countries. In Brazil, there are approximately two working-age adults for every school-age child. Public investment per youth in Brazil is about 10 percent of the average wage, or a lifetime educational investment of about a year and a half of annual wages. The governments of all three countries are investing approximately the same relative amounts in educating the next generation—approximately 4.5 percent of GDP—but with very different investment levels per youth on account of difference in the age structure of populations. Based on this cross-national sample for 2005–06, it appears that there is very little variation in aggregate public spending in response to the size of the young population—so that educational investments per student are inversely related to population size.

Using equation 1, aggregate spending on public pensions is decomposed into two components: the size of the elderly population relative to the working-age population and the generosity of the public pension, which reflects both pension coverage and the average pension benefit relative to GDP per working-age adult. Figure 6.4 presents the decomposition results for spending on national pension systems (excluding civil

Figure 6.4   Elderly Population and Public Pension Spending per Older Adult by Country, 2005–06

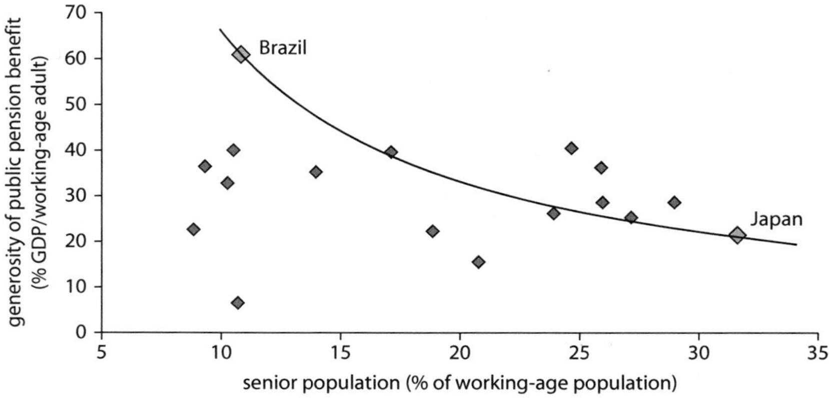

Source: Miller and Castanheira (2010) based on population data from CEPAL (2008) and expenditure data from NTA (2010) and OECD (2009b).

servant pension systems) for several OECD (Organisation for Economic Co-operation and Development) and Latin American countries. Brazil is a clear outlier: it has by far the most generous public pension system in the world. In OECD countries, average public pension benefits hover in the range of 20 to 40 percent of GDP per working-age adult, while in Brazil the pensions are about twice as generous as those in the OECD group. Of particular note is the dramatic difference between Japan and Brazil. Governments in both countries are equally involved in financing pensions, accounting for 7 percent of GDP, yet the relative share of older adults in Brazil is only one-third that of Japan.

Education and pension benefits are directed to clearly defined demographic groups, for which in this calculation, a simple decomposition of aggregate spending into two scalar quantities (equation 1) works well as a heuristic device. In the case of health spending, it is difficult to define a particular demographic group to whom health spending is directed; therefore, the decomposition of spending into demographic and economic scalar values works less well than in the case of education or pensions. In the forecast model, discussed later in this chapter, a more robust analysis is presented using age-specific vectors rather than scalar values, which overcomes this limitation. In keeping with the simple decomposition method of equation 1, a population is defined for which most health care spending is directed: the population whose age makes them close to death.

Many studies of OECD countries have shown that most health costs for individuals occur in the final decade of life, and within that decade, in the final year of life (Miller 2001). This means that most health systems devote a large percentage of their resources to curative and palliative services rather than preventive services. To estimate the number of persons close to death in the population, Miller and Castanheira (2010) use estimates and projections of the number of deaths over the next decade of the original cohort using population estimates and projections from CEPAL (2008) (Comisión Económica para America Latina y el Caribe, the Latin American Economic Commission). This is an approximation of the number of people who are likely to use a high proportion of all health care services consumed within the year, at least in developed countries.

The generosity ratio for public health benefits is calculated by dividing public expenditures on health as a percentage of GDP (from WHO data) by the health dependency ratio (that is, the near-death population as a proportion of the working-age population). Under the assumption that all health care spending is directed toward those in their last decade of life, the benefit generosity ratio measures the average annual expenditures on health care for these individuals relative to the average wage.

Figure 6.5 presents estimates of the near-death population and the generosity of public health benefits around the world. South Africa and Costa Rica lie at opposite extremes. South Africa has one of the highest

Figure 6.5   The Near-Death Population and Public Health Spending per Capita by Country, Circa 2006

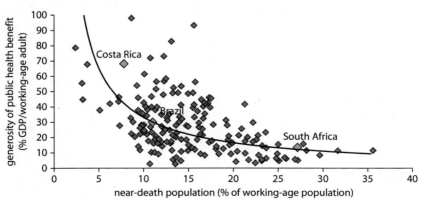

Source: Miller and Castanheira (2010) based on population data from CEPAL (2008) and expenditures data from WHO (2010).

health dependency ratios in the world. The number of people who will die within the next decade is nearly one-fourth the size of the working-age population. Despite this large health dependency ratio, aggregate public health spending is low, about 3.6 percent of GDP, and the resulting generosity of average health benefits is quite low: less than 10 percent of the average wage. Costa Rica lies at the opposite extreme. Thanks to its high life expectancy and relatively young age structure it has one of the lowest health dependency ratios in the world: with a near-death population only 7 percent the size of the working-age population. Health spending in Costa Rica is rather generous: amounting to 90 percent of the average annual wage. In Brazil, the health dependency ratio is slightly higher than that of Costa Rica. But owing to lower aggregate expenditures on health, the average generosity of the health care benefit is lower than Costa Rica, amounting to about 65 percent of the average wage.

Table 6.2 compares Brazilian public-sector spending to that of OECD countries. Brazil's public-sector spending on education and pensions resembles that of OECD countries (as percent of GDP) but its population age structure is much younger. This results in markedly lower public education investment in youth (9.8 percent of average wages in Brazil vs. 15.5 percent in OECD) and markedly higher average public pension benefits (66.5 percent of average wage in Brazil vs. 30.4 percent of average wage in OECD). Aggregate public health care expenditures in Brazil are much below the OECD average, and average health benefits are somewhat lower.

How quickly might these changes in average benefits be expected to take place? In the projections several plausible scenarios are considered for each sector. For education, two scenarios are evaluated. In the first, aggregate public spending is maintained at its current level for the next

Table 6.2   Summary of Brazilian and OECD Spending in 2005

	Public education		Public pensions[a]		Public health care	
	Brazil	OECD	Brazil	OECD	Brazil	OECD
Aggregate Spending	4.4%	4.8%	6.6%	8.0%	3.3%	6.9%
Benefit generosity	8.7%	15.5%	61.1%	30.4%	30.0%	44%
Dependency rate	50.5%	31.1%	10.8%	26.3%	11.0%	15.9%

Sources: Miller and Castanheira 2010, based on various data sources: population, CEPAL 2008; expenditure on public education, UNESCO 2010; expenditure on public pensions, NTA 2010; OECD 2009b; expenditure on public health care, WHO 2009.
a. Excludes civil servant pensions; in Brazil, pension payments to civil servants were 3.8% of GDP in 2005.

few decades. Over time, as the school-age population declines, investments per student gradually climb toward OECD levels. In a second scenario, the more ambitious goal is set of reaching OECD levels of investment per student within a decade, by 2020.

For pensions, three scenarios are explored. The first is a counterfactual experiment that assumes no changes in average pension benefits. It represents the hypothetical Brazilian future in which the pension reforms of 1998 and 2004 were never implemented. The second scenario models the changes in benefits that are likely to result from these newly legislated pension reforms. The third scenario ignores the recent reform legislation and instead predicts a set of future reforms that gradually and continuously reduce pension benefit generosity toward OECD levels. The rate of this reduction is set so that once Brazil reaches the levels of GDP per worker currently observed in OECD countries, its pension benefits will also reach OECD levels.

For health care, two scenarios are forecast. As was the case with pensions, one scenario assumes that average benefits remain constant relative to wages. In the second scenario, average benefits are assumed to rise relative to wages as GDP per worker rises.

This study's projections of public spending are derived from equation 1 based on forecast of the population, $P(x,t)$, and average benefits, $b(x,t)$.[3] The population forecasts are derived from data from CEPAL for 2005 through 2050. A single population forecast based on the cohort component method is used in which a single trend in mortality rates, in fertility rates, and in migration rates are combined to generate a forecast of the age structure of the population. There is considerable uncertainty about the particular path of future mortality, fertility, and migration in Brazil; also taken into account is the added uncertainty of knowing the current levels of these factors.

Miller, Bay, and Ruiz (2009) produced probabilistic population forecasts for the population of Brazil based on random sampling from the historical time series of UN member countries. The results show the highest level of uncertainty for the school-age population, reflecting the large uncertainty about how low and how fast fertility will fall in the future, but they have considerably lower levels of uncertainty for the old-age population. While uncertainty over the future course of population will affect the timing of the impacts discussed here, it does not affect the general conclusions regarding the overall demographic uncertainty.

The forecasts of average benefits should also be considered highly uncertain. When faced with this challenge, many forecasters prefer to assume that average benefits remain constant through time. Therefore, their forecasts reflect the impact of demographic pressures under the assumption that current policy remains unchanged. In the cases of education and health care, these sorts of forecasts ignore likely policy changes, such as increases in school enrollment rates and increases in utilization of health services by the elderly. Hence, those forecasts greatly understate the likely fiscal impacts of population change in these sectors. In the case of pensions forecasts, holding the age profiles constant at current levels in Brazil ignores the future impact of reforms that have already been enacted into law (for example, increases in retirement age or changes in benefit formulas).

Average public and private spending on education, health care, and pensions by age in Brazil and that of OECD countries are taken from the National Transfer Accounts (NTA) project (see chapter 1, box 1.1 for a brief description of the NTA project). The next three sections present and discuss this study's projections of public expenditures in the three sectors: education, pensions, and health care.

Education

With the sharp decline in fertility in Brazil over the past few decades, the size of the school-age population has dramatically declined, as shown in figure 6.6. In 1950, the school-age population was 85 percent as large as the working-age population, a ratio higher than that observed in Burkina Faso at the time. By 2010, the school-age population was half the size of the working-age population. If fertility rates remain low in Brazil, it is expected that by 2040 the school-age population would be about 30 percent of the working-age population, a ratio currently observed in Italy and several other European nations. This long-run decline in the school-age population substantially reduces the demographic pressures in the education sector in Brazil.

As with the discussion of demographic dividends for growth (see chapter 2), this process of a reduced ratio between the school-age population relative to the working-age population can also be divided in two phases, as illustrated by Soares (2008). The first phase, called "Relative Bonus," occurs when the working-age population and the school-age population are both increasing, but the working-age population is increasing faster. The second phase, called "Absolute Bonus," is characterized by school-age population decreasing and working-age population increasing. Brazil is the only country in LAC that has already entered this second

Figure 6.6   School-Age Population vs. Working-Age Population in Brazil, Italy, and Burkina Faso, 1950–2050

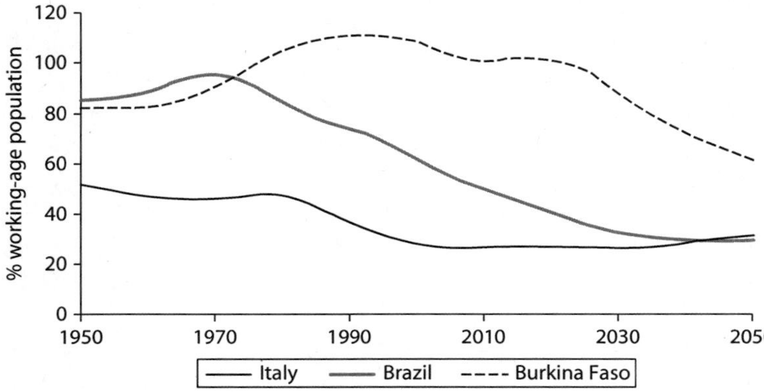

Source: Miller and Castanheira 2010, based on population data from CEPAL 2008.

phase, which started at the beginning of the 1990s. The increase in the share of working-age adults relative to school-age youth generates more resources available to finance public programs targeted at children, or for other fiscal purposes, as the economy grows faster.

Education investment per student depends not only on the amount of resources (as percentage of GDP) that countries allocate on education but also on the number of students. A good measure of expenditure per student is the education benefit ratio, as described in equation 1.

A good example is comparing education spending in LAC and OECD. On average, both groups of countries currently assign about 5 percent of GDP to educating the next generation. A closer inspection using the framework presented above shows that this seemingly similar allocation implies vastly different levels of generosity because of the significantly higher proportions of children in most LAC countries. The student-age population in LAC is about two-thirds the size of the working-age population, while in the OECD countries it is only about two-fifths. In terms of generosity, this means that OECD secondary education spending per youth is about twice as high as in LAC. Within LAC there are significant differences that are often not appreciated. Comparing LAC countries that spend similar amounts of GDP on education—say Brazil and Nicaragua at about 5 percent of GDP or Peru and Uruguay at about 3 percent—the model makes it clear that because there are higher school dependency rates in Nicaragua and Peru, the same investment in education implies significantly lower generosity in spending per student. Brazil and Mexico spend about twice as much per student as a proportion of GDP per worker as Peru does (World Bank forthcoming).

Figure 6.7 shows that Brazil's current level of public spending is above the OECD average. However, given the larger share of school-age population in Brazil than in OECD countries, Brazilian expenditures per student are less than those observed in OECD countries for all types of education, with the exception of higher education (see table 6.3). In particular, Brazilian current public expenditures per student in high school, elementary, and infant education are still very low compared to higher education (Tafner 2010). As a consequence, the higher-to-elementary ratio is 1.2 in OECD and 6.1 in Brazil.

Projections

Two scenarios are presented for projecting future public spending on education in figure 6.8. In the "status-quo scenario," the government maintains its current levels of aggregate spending on education. As the population of students declines over time, the average benefit per student would gradually rise toward OECD levels, but it would never reach these levels over the next four decades. An "alternative scenario" considers an ambitious expansion of educational spending to reach OECD levels of investment per student within a decade. In this scenario, spending as a percentage of GDP increases sharply over the decade, reaching 6.3 percent by 2020. Once it reaches this target level of investment per student, the share of GDP devoted to education would then gradually decline in concert with the decline in the school-aged population, while maintaining investment levels per student equivalent to those of OECD countries.

What would it mean to reach OECD levels of investment per student? This investment is measured relative to the average wage in the economy. To the extent that education is a product solely of teachers' salaries and average classroom sizes, then reaching OECD levels of investment per student would mean that Brazil had achieved the same level of "quantity," as measured by enrollment rates, and "quality," as measured by class sizes and average teacher salaries, as the OECD countries. Such an ambitious increase in educational investment would likely have profound implications for both economic growth and inequality in Brazil. Indeed, Lee and Mason (2010) present simulation results that suggest that such investments in human capital can offset the costs of population aging.

Figure 6.7   Public Expenditure on Education as a Percentage of GDP, OECD Countries, and Brazil, 2007

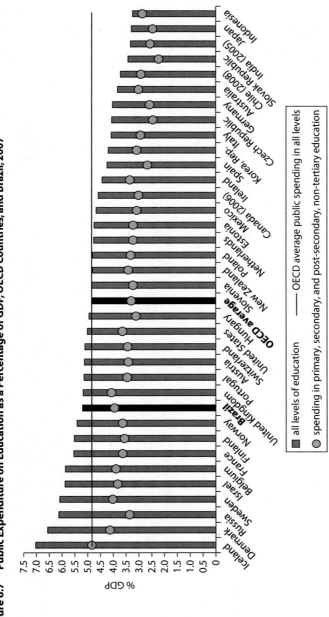

Source: World Bank forthcoming.

Table 6.3   Expenditures per Student (PPP-GDP US$), 2006

Countries	Preschool education	Basic Education			Higher education	Higher ed-to-elementary ratio
		Elementary				
		1st–4th gr	5th–8th gr	High school		
OECD average	5,260	6,437	7,544	8,486	8,455	1.2
Brazil	1,315	1,566	1,726	1,225	10,067	6.1

Source: OECD 2009a.

Figure 6.8   Public Spending on Education as Percentage of GDP, Brazil, 2005–50

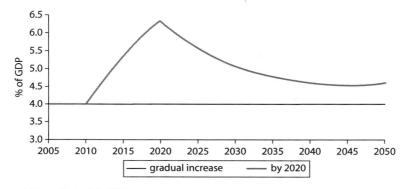

Source: Miller and Castanheira 2010.

It seems that Brazil has made a great effort to universalize primary education, but this effort is not yet followed by either an improvement in quality or improvements in early childhood development and high school coverage. Now the country has the chance to pay more attention to the construction of nurseries, to the quality of primary education, and to the universalization of middle school. Some resources today applied to higher education could be reallocated to these improvements in other levels of education, as spending on higher education per student in Brazil is much higher than in OECD countries. And with only a few more resources, it will be possible to increase per student spending, because there will be far fewer students enrolled than in the past.

Pensions

This section focuses on the likely implications of aging for pension expenditure, given the structure and recent developments in pension finance in Brazil.

In 2005, the Brazilian government was spending a tenth of its GDP on its two main pension programs: 6.6 percent on RGPS (*Regime Geral de Previdencia Social*), paying retirement benefits to former private sector workers, and 3.8 percent on RPPS (*Regime Proprio de Previdencia Social*), paying retirement benefits to former civil servants. The last few decades have seen relatively little change in the proportion of elderly population relative to the working-age population in Brazil. Thus, the large expansion of public pension benefits in Brazil took place under very little demographic pressure. There will be a dramatic change in this situation in the coming decades, as shown in figure 6.9. In 2010, the elderly population in Brazil was about 11 percent the size of the working-age population. By 2050, this ratio will more than triple, with the elderly population in Brazil at about 39 percent of the size of the working-age population. Sometime during the 2040s, the proportion of elderly population of Brazil is projected to surpass that of youth.

Aggregate spending on pensions in Brazil is slightly below the OECD average, but the benefit generosity is more than twice as large—and this is the case even considering that the dependency ratio in Brazil is currently less than half of the OECD average (table 6.2). See chapter 3 for a more extensive review of public spending on pensions in Brazil.

Projections

Three scenarios are presented here for future public spending on pensions.[4] The "status-quo scenario" assumes no change in the current

Figure 6.9   Elderly vs. Working-Age Population in Brazil, Nicaragua, and Spain, 1950–2050

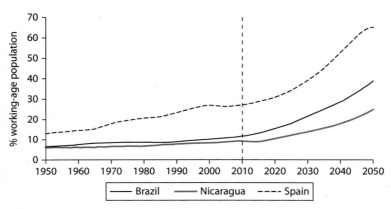

Source: Miller and Castanheira (2010) based on population data from CEPAL 2008.

generosity of pensions. In this case, the rapid increase in the ratio of older adults to working-age adults directly translates into dramatic and unsustainable increases in public spending, with spending on pensions rising from 10 percent of GDP in 2004 to an astounding 37 percent of GDP by 2050. Clearly this path would not be sustainable.

The "legislated reform scenario" models the impact of several recent pensions reforms (1999 and 2003), which resulted in significant reductions in the generosity of pensions, both in the short and long run.[5] This study's post-reform projections are calculated by a slight revision to equation 1, shown below as equation 2.

$$B(t)/GDP(t) = \text{sum over } x \{ b(x,t) * o(x,t) * P(x,t)/P(20\text{–}64,t) \} \quad (2)$$

A measure of the impact of these reforms was developed by calculating an "obligation matrix," $o(x,t)$, which measures the ratio of post-reform to pre-reform benefits. The obligation matrix measures the extent to which the pre-reform obligations are honored. It has values ranging from 1 (meaning benefits are maintained at pre-reform levels) to 0 (meaning benefits are completely eliminated).

A full modeling of the impact of these rules is beyond the scope of the current research and would require information on wage distributions, predictions of the future course of minimum wage relative to average wage, and prediction of behavioral responses to the new rules such as switching from retirement based on age to retirement based on contribution period, among other calculations. This scenario simply presents a stylized version of the reforms by examining their impact on the "typical" retiree in each system. In the RGPS system, payouts based on contribution period exceed payouts based on age, so the typical worker is assumed to retire based on contribution time. The main RGPS reform was the introduction of a new social security factor that would reduce benefits to those retiring at age 52 by 29 percent. This factor is taken from Miessi and Portela Souza (2007), which bases it on an average age of retirement of 52 and average length of contribution of 33 years. This transition is assumed to take place over the course of five years beginning in 1999. In addition, the new social security factor automatically reduces benefits of future cohorts as life expectancy increases. The reduction in benefits is based on projected changes in life expectancy at age 52 from 2005 to 2050.

For the RPPS system, the typical civil servant is assumed to retire based on age. Four distinct rule changes are modeled. In 1998, it was assumed that all new hires cannot retire until age 57.5 (the simple average of minimum ages for men and women of 60 and 55, respectively); while those currently insured as of that date have a minimum retirement age of 50.5 (the simple average of minimum ages for men and women of 53 and 48, respectively).[6] Since data on new hires are not available, it is assumed that 100 percent of 20-year-olds and 0 percent of 50-year-olds are new hires, and there is a linear transition in between. In 2005, three new reforms were introduced, which are assumed to apply only to new hires: an increase in the minimum retirement age from 60 for men and 55 for women to 65 for men and 60 for women, benefits based on average of 80 percent of highest wage contributions rather than wage in year of retirement, and use of price-indexing rather than wage-indexing for post-retirement benefit increases.[7]

These reforms served to delay the onset of the rapid increases in pension costs due to population aging (comparing the blue and red lines in figure 6.10). The reforms—while implying substantial cuts in benefit generosity over the coming decades—were not enough to blunt the enormous public finance impact of a more than tripling of the size of the elderly population relative to the working-age population. Even in the reform scenario, projected pension costs rise substantially over the period, reaching 22 percent of GDP by 2050.

In the third "predicted reforms scenario," the impact of the legislated reforms on pension benefits is ignored. Instead, the benefits are assumed to decline toward OECD values as the Brazilian economy grows. Specifically, it is assumed that the GDP per worker will grow at

Figure 6.10   Public Spending on Pensions as Percentage of GDP, 2005–50

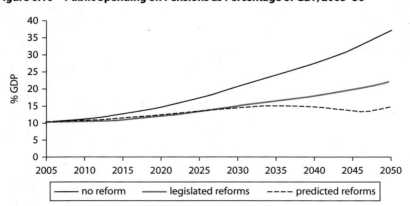

Source: Miller and Castanheira 2010.

2.5 percent over the next 40 years and that the generosity of public pension benefits will fall toward OECD levels. In this scenario, specific reforms are not modeled; instead, it assumes reforms will be carried out in a continuous manner to lead to a smooth reduction in benefit generosity as the economy grows over time. Interestingly, projected expenditures in this scenario are broadly similar over the next 15 years to the projections based on the specific reforms recently legislated. In this scenario, pension costs rise modestly to about 15 percent of GDP (on par with that observed in several European countries). Given that the recent set of reforms is not sufficient to curb the growth of pension spending, future sets of reforms can be expected. To insure fairness, such reforms would need to be implemented incrementally, which is what this third scenario attempts to imitate.

Figure 6.10 presents the findings of projections under the three scenarios. The costs projected under the legislated reform are below those of the third scenario up until 2027. Beyond 2027, the costs projections in the two scenarios sharply diverge. The scenario in which benefits continue to decline until reaching OECD levels serves to postpone the sharp increase in pension expenditures that accompany aging until the late 2040s.

Health Care

The government of Brazil is heavily involved in the provision and financing of health care.[8] The current Brazilian public-sector health system was introduced under the new 1988 constitution, which, inspired by the idea of a national health system, created the Sistema Único de Saúde (SUS, or Unified Health System), whose principles are free and universal access to health care, comprehensiveness, and public financing. The SUS functions across Brazil's three levels of government (central, state, and municipality). Brazil's constitution allows the existence of a private sector in health, so the Brazilian health system is composed of a mix of public-system and the private-sector providers. In practice, the statutory system is the public one, and the private sector, which comprises both private voluntary health insurance and private providers, operates alongside the public system. In the private sector, people pay private providers using private health insurance or out-of-pocket payments.

Health care spending is a major, ever growing source of fiscal pressure. In 2000, Constitutional Amendment No. 29 (EC 29) introduced important changes in the public financing of health care services. EC 29 determines the minimum percentage of the federative entities' revenue allocated to public expenditure on health.[9] As expected, states' compliance with the maximum limits imposed by EC 29 on public expenditure financing on health produced an increase in spending.[10] Table 6.4 shows expenditures on health by all levels of government. Between 2000, the EC 29 approval year, and 2006, federal expenditure on health using the federal funds only grew 10.4 percent in actual terms. In addition, state and local governments show an actual growth of 73 percent and 75.6 percent, respectively. Thus, spending through state and local governments' own resources stimulated a total growth of 36.1 percent in the period. The total increase in spending per capita was 24.5 percent and as a percentage of GDP was 24.6 percent.

Projections

As countries move through the demographic transition, the health sector dependency ratio follows a U-shaped curve. Initially, declines in mortality rates lead to declines in the proportion of the population near death. As evident in the case of Nicaragua, as shown in figure 6.11, such declines can be quite rapid and substantial. The near-death population was about one-third the size of the working-age population in 1950 in Nicaragua. Over five decades, the near-death population declined to about one-tenth the size of the working-age population. Eventually as the demographic transition proceeds, the age structure of the population shifts substantially toward older persons and the near-death population begins to increase relative to the working-age population.

In virtually all LAC countries the near-death population will grow more quickly than the population of working-age adults, which will tend to increase the financial burden associated with financing health care. In the case of Brazil, the near-death population has been declining since 1950, when it was about one-fifth of the working-age population. It reached a nadir of about 11 percent of the working-age population in 2006 and is projected to continue increasing. After decades of favorable demographic chance, the health system in Brazil is set to experience increasing demographic pressures over the coming decades.

There are striking differences in health care expenditures by age between high-income and middle-income countries. Figure 6.12 shows health care expenditures per person of each age as a fraction of GDP per-working-age adult based on the authors' calculations using data taken from National Transfer Accounts. For those below age 40, health spending in high-income and middle-income countries is surprisingly similar. This

Table 6.4   Federal, State, Municipal, and Total Health Care Spending, 2000–06

Year	Central government			States			Municipalities			Total		
	A	B	C	A	B	C	A	B	C	A	B	C
	R$ millions	R$	% GDP	R$ millions	R$	% GDP	R$ millions	R$	% GDP	R$ millions	R$	% GDP
2000	44,197	119.86	1.73	13,710	37.18	0.54	16,006	44.71	0.62	73,916	200.44	2.89
2001	44,224	130.37	1.73	16,270	47.96	0.63	18,281	54.79	0.71	78,774	232.22	3.07
2002	42,884	141.65	1.67	17,818	58.86	0.70	20,838	70.17	0.81	81,540	269.34	3.18
2003	38,376	153.67	1.60	17,147	68.66	0.71	19,771	81.35	0.82	75,294	301.51	3.14
2004	42,206	182.59	1.68	20,686	89.49	0.83	21,163	94.51	0.84	84,056	363.64	3.35
2005	44,448	198.15	1.70	20,992	93.58	0.80	24,677	111.88	0.94	90,118	401.73	3.45
2006	48,786	218.18	1.75	23,703	106.01	0.85	28,115	128.13	1.01	100,605	449.93	3.60

Source: Ministry of Health 2009.

A. financed by own resources in Jan. 2010 R$ millions.

B. per capita health care spending.

C. health care spending as percentage of GDP.

Figure 6.11   Near-Death Population vs. Working-Age Population: Brazil, Nicaragua, and United States, 1950–2040

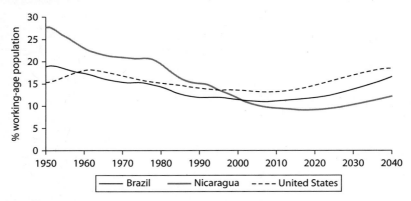

Source: Miller and Castanheira 2010, based on population projections from CEPAL 2008.

Figure 6.12   Average Health Spending per Person by Age in Middle- and High-Income Countries, 2005

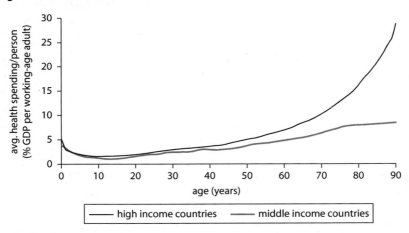

Source: Miller and Castanheira 2010, based on data from the National Transfer Accounts project 2010.

cross-section of data implies that health care spending at these ages increases proportionally with income. Above age 40, the pattern is very different. In high-income countries, health care expenditures per older adult are significantly greater than in middle-income countries. That is, as incomes rise, health care expenditures after 40 increase more rapidly than income. This means that in high-income countries health care for the aged is a "luxury good," that is, a good for which demand increases more than proportionally as income rises; whereas health care for those under 40 is a "normal good," that is, a good for which demand increases when income increases and falls when income decreases, but price remains constant.

It is very much an open question as to why societies seem to choose this pattern of higher health expenditures above age 40 more in high-income than in middle-income countries. Some possible explanations include:

- Shifts in medical protocol in which chronic diseases are more aggressively treated;
- Age-biased technological change, wherein advances in medical care favor the sorts of chronic medical problems common among older people;
- Political power, since these are mainly public expenditures, it could represent the rising political power of older people as societies age (and simultaneously become wealthier); and
- Data measurement anomalies, that is, older and wealthier countries may provide some care for senior citizens in the market, whereas in poorer countries such goods are home produced.

Whatever the reasons for this pattern, the shift to higher expenditures at older ages as countries become richer magnifies the impact of population aging and is projected to lead to significant increases in health expenditures as a share of GDP in Brazil.

As in the case for pensions, two alternative scenarios are presented for future public spending on health. In the "status quo scenario," age-specific public spending on health remains constant relative to GDP per working-age adult. In this scenario, only demographic change drives public health expenditures. In Brazil, this results in about a 1.6 percentage points increase in spending through 2050: rising from 3.3 percent in 2005 to reach 4.9 percent in 2040. In the "alternative scenario," public expenditures on health care move toward the patterns observed in high-income economies—with large increases in the older ages, as GDP per worker increases (at a fixed rate of 2.5 percent per year). In this scenario, the fiscal impact of growing numbers of elderly is multiplied by this shift toward increasing levels of medical treatment of the elderly. Public expenditures increase by 4.4 percentage points of GDP by 2050, reaching 7.7 percent of GDP (see figure 6.13). This increase is on par with that observed for pensions under the "predicted reforms" scenario.

Figure 6.13   Public Spending on Health as Percentage of GDP, 2005–50

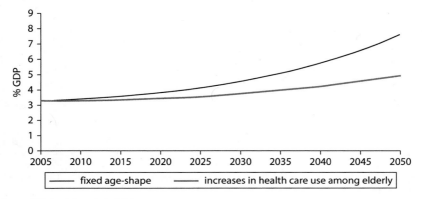

Source: Miller and Castanheira 2010.

Overall Fiscal Impact of the Aging Population

The age structure of Brazil's population will change dramatically over the coming decades. The elderly population is projected to increase from about 11 percent of the working-age population to 49 percent by 2050, while the school-age population is projected to decline from about 50 percent of the working-age population to 29 percent by 2050. These shifts in population age structure are likely to lead to substantial additional fiscal pressures on publicly financed health care and pensions, along with substantial reductions in fiscal pressures for publicly financed education.

Having assessed the impact of population aging in each sector, this chapter concludes by presenting an assessment of the overall impact on government spending. In 2005, total public spending on education, pensions (including those for civil servants), and health care amounted to 17.7 percent of Brazil's GDP. The authors' projection shows an increase of 9.5 percentage points of GDP, such that by 2050 public spending in these sectors would reach 27.2 percent of GDP. This projection combines three sector forecasts: (1) for education, an ambitious program is assumed of increased expenditures to reach OECD levels of investment per student by 2020; (2) for pensions, a program of pension reforms is assumed that gradually reduces benefits to those of OECD by 2050; and (3) for health care, it is assumed that the impact of increasing numbers of elderly is multiplied by an increase in the costs of care for this age group. Figure 6.14 shows the path of public spending 2005–50 in this scenario.

Figure 6.14   Public Spending on Education, Pensions, and Health as Percentage of GDP, 2005–50

investment per student at OECD levels

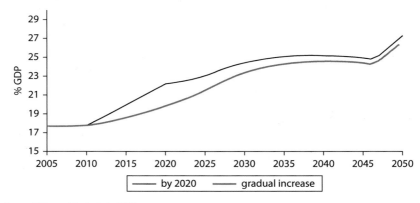

Source: Miller and Castanheira 2010.

As an alternative, a scenario is shown in which aggregate expenditures in education remain constant over the projection and investments per student gradually approach OECD levels.

The costs of these two alternative scenarios are evaluated by taking the present value of future cost increases as a share of current GDP. In the first scenario, the future cost increases amount to two times current GDP under an assumption of a 4 percent discount rate. These costs can be decomposed by program, as shown in table 6.5.

The largest contributor to future costs increases are pensions, which will see cost increases amounting to half the overall increase in public spending: 99 percent of current GDP. The remainder is split between health cost increases (50 percent of current GDP) and education increases (39 percent). It is worth stressing that the very ambitious program of increasing educational spending to reach OECD levels of student investment within a decade is far less costly than the projected increases in health care and pensions.

In terms of public health care, one of the key findings from this study's projections is that heath care expenditures are likely to increase substantially in Brazil. An increase is projected of more than 4 percentage points of GDP, about the same increase as in pensions. These increases in health spending come relatively later in the projection period as compared to pensions; thus, the present value of cost increases in health care is about half that of pensions. There are two driving forces behind this increase in

Table 6.5   Projected Increases in Public Spending, 2005–50

Sector	Scenario	Costs of future increases in spending relative to current GDP (%)	Spending as % of GDP		
			2005	2050	Difference
Education, pensions, and health care	Rapid increase in education investment; decline in pension benefits according to current reforms through 2027 and then continued declines to OECD levels thereafter; increasing health expenditures at older ages	188	17.7	27.2	9.5
	Gradual increase in education investment; decline in pension benefits according to current reforms through 2027 and then continued declines to OECD levels thereafter; increasing health expenditures at older ages	149	17.7	26.6	8.9
Education	Rapid increase in student investment, reaching OECD levels by 2020	39	4.0	4.6	0.6
Pensions	Average pension benefits fixed at current levels relative to average wage	357	10.4	37.2	26.8
	Average pension benefits reduced according to recently legislated reforms	156	10.4	22.4	12.0
	Gradual decline toward OECD levels	107	10.4	14.9	4.5
	Average pension benefits cut according to current law through 2026 and future reforms reduce values toward OECD	99	10.4	14.9	4.5
Health care	Increasing health expenditures at older ages	50	3.3	7.7	4.4
	No change in health expenditures by age	18	3.3	4.9	1.6

Source: Miller and Castanheira 2010, based on fiscal projection model.

health costs: the increasing proportion of elderly in the population and a growing intensity of formal health care use among the elderly. Therefore, health care is likely to emerge as a major fiscal challenge in the coming decades in Brazil.

Without the public pension reforms that were carried out in the late 1990s through early 2000s, the projected increase in costs through 2050 would have amounted to more than 3.5 times current GDP. Clearly, the old system was unsustainable. The stylized model presented here of the recent set of pension reforms projects future increases amounting to 156 percent of current GDP—with pension expenditures projected to double to 22.4 percent of GDP by 2050. The model presented here is admittedly a crude estimate of the impact that tends to overstate the amount of savings from the reform. Therefore, the estimate should be taken as a lower bound on future increases. The current set of reforms more than halved the projected cost increases in the absence of reform. At the same time, the projections have not solved the problem of increasing pension benefits. In the alternative predicted reforms scenario, a series of reforms is forecast intended to gradually bring Brazil pension benefits into line with those of OECD countries. Even in this optimistic scenario, increases in pension expenditure dominate the fiscal outlook for Brazil.

In summary, Brazil is entering a new demographic phase in which changing population age structure will lead to increasing cost pressures on health care and, especially, on pensions. The projections here show that beginning around 2015, after a respite due to the recently enacted pension reforms, pressure on public spending will begin a sustained and rapid increase lasting several decades. The need for increased investment in students will compete against those of sustaining pension benefits and increasing demands for health care—especially among the elderly.

Annex 6.1

Table A6.1   RGPS (Private Worker System) Retirement Rules by Retirement Type

Type of retirement	Old age		Length of contribution		Length of contribution + age	
	Men	Women	Men	Women	Men	Women
Minimum age	Urban worker: 65 Rural worker: 60	Urban worker: 60 Rural worker: 55	n.a.	n.a.	53	48
Minimum contribution length	n.a.	n.a.	Men: 35 years Women: 30 years		30 years + 40% of the time missing to complete 30 years of contribution in December 16, 1998	25 years + 40% of the time missing to complete 25 years of contribution in December 16, 1998
Benefit value	70% of salary-benefit + 1% to each group of 12 contributions until it reaches the maximum of a 100% of the salary-benefit. The benefit value will not be less than the official minimum wage.		100% of the salary-benefit		70% of the salary-benefit + 5% for each contribution year after the minimum length of contribution (30 if male and 25 if female)	
Salary-benefit	Insured in the system until November 28, 1999: simple average of 80% highest wages since July 1994		Insured in the system until November 28, 1999: Simple average of the 80% highest wages since July 1994 multiplied by the social security factor		Insured in the system until November 28, 1999: Simple average of the 80% highest wages since July 1994 multiplied by the social security factor	

(continued next page)

Table A6.1 *(continued)*

Type of retirement	Old age		Length of contribution		Length of contribution + age	
	Men	**Women**	**Men**	**Women**	**Men**	**Women**
	Insured in the system after November 29, 1999: simple average of 80% highest wages of the complete contribution period		Insured in the system after November 29, 1999: simple average of 80% highest wages of the complete contribution period multiplied by the social security factor		Insured in the system after November 29, 1999: simple average of 80% highest wages of the complete contribution period multiplied by the social security factor	
Social Security Factor[1]		Can be applied if advantageous	Mandatory		Mandatory	
Penury period to retire	Insured in the system after 1991: 180 contributions. Insured in the system before 1991: depends on the year of retirement requirement. If the requirement is in 1992, it is 60 contributions, for each additional year it is 6 additional contributions until it reaches 180 in 2011. The exception is 1995–96—that one year adds 12 contributions (from 78 to 90 contributions).					

Source: Miller and Castanheira 2010.

Notes:

1. Transition rule to Social Security Factor: To people in the system before December 15, 1998, the Social Security Factor is applied to only 1/60 of the average 80% highest wages for people who retire in the first month after the reform. In the second month, the Social Security Factor is applied to 2/60 of the average highest 80% wages. It keeps on like this until it reaches 100% after five years of reform.

2. To people enrolled in the system but with no contribution since July 1994, the benefit value will be the official minimum wage.

3. Teachers of infant, basic, and secondary education receive a discount of five years in the retirement minimum age and in the contribution length.

n.a. = not applicable.

Table A6.2 RPPS (Civil Service System) Retirement Rules

for those enrolled in the system after or before Constitutional Amendment 41 of 2003

Type of retirement	Old age		Length of contribution	
	Men	*Women*	*Men*	*Women*
Minimum age	65	60	60	55
Minimum contribution length	n.a.	n.a.	35 years	30 years
Benefit value	Proportional to time of contribution		100% salary-benefit	
Salary-benefit	Average of 80% highest wages of the career with a ceiling of (R\$2,500) if a private additional regime (RPC) is available. The salary-benefit will not be less than a minimum wage.			
Penury period to retire	10 years of performance in the public sector and five years in the retirement work occupation			

Source: Miller and Castanheira 2010.

n.a. = not applicable.

225

Table A6.3 RPPS (Civil Service System) Retirement Rules

for those enrolled in the system before Constitutional Amendment 20 of 1998

Type of retirement	A		B		C¹	
	Men	Women	Men	Women	Men	Women
Minimum age	53	48	Minimum age (60) will be reduced by 1 year for each contribution year that exceeds the minimum contribution length (35 years)	Minimum age (55) will be reduced by 1 year for each contribution year that exceeds the minimum contribution length (30 years)	60	55
Minimum contribution length	35 years + 20% of the time missing to complete 35 years of contribution by December 16, 1998	30 years + 20% of the time missing to complete 30 years of contribution by December 16, 1998	35 years	30 years	35 years	30 years
Benefit value	3.5% of salary-benefit reduction for each year less than 60 if the person reached those retirement requirements before December 31, 2005	3.5% of salary-benefit reduction for each year less than 55 if the person reached those retirement requirements before December 31, 2005	100% salary-benefit		100% salary-benefit	

226

	5% of salary-benefit reduction for each year less than 60 if the person reached those retirement requirements after January 1, 2006	5% of salary-benefit reduction for each year less than 55 if the person reached those retirement requirements after January 1, 2006	100% of last wage actualized by the wage of active people in the retiree's last occupation or function
Salary-benefit	Average of 80% highest wages since July 1994	100% of last wage actualized by the wage of active people in the retiree's last occupation or function	
			20 years enrolled in the public sector, 10 years of career, and 5 years in the retirement work occupation
Career condition	5 years in the retirement work occupation	25 years enrolled in the public sector, 15 years of career, and 5 years in the retirement work occupation	

Source: Miller and Castanheira (2010).

Notes:
1. Retirement type C is for people enrolled in the system before Constitutional Amendment 41 in 2003.
2. The retirement in RPPS (Public Employee Pension System) is mandatory when the worker reaches 70 years old.
3. Civil servants who are teachers will have an addition of 17% (if male) and 20% (if female) in their length of contribution if they are enrolled in RPPS before the Constitutional Amendment of 1998.
4. Inactive people already retired within RPPS will have to pay contributions to the government in the same proportion as actives employees (11% of the wage) if their retirement benefit is 50% more than the RGPS (Private Worker Social Security) ceiling (R$2400,00) to retired civil servants of states, municipalities, and the Federal District; or 60% more than the RGPS ceiling (R$2400,00) to retired civil servants of the federal government.
n.a. = not applicable.

Notes

1. Data on spending on health by all levels of government (federal, state, and municipal) became available only in 2000. Figure 6.1 reports both total public spending during 2000–08 and federal spending on health during 1980–2008.
2. Most educational spending occurs in this age group, although increasingly expenditures are being directed to early education and continuing education.
3. The equation used for projections of spending is simply the vector version of equation 1, which was used for our international cross-sectional comparisons.
4. The assumptions behind each scenario are presented in the annex.
5. The annex lists the pension rules for the two programs and highlights the recent reforms.
6. This impact is modeled as the ratio of life expectancy at these ages, e (57.5)/e (50.5) = 0.81.
7. The change in benefits is modeled as 0.81 (based on change in expected length of retirement) using e (62.5)/e (57.5)* 0.74 (assuming a real wage growth of 2.5% per year and an average retirement period of 20 years)* 0.75 (use of 80% highest rather than last year wage), or a benefit that would be 45% of the benefit prior to the reform.
8. This reflects a shared view of the economic rationale for public-sector involvement in health care markets based on efficiency and equity consider-ations. Health care markets suffer from the typical problems of insurance markets, such as adverse selection (which may make it difficult for persons with higher health risks to obtain affordable coverage, leading to a suboptimal consumption of health care services); moral hazard (whereby insured persons may have an incentive to overconsume health care services because they do not bear the full cost); and other asymmetric information (whereby health care providers may be in a position to induce the demand for treatment and extract economic rents).
9. For the federal government, in the year 2000, this minimum amount was to be equivalent to the amount spent on health public services in fiscal year 1999 plus 5 percent. From 2000 on, it was to equal the value obtained in the previous year, plus the nominal GDP variation. For states (including the Federal District) and local governments, the minimum amount of resources applied to health was to be increased gradually—up to one-fifth of the difference—until the fifth year after approval of EC 29. Until 2004, such resources would reach 12 percent at state level and 15 percent at municipal level. After that, they would stabilize at least at that threshold.
10. In 2000, when the minimum percentage was 7 percent, only 63 percent of the states fulfilled the commitment. In 2008, when this minimum value had

already reached 12 percent, 85 percent of the states spent as much or more than what was mandatory.

References

CEPAL (Comisión Económica para America Latina y el Caribe). 2008. *Transformaciones demográficas y su influencia en el desarrollo en América Latina y el Caribe*. CEPAL: Santiago de Chile.

Lee, Ronald, and Andrew Mason. 2010. "Fertility, Human Capital, and Economic Growth over the Demographic Transition." *European Journal of Population* 26 (2): 159–82.

Miessi, F., and A. Portela Souza. 2007. "(Un)Sustainability and Reform of the Social Security System in Brasil: A Generational Accounting Approach." *Revista Brasileira de Economia* 61 (3): 379–404.

Miller, T., G. Bay, and M. Ruiz. 2009. "The Random Country Model: An Examination of Likely Demographic Surprises in Latin America and Their Fiscal Impact." Paper presented at the XXVI IUSSP International Population Conference, Marrakech, Morocco, September 27–October 2.

Miller, T. 2011. "Increasing Longevity and Medicare Expenditures." *Demography* 38 (2): 215–26.

Miller, T., and H. C. Castanheira. 2010. "The Fiscal Impact of Population Aging in Brazil." Background paper prepared for the Workshop on Aging in Brazil, World Bank. Brasilia, April 6–7, 2010.

Ministry of Health (Brazil). 2009. Information System on Health Public Expenditures (SIOPS). Online database. http:\\siops.datasus.gov.br.

OECD (Organization for Economic Co-operation and Development). 2009a. *Education at a Glance 2009: OECD Indicators*. OECD, Paris, France.

———. 2009b. Social Expenditure Database. Online database: http://oberon. sourceoecd.org/vl=2355160/cl=17/nw=1/rpsv/ij/oecdstats/1608117x/ vl35n1/s1/p1.

Soares, S. 2008. "O Bônus Demográfico Relativo e Absoluto no Acesso à Escola." Texto para discussão 1340. IPEA *(Instituto de Pesquisa Econômica Aplicada)*, Rio de Janeiro.

Tafner, P. 2010. "Public Expenditure Review for Health, Education and Social Security in the Context of Population Aging in Brazil." Unpublished report, World Bank, Brasilia.

UNESCO (United Nations Educational, Scientific and Cultural Organization). 2009. UNESCO Institute for Statistics Data Centre. Online database: http:// stat.uis.unesco.org.

WHO (World Health Organization). 2009. WHO Statistical Information System. Online database: http://www.who.int/whosis/en/index.html.

World Bank. 2009. *World Development Indicators 2009*. Washington, DC: World Bank.

World Bank. Forthcoming. "Achieving World Class Education in Brazil: The Next Agenda." Latin America and the Caribbean Region. Washington, DC: World Bank.

CHAPTER 7

Financing Brazil's Aging Population: Implications for Saving and Growth

Population aging in Brazil is an inevitable consequence of its demographic transition from young to old. Economic behavior and macroeconomic outcomes change both systematically and endogenously with aging. Therefore, Brazil is bound to experience pressure on fiscal sustainability, while saving and investment are in danger of falling short of what is needed to keep capital accumulation, wealth, and welfare at desirable levels.

Sufficient saving is important in an economy in order to generate a high per capita income. Population aging has two direct effects on saving: First, aging is traditionally believed to reduce aggregate saving rates because the working-age (elderly) share of the population—who generally have high (low) saving rates—will decrease (increase) as implied by the life cycle hypothesis (LCH) that people tend to save relatively more in their working years than in their youth and old age (Modigliani and Brumberg 1954). All other things being equal, this effect will lead to lower economic growth (Solow 1956; Weil 1997). Second, aging will probably increase the saving rate since life expectancy is increasing and people consequently anticipate a longer retirement period to be financed partly by private saving (Jorgensen and Jensen 2010). These two effects may have offsetting impacts on saving, and thus on growth. Therefore, which effect dominates is clearly an empirical matter, as is whether the assumptions behind the LCH are valid in the context of Brazil.

To further point out the complexity of this issue, what if age-specific saving rates do not decline in old age, as posited by the LCH? That could entail completely different macroeconomic effects of aging than would be expected. There may be a desire on the part of the elderly to leave bequests (Kotlikoff and Summers 1981; De Nardi, French, and Jones 2009) or to share their pension income with their children (Barro 1974). In addition, aging has countless indirect effects on saving. For example, the intensity of the labor supply might fall when statutory retirement ages are increased often as a policy response to aging, which results in a decline in people's lifetime leisure (Jorgensen and Jensen 2010). Furthermore, the way in which the Brazilian government decides to finance the inevitably increasing costs for social security and health will also have major implications for the behavioral economic responses of Brazilians.

This chapter, which builds on Jorgensen (2011), presents an analysis of the macroeconomic implications of population aging in Brazil using four alternative yet complementary methodologies. First, the international and Brazil-specific econometric evidence on the aging-saving transmission channel is analyzed. Second, a partial equilibrium model is developed to exploit the rich household data on exogenous age-specific saving rates in Brazil. Third, because partial equilibrium analyses do not take into account the potentially endogenous behavioral responses to aging (Acemoglu 2010), a general equilibrium framework is presented—under which a reduced form and a full-fledged version of the general equilibrium model are analyzed. Simulations are performed for different scenarios of poverty reduction and fiscal policies, and the implications for key macroeconomic aggregates, such as saving, wealth, and demographic dividends, are analyzed and discussed in light of the advantages and disadvantages of the different models.

The main findings of the four complementary analyses follow. In relation to the econometric evidence for Brazil, a higher saving rate is found to lead to higher income growth. This is an empirically well-established relationship for most countries. What is more controversial is the econometric finding that an increase in the old-age dependency ratio has, so far, led to an increase in the private saving rate—suggesting that aging may lead to higher growth in the future due to higher saving rates. The econometric evidence is paired with a literature review that places Brazil in international context regarding the relationship between population dynamics and saving—revealing that Brazil is not the only developing country that has experienced such unexpected dynamics.[1] Ultimately, there is no econometric evidence suggesting that an increasing old-age dependency ratio has led to reductions in saving and growth.

The partial equilibrium results suggest that saving rates in Brazil depend crucially on public pensions. The elderly tend to save a large fraction of public pensions, effectively leading to just as high saving rates for elderly as for workers. If Brazil maintains relatively high public pensions, it is therefore likely that the saving rate will increase, since the population structure will comprise a larger fraction of high-saving workers and elderly—rather than low-saving young. On the other hand, it should be taken into account that high pensions themselves crowd out savings; if people are sure that they will receive high public pensions, why should they save for their retirement? Consequently, these forces counteract each other. Moreover, if poverty levels fall further, there will be more high savers because the non-poor tend to save more than the poor—thus promoting saving even further.

In terms of financing the costs associated with aging, this chapter compares in the full-fledged general equilibrium model three financing options: First, "Tax-Financing," where taxes for health and pensions increase to finance an unchanged level of health and pension benefits as debt is left untouched; second, "Benefit-Financing," where debt and taxes are unchanged while pension benefits per elderly decline; and third, "Debt-Financing," where public debt is allowed to absorb all costs while the pensions and health contributions and benefits remain constant. Clearly, the different financing scenarios will have different effects on economic behavior and fiscal costs, and the chapter analyzes their respective implications for saving, capital accumulation, and demographic dividends.

The key driver of the general equilibrium results is endogenous capital accumulation—signifying the catalyst for the second demographic dividend.[2] The key finding is that Benefit-Financing will be strongly preferable as a financing method because capital accumulation and growth-dividends would increase under this scenario when the population ages—while capital accumulation and growth-dividends are expected to fall under Tax-Financing or Debt-Financing scenarios. Consequently, with appropriate policies, there is scope for promoting the second demographic dividend over the period 2010–50. A possible reform of the relatively generous Brazilian social security system should consider the advantages involved with indexing the age of eligibility for pension benefits (the statutory retirement age) to the life expectancy. Such a policy response is analytically formulated by Jorgensen and Jensen (2010) and has informed policy debates across OECD countries in particular.

The scope of this chapter does not encompass all the transmission channels through which aging will lead to macroeconomic changes. Decisions about labor force participation and endogenous changes in effective retirement ages are not explicitly considered here.[3] The next section presents new econometric evidence for Brazil on the aging-saving relationship and reviews the literature to view Brazil in an international context. After that, the chapter builds and simulates a partial equilibrium model to evaluate the likely implications that aging will have for household saving rates depending on scenarios for poverty headcounts. The final section concludes the triad of methodologies applied to analyze the macroeconomic implications of aging by constructing both a reduced form and a full-fledged general equilibrium model where saving, capital accumulation, and demographic (growth) dividends all can be analyzed empirically for Brazil.

Aging, Saving, and Growth: The Empirical Evidence

Will population aging affect growth through saving in Brazil? The traditional view is that growth should be negatively associated with aging because aging would reduce saving—and lower saving would reduce growth. But is this really what aging has in store for Brazil? To address this question, it is necessary to econometrically analyze the aging-saving and saving-growth relationships, respectively.

Before focusing on the aging-saving relationship, which is the main focus of this chapter, the saving-growth relationship needs to be firmly econometrically established in the case of Brazil. Rodrik (2000) argues that the accumulation of physical capital is the proximate source of economic growth, and, in the context of growth theory, saving is critical to maintaining a high per capita income (Solow 1956). Jorgensen (2011) provides significant and robust evidence that saving is an important determinant of growth.[4]

As a further support for this finding, private saving is found to positively but insignificantly affect investment; growth is significantly increasing investment; and, if investment increases in the short term, growth may fall since output is used for long-term investment rather than consumption; thus, over the long term, investment positively affects growth. These relationships for Brazil conform well to the established macroeconomic literature, and all relationships (except one) confirm the conclusion by Attanasio (2000)—that private saving and growth is positively correlated—thus making an even stronger case for private saving causing growth.[5]

The international evidence on whether saving follows the LCH is quite clear—but mainly for industrialized countries. Cross-country econometric studies using aggregate time-series data reveal correlations between demographics and saving rates that broadly confirm the LCH (Graham 1987; Koskela and Viren, 1992; Masson, Bayoumi, and Samiei 1998; Miles 1999). The international evidence is mixed, however, if low- and middle-income countries are also considered; and it is highly dependent on how income is estimated. Households do not seem to run down their stocks of wealth in retirement at the rate predicted by the LCH (Poterba 1994; Gregory, Mokhtari, and Schrettl 1999). Miles (1999) clarifies that a key error in traditional estimations is to count all of pension receipts as income; they must be adjusted for private pension savings.[6]

The literature review presented in table 7.1 reveals that the expected correlation between the dependency ratio and private saving may be insignificantly positive for "transition" countries (including Brazil) from a developing to a developed economy, though it would be expected to display a negative relationship for developed countries.[7] The likely cause of a positive link between the saving rates and the dependency ratio is the simple fact that household saving rates remain high in old age, which indeed is the case for Brazil, as will be shown. Also, the old-age dependency ratio is likely to be insignificantly positive for Latin American and Caribbean (LAC) countries as a subgroup. An additional element of aging is increased life expectancy, which may raise the rate at which individuals save during working life. Life expectancy is specifically found to positively impact private saving, as shown in table 4.1, and this is supported for LAC countries.

As far as the econometric evidence for Brazil, Jorgensen (2011) finds that the old-age dependency ratio positively (Granger) causes private saving, both in the short and long term (annex 7.1, table A2). This is contrary to the international literature on developed countries, but not necessarily contrary to what is observed in middle-income developing countries. Furthermore, it is found that public saving crowds out private saving, which is consistent with findings in Paiva and Jahan (2003) in the case of Brazil.[8]

OLS (ordinary least squares) estimations further reveal that the private saving rate is significantly and positively correlated with the total dependency ratio. In addition, life expectancy is found to contribute

Table 7.1 Determinants of the Private Saving Rate (in panel studies)

Variable category	Specific variable	Expected sign	Empirical finding (cross country)
Demographics	Dependency ratio	−	− (3, 6) 0 (1, 7, 9, 10) +(17 (insignificantly positive for transition economies incl. Brazil))
	Old-age dependency ratio	−	− (1, 4, 5, 6, 12, 14 (insignificantly positive for LAC)) 0 (7, 9, 13))
	Youth dependency ratio	−	− (1, 4, 6, 12, 14 (insignificantly negative for LAC)) 0 (7, 13)
	Life expectancy	+	+ (15, 14 (insignificantly positive for LAC))
	Urbanization	Ambiguous	− (1, 4) + (17 (transition economies incl. Brazil))
Fiscal policy	Gross public saving to GDP	−	− (3, 4, 5, 8, 9, 10, 11, 17 (transition economies incl. Brazil))
	Government net lending	−	− (1, 6, 7)
	Public surplus	−	− (6, 13, 7) 0 (12)
	Public consumption	Ambiguous	− (6, 7)
Rate of return	Real interest rate	Ambiguous	− (1, 8) 0 (1, 3, 4, 7, 9, 10, 11, 13) + (5, 6, 7)
Uncertainty	Inflation rate	+	0 (3, 5, 7, 8, 10) + (1, 6, 9)
	Gini coefficient	+	
	Measures of political stability	+	− (12) 0 (11, 6, 4) + (1)
Income	GDP	0 or +	+ (11, 6, 4, 12, 1, 17 (transition economies incl. Brazil)) 0 (13, 7)
	Growth rate of GDP per capita	Ambiguous	+ (3, 6, 4, 1, 10) 0 (9, 12, 13, 7)
	GDP growth	0 or +	+ (5) 0 (6, 7)
	Labor productivity growth	0 or +	+ (8)
Competitiveness	Terms of trade	0 or +	+ (1, 6, 7, 8, 9, 12, 17 (transition economies incl. Brazil))
	Current account to GDP	+	

Domestic borrowing constraints	Private credit flows	–	+ (3, 4) – (1)
	Credit to GDP ratio	Ambiguous	0 (9, 10)
Foreign borrowing constraints	Current account deficit	–	– (1, 11, 4, 6)
Financial depth	Private or domestic credit stock	Ambiguous	– (13)
	Money stock to GDP	Ambiguous	+ (11, 4, 12) 0 (1)
Pension system	Pay-as-you-go transfers	0 or –	– (4, 12, 13)
	Mandatory funded pension contributions	0 or –	+ (12)
	Fully funded pension assets	Ambiguous	0/+ (13)
Distribution of income and wealth	Income concentration	Ambiguous	0 (4)
	Gini coefficient	Ambiguous	

Source: The compilation was done by Jorgensen (2011).

Note: Results under empirical findings summarize the significance of saving regressors in the following studies, where only statistically significant findings are reported: (1) Loayza, Schmidt-Hebbel, and Servén 2000; (2) Fletcher et al. 2007; (3) Edwards 1995; (4) Edwards 1996; (5) Callen and Thimann 1997; (6) Masson, Bayoumi, and Samiei 1998; (7) Haque, Pesaran, and Sharma 1999; (8) De Serres and Pelgrin 2002; (9) Ozcan, Gunay, and Ertac 2003; (10) Schrooten and Stephan 2005; (11) Corbo and Schmidt-Hebbel 1991; (12) Dayal-Gulati and Thimann 1997; (13) Bailliu and Reisen 1997; (14) Doshi 1994; (15) Bloom, Canning, and Fink (2009); (16) Paiva and Jahan 2003; (17) Rodrik 2000.

positively to private saving, and this is true to a significant extent when pension benefits are included in the estimations. On the other hand, in the OLS estimations, the effect from the old-age dependency ratio is negative—a finding that supports the LCH, but counters the error-correction approach followed above, revealing some ambiguity in the econometric evidence. Higher inequality, as measured by the Gini-coefficient, is seen to positively affect the precautionary saving motive because it increases the private saving rate. This is also true in estimations where inflation is excluded and the Gini-coefficient is included in order to avoid double-counting the precautionary saving motive.[9] Future econometric research on Brazil could address this ambiguity of double-counting in the econometric approach.

An important insight by Jorgensen (2011) is that, in the future, the dependency ratio will be driven mainly by the old-age dependency ratio rather than the youth dependency ratio. Could such demographic dynamics cast doubt upon the empirical results found in this section? In the simple OLS regressions (over the period 1970–2008), the youth dependency ratio was found to positively and significantly increase the private saving rate, while the old-age dependency ratio was found to lower the private saving rate. Since the total dependency ratio was found to increase the private saving rate—and because the total dependency ratio was mainly driven by changes in the youth dependency ratio—a stronger future role of the old-age dependency ratio in driving the total dependency ratio may reverse the relationship between the total dependency ratio and the private saving rate.[10]

The econometric evidence above is valuable to establish a historical relationship between population dynamics, saving, and growth. However, for the purpose of projecting these relationships into the future, there remains some ambiguity as a result of the shift in the main driver of the total dependency ratio from being the old-age to the youth dependency ratio.[11] Therefore, the aim of the remainder of this chapter is to dig deeper into the relationships between population dynamics and economic behavior.

Aging and Saving

It is well known that population aging is likely to reduce the saving rate because there will be a larger share of elderly in the population who may not have much incentive to save. What if, however, the LCH is not supported in Brazil if elderly also save? This is exactly the case, as this section will demonstrate, so a larger share of elderly will *not* necessarily reduce the saving rate. In fact, aging may even increase the saving rate—an effect that will be amplified by the expected fall in the share of children in the population in Brazil.

This section has two main purposes: to confirm or reject the LCH for Brazil, and to project the most likely trajectory for the future saving rate. A partial equilibrium treatment is offered for dynamics of household saving rates over the period 2010–50, which simulates the implications for the saving rates under various scenarios for income inequality, building on the latest 2008 POF (*Pesquisa de Orçamentos Familiares*) household expenditure survey and the 1995–2008 PNAD (*Pesquisa Nacional por Amostragem a Domicílios*) household surveys. The analysis assumes that age-specific saving rates do not change as a response to aging, but that the aggregate household saving rate will change as the population structure changes. Clearly, the assumption of constant age-specific saving rates is rather strong, so in the next section of this chapter the partial equilibrium present findings will be complemented with a general equilibrium analysis, where the saving rate is endogenous to macroeconomic and population dynamics.

A key finding is that age-specific saving rates increase to about age 40, after which they remain virtually unchanged—but this is on average. As is evident in figure 7.1b, it matters greatly to the measurement result whether or not public pensions are included as part of income. The literature is quite clear: private pensions should be deducted from the measure of income but public pensions should not (Bosworth, Burtless, and Sabelhaus 1991; Miles 1999). Mason and Lee (2010) further argue that pensions paid to public workers are components of labor income and simply a cost of producing public goods. As a result, they should be included in the income measure. This model therefore adjusts gross income for private pensions, all taxes, and pension contributions but not public pensions. Figure 7.1b illustrates the trajectories of the saving rate where income either includes or excludes public pensions, respectively.[12]

As figure 7.1b shows, the LCH is contradicted in the case of Brazil with the key implication that saving rates (and potentially economic growth through the channel of saving) will not necessarily be depressed by population aging as would usually be expected. This pattern of saving is not unique to Brazil; rather, in several developing countries the saving rates do not decline in old age as they do in most developed countries (Gregory, Mokhtari, and Schrettl 1999; Miles 1999; Poterba 1994; Weil 1997). In particular, Attanasio and Székely (2000, 38) note in a

Figure 7.1   Population Projections and Saving Rates in Brazil, 2008

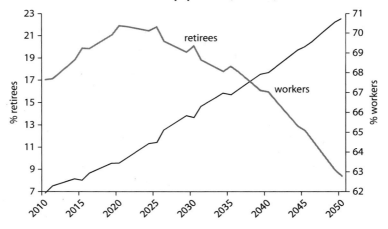

a. Fewer people age 15–65, and more of the age 65+ in the future Brazilian population (2010–50)

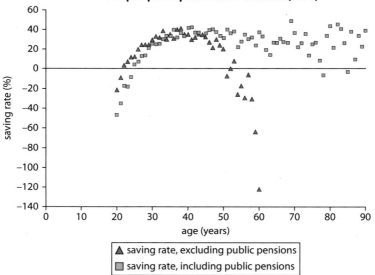

b. Average saving rates virtually unchanged after age 40, except if public pensions are excluded (2008)

▲ saving rate, excluding public pensions

☐ saving rate, including public pensions

Sources: UN Population Division (2008 rev.); Jorgensen 2011 based on POF (*Pesquisa de Orçamentos Familiares*) 2008.

Note: After age 63 the saving rates for both the rich and the poor become extremely low, varying between –500 and –3,000 percent. These savings are represented by very few households and therefore not shown, but are included in subsequent simulations with the partial equilibrium model.

cross-country study including LAC countries, that "a common feature across countries is that we do not find strong evidence of negative saving or even declining saving in the last part of the life cycle in any country."

There are several possible explanations why people save in old age. First, elderly may desire to leave bequests for their working-age children or their grandchildren (Barro 1974; Stokey 1979). In the case of Brazil, however, analytical work on this issue is lacking, but there is evidence suggesting that intra-household transfers run from retired elderly to their adult children with whom they often cohabitate. Therefore, public pensions indirectly become a transfer that covers the entire household. The economic implications of such two-sided, intra-household transfers are also explored theoretically, for example, by Nerlove and Raut (1997). However, in Brazil this remains an issue for future research.

Implications of Income Inequality

On average, age-specific saving rates remain virtually unchanged after age 40, but this aggregate view on age-specific saving may hide some important heterogeneity among households in Brazil. In particular, the high income inequality in Brazil may lead to differential saving behavior by income group.

The difference between age-specific saving rates among the "non-poor" and the "poor" is illustrated in figure 7.2, which shows a crucial difference in their respective saving behavior.[13] Despite the fact that their overall saving pattern is the same, the poor save much less at most ages. The poor also tend to display negative saving after the age of 45 until 65, while the non-poor have positive saving rates in the same age interval. This has a very important effect on the weighted average of the aggregate saving rate, since a large fraction of the population in Brazil is between 45 and 65. The negative saving rates among the poor may be difficult to explain, but could be a result of informal credit possibilities for the poor that are not part of the established financial sector ("*agiotas*"), which may explain the possibility of negative saving.

The simple division of age-specific saving rates across the population above and below the poverty line would therefore suggest the saving rate would be positively affected in the future if the share of the population below the poverty line were to continue to fall, as has been the recent trend. In fact, it does not make sense to speculate about future saving behavior without taking income inequality into consideration. Such dynamics are therefore incorporated into the partial equilibrium model employed below.

Figure 7.2   Saving Rates for Non-Poor and Poor in Brazil, Including and Excluding Public Pensions

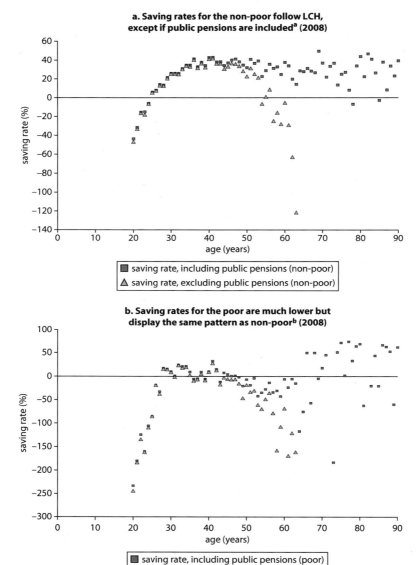

Source: Jorgensen (2011) based on POF 2008.
Notes: a. See endnote 5.
b. The "non-poor" and "poor" are classified according to the $2 PPP (Purchasing Power Parity) per day national poverty line.

In 2008, 41 percent of Brazilian families had negative savings, which is 8 percentage points less than in 2002 (figure 7.3a). What lies behind this change in saving patterns? Positive savings started at the 74th percentile in 2008 and at the 61st percentile in 2002. The main driver of the increase in saving rates is the decrease in the inequality of Brazilian income distribution, which occurred between 2002 and 2008. Figure 7.3b supports this argument by illustrating that there are fewer poor elderly than poor young. Since poverty is declining and the poor generally save less than the non-poor, it can be expected, everything else being equal, that aging will increase the weighted average of the saving rate.[14] Such dynamics are incorporated into the partial equilibrium model presented in the next section.

Partial Equilibrium Implications of Population Aging

This section will present the partial equilibrium approach to determining the implications of population aging for the household saving rate. The methodology is outlined in Weil (1997), but is extended here to include the important feature of differential saving behavior across income groups.[15] To determine the projected trajectories for the weighted average household saving rate, the advantage of the partial equilibrium approach is to exploit the combination of detailed age-specific population projections and detailed age-specific saving rates available for Brazil—performed across income groups by using scenarios for different poverty headcount levels.

Of course, the question is whether the saving rate is expected to rise or fall in the future when the population ages, since this will affect economic growth in the same direction. Population aging implies that older age groups increase in size and that they possibly live longer due to increased life expectancy. Depending on the size of saving rates of the young, middle-aged, and old people, such demographic changes are likely to change the weighted average of the saving rate.

By combining three types of projections for (1) age-specific saving rate, (2) age-specific population changes, and (3) the shares that are non-poor and poor, it is possible to project the weighted average household saving rate in Brazil. Figure 7.4a shows the two scenarios for the poverty headcount assumed in the projections of the saving rate. First, no change is assumed across any age group in the poverty headcount; second, the trend poverty headcount of 8.93 percent per year is assumed. The simulations in figure 7.4a then show that the household saving rate in Brazil is likely to increase over the medium and long term, from 4.84 percent

Figure 7.3   Projections of Household Saving and Poverty Rates in Brazil

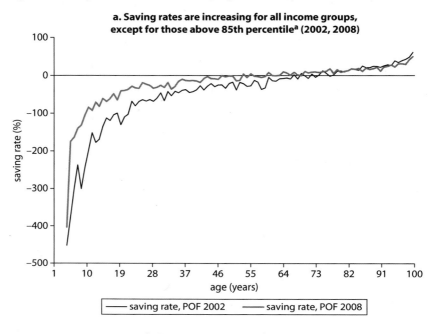

**a. Saving rates are increasing for all income groups,
except for those above 85th percentile[a] (2002, 2008)**

— saving rate, POF 2002   — saving rate, POF 2008

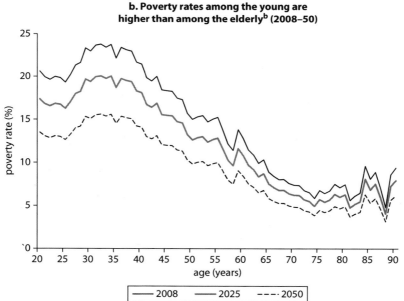

**b. Poverty rates among the young are
higher than among the elderly[b] (2008–50)**

—— 2008   —— 2025   ---- 2050

Sources: Jorgensen (2011) based on POF 2002, 2008; Jorgensen (2011) based on POF 2008.
Notes: a. The tendency for higher age-specific saving rates could lead to higher future growth.
b. The projections are uniform when the share below the $2 PPP per day national poverty line falls by 1 percent.

Figure 7.4   Poverty and Saving Rate Projections, 2010–50

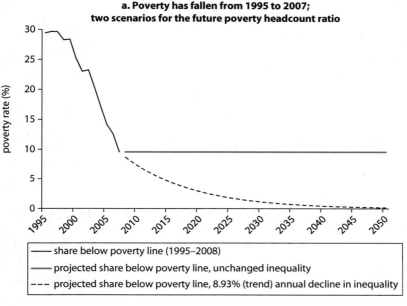

**a. Poverty has fallen from 1995 to 2007;
two scenarios for the future poverty headcount ratio**

—— share below poverty line (1995–2008)

—— projected share below poverty line, unchanged inequality

--- projected share below poverty line, 8.93% (trend) annual decline in inequality

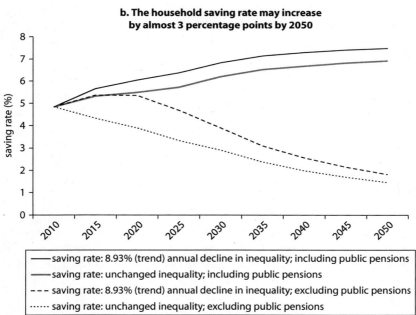

**b. The household saving rate may increase
by almost 3 percentage points by 2050**

—— saving rate: 8.93% (trend) annual decline in inequality; including public pensions

—— saving rate: unchanged inequality; including public pensions

--- saving rate: 8.93% (trend) annual decline in inequality; excluding public pensions

······ saving rate: unchanged inequality; excluding public pensions

Sources: Estimations by Jorgensen (2011) based on PNAD survey 1995–2008 for the poverty line of less than $2 in income per day; simulations by Jorgensen (2011) for the saving rate depending on scenarios for poverty and the exclusion or inclusion of public pensions in income.

in 2010 to 7.49 percent in 2050. Figure 7.4b illustrates four trajectories, where the solid line is the main baseline projection of trend change in the poverty headcount and the remaining three scenarios are presented for robustness purposes. If the poverty headcount remains unchanged, the trajectory for the saving rate will take a parallel shift downward and reach 6.92 percent in 2050.

The projected increase in saving rate is the result of two main factors. First, the change in the population structure leaves larger shares of the population in age groups that save relatively more. Second, because the share of poor falls with age, the share of the population that is non-poor will increase with time (solid line in figure 7.4b)—and this will lead to a higher weight by the non-poor in the average weighted saving rate. If the poverty headcount (inequality) then falls, there will be even fewer poor people across all age groups, and therefore also for the population as a whole, leading to an even higher weight on the non-poor's saving rates in the average weighted saving rate.[16]

Robustness and Sensitivity

When fertility is assumed to be higher (lower) than projected by the UN Population Division's medium fertility variant, there will be a larger (smaller) share of the population in younger age groups who save relatively less (more), thus reducing (increasing) the weighted average of the saving rate. On the other hand, if the age-structure of mortality changes, the share of "low-savers" to "high-savers" will also change. In that context, it is more likely that mortality decreases relatively more for older age groups than for younger age groups, thus increasing the saving rate.

The same argument holds for the share of the population below the poverty line: If the share below the poverty line falls for older age groups, there will probably be a larger effect on the saving rate than if poverty in youth falls. However, if poverty uniformly falls at the same rate over the entire age spectrum, there will be a relatively larger increase in the saving rate from young savers, since a relatively larger share of young live in poverty.

The age-specific saving rates might also be expected to endogenously change in one or the other direction, an issue that will be addressed in the next section. If an increase in the saving rate occurs, that would translate into increases in the age-specific saving rates used in this section. This may already be occurring, as illustrated in figure 7.3a where age-specific saving rates increased to a non-negligible extent from 2002 to 2008.

In the case that saving rates increase relatively more for older age groups, the weighted average of the saving rate is likely to increase substantially, since the elderly will constitute a larger share of the population and thus be assigned a larger weight in the average saving rate. If the saving rate increases mainly for younger age groups, on the other hand, there may not be a marked difference in the average saving rate.

In conclusion, more research is needed on this topic for Brazil in order to determine the likely implications for saving of changes in age structure and poverty. However, the main finding from the partial equilibrium analysis is that the saving rate is likely to increase in the future, especially if poverty falls. However, this finding depends crucially on whether there will be endogenous changes in age-specific saving rates, the topic of the next section.

Aging, Capital Accumulation, and Demographic Dividends

This section provides a general equilibrium analysis of the policy challenges and trade-offs the Brazilian government faces in the context of aging. This analysis complements the partial equilibrium analysis of the previous section. The partial equilibrium model does not allow households to change their saving behavior as a response to aging or its possible economic implications.[17] However, aging is likely to have major general equilibrium implications for household behavior, for example, in terms of consumption, saving, human capital investments, and labor supply.

Since people's economic behavior is strongly associated with their life cycle stage—as clearly evidenced by the partial equilibrium model above—changes in age structure tend to have a major impact on economic development (Bloom and Williamson 1998; Lee and Mason 2006).[18] The "demographic bonus"—when the labor force far outsizes the dependent population—may therefore lead to a "demographic dividend," an opportunity for growth rather than a challenge (Cutler et al. 1990). While the demographic bonus is a purely demographic phenomenon, the demographic dividend refers to economic returns related to the demographic bonus.

The demographic dividend operates through several channels. Bloom, Canning, and Sevilla (2003) mention three major channels: labor supply, savings leading to increases in physical capital, and investments in human capital. As for labor supply, the generations of children born during periods of high fertility are now becoming workers. Furthermore, women now have fewer children and tend to be better educated than older cohorts and are therefore more productive. In terms of saving, the shift away from a very young age distribution favors greater personal and national savings, as discussed in detail above. Finally, regarding human capital, having fewer children enhances the women's health and there is less stress on parents to provide for many children. Thus, many factors interact and promote the demographic dividend.

The demographic dividend comprises two dividends that are sequential and overlapping: the first initiates the process and later comes to an end; the second begins somewhat later and continues indefinitely. In short, the first dividend signifies a transitory economic return, while the second transforms the first dividend into greater assets and potentially sustainable development. These outcomes are not automatic but depend on the implementation of effective policies. Thus, the dividend period is a window of opportunity rather than a guarantee of improved standards of living.

The First Demographic Dividend

The first dividend has been described by Lee and Mason (2006), who provide empirical evidence for both the first and second demographic dividends using a "reduced form" general equilibrium framework calibrated for Brazil. The first dividend is measured as the increase in GDP growth caused by the growth of working-age population. Their model (annex 7.4) offers an empirical, but not particularly rigorous, analytical framework for studying the potential dividends that may arise due to aging.

The contribution of both the first and second demographic dividends to growth in GDP per effective consumer is presented in table 7.2.[19] The table shows Brazil having experienced a large first dividend compared to other regions in the world (see table 2.9). Furthermore, the two sets of estimations of the first dividend by Mason (2005) and Queiroz and Turra (2010), respectively, are close in magnitude. In the future, however, projections show that Brazil will experience a very small, and possibly negative, first dividend since the growth of workers as a share of the total population slows down and the population starts aging.[20]

The Second Demographic Dividend

The second dividend arises to the extent that anticipated changes in the share of the population concentrated in the retirement ages induce individuals, firms, and governments to accumulate capital. A crucial point is that only in societies where capital deepening prevails will the effects of

Table 7.2   First and Second Dividends for Brazil and in International Context
GDP growth per effective consumer

Brazil and world regions	Period	Demographic dividends (% contributions to GDP growth)		
		First	*Second*	*Total*
Historical estimates	1970–2000			
Brazil (Mason 2005)		0.64	1.30	1.94
Brazil (Queiroz and Turra 2010)		0.55	1.73	2.28
Projections	2000–2045			
Brazil (Mason 2005)		−0.01	2.49	2.48
Brazil (Queiroz and Turra 2010)		0.08	2.19	2.29
Regions (Mason 2005)	1970–2000			
Industrial		0.34	0.69	1.03
East Asia & Southeast Asia		0.59	1.31	1.90
South Asia		0.10	0.69	0.80
Latin America		0.62	1.08	1.70
Sub-Saharan Africa		−0.09	0.17	0.08
Middle East and North Africa		0.51	0.70	1.21
Transitional		0.24	0.57	0.81
Pacific Islands		0.58	1.15	1.73

Source: World Bank staff estimations based on raw data supplied by A. Mason, B. Queiroz, and C. Turra. Estimates of dividends are annual, and the aggregate dividends presented in the table are calculated as the simple average across the time period covered. Estimated dividends signify the contribution to output growth per worker to which the two dividends, and in total, contribute.

aging ultimately increase the output per effective consumer (Bloom and Williamson 1998; Jorgensen and Jensen 2010).

During the later stages of the transition to lower fertility, a growing share of the population consists of individuals who are nearing the completion of their productive years. They must have accumulated wealth in order to finance consumption in excess of labor income for many of their remaining years.[21] Furthermore, the rise in life expectancy, and the accompanying increase in the duration of retirement, lead to an upward shift in the age profile of wealth (Jorgensen 2011; Jorgensen and Jensen 2010).

The second dividend is found to be positive by Mason (2005) and Queiroz and Turra (2010) for all regions, and substantially larger than the first dividend for the period 1970–2000 (table 7.2). In East and Southeast Asia, the second dividend was 1.31 percent per year in additional income growth—the largest of any region. Brazil is seen to display remarkable first and second dividends. Clearly, Brazil drives up the average for LAC countries for the second dividend, while the two sets of estimates suggest that the first dividend should be somewhere around the LAC average.

The total demographic dividend will fall between approximately 2.29 and 2.48 percent of additional income growth.

Mason (2005) and Queiroz and Turra (2010) conclude that the second dividend does not turn negative to any important degree—the result being a permanent increase in the capital intensity of the economy and a permanent increase in output per worker. However, the Brazilian economy has so far failed to take full advantage of the second dividend, just as the country failed to take advantage of the first dividend (Queiroz and Turra, 2010). These authors show that for the last two decades the growth rate of GDP per effective consumer was lower than what the demographic dividends would predict.[22] However, population change does still seem to be favorable to economic growth in Brazil for the near future. From 2010 to 2045, the demographic dividends could raise GDP growth per effective consumer by 2.48 percent per year on average, according to Queiroz and Turra (2010).[23]

Promoting the Demographic Dividends

In terms of policies to harvest the demographic dividends, the Brazilian economy has in the last few decades grown at much slower rates than what the demographic dividends alone would predict, in contrast to the experience of other developing countries, for example, East Asian countries (World Bank 1993). Unfortunately, therefore, the demographic dividends are not automatic and depend on institutions and policies to transform changes in population age structure into economic growth (Bloom and Canning 2003). For example, it is fundamental that the labor market creates enough opportunities for the growing working-age population, and that a developed financial market exists to fulfill the individual's willingness to save (Mason 2005).

To the extent that countries meet the challenge of aging by expanding unfunded familial or public transfer programs, asset growth will be reduced, and the second dividend will be diminished. By contrast, if workers are encouraged to save and accumulate pension funds, population aging can boost capital per worker, productivity growth, and per capita income. Thus, policy makers in Brazil will need to focus on establishing financial systems that are sound, trusted, and accessible to the millions who wish to secure their financial futures. The time to do so is now so that, as the population ages, its growth-inducing potential will be realized.

In the case of Brazil, Queiroz and Turra (2010) argue that low investment in human capital and the lack of proper social and economic institutions are responsible for jeopardizing the demographic dividends in the country. It is important that public policies in Brazil create incentives to private savings and that institutions are reliable for investors. Making public pension systems large and generous might crowd out the propensity to save, thus jeopardizing the second demographic dividend and reducing the capacity to invest. A population concentrated within older working ages and facing an extended period of retirement has a powerful incentive to accumulate assets—unless it is confident that its needs will be provided for by families or governments.

One of the main findings by Queiroz and Turra (2010) is that the demographic dividends explain a large degree of GDP per effective consumer growth from 1970 to 2010. However, their results also indicate that the economic growth rate could have been greater if the country had taken advantage of the changes in population age structure. While they find that most of the contribution to dividends happened in the 1970s, the last two decades have seen economic growth rates much smaller than what demographic changes would predict. These findings reveal that Brazilian policy makers have not made necessary decisions to transform changes in population age structure into economic growth. Moreover, if such policies are not adopted, future benefits of the dividends will also be lost.

The empirical evidence using a "reduced form" model with capital accumulation suggests that great economic dividends may emerge as a consequence of aging. In the following section, these findings are put to the test in a full-fledged general equilibrium model in order to go even deeper into the behavioral and macroeconomic responses of aging.[24]

General Equilibrium Implications of Population Aging

Since aging, broadly speaking, comprises two elements—(1) lower population growth due to reductions in fertility; and (2) changes in life expectancy due to reductions in mortality—these should be considered the two factors in a composite demographic development in any general equilibrium analysis on the economic implications of aging. These two demographic changes have differential economic implications; however, it is important to distinguish these demographic changes in order to identify what drives the aggregate results of the general equilibrium analysis.[25]

Economic Implications of Lower Fertility and Lower Population Growth

The general equilibrium implications of an isolated drop in the population growth rate, which changes the age-structure of the population over the demographic transition and leads to future aging, is that the capital-labor ratio increases and makes labor a more scarce production factor. This may cause factor prices to change, leading to upward pressure on wages and downward influences on the return to capital.

A reduction in the population growth rate may also lead to transitory changes in saving behavior, as well as in labor supply decisions, in which case the capital-labor ratio may change even further and amplify the direct effect originating from fewer workers. This effect on saving rates is not present in the simulation of saving rates in the partial equilibrium analysis. Importantly, this effect in part leads to the potential second demographic dividend, which was found to be positive for Brazil, as documented above.

Additional dynamics appear when the government manages systems that are influenced by the population structure, in particular pay-as-you-go (PAYG) pensions systems, but also health and education systems.[26] If the model includes more features, such as human capital and intrahousehold bequest dynamics, the aggregate effect of changes in population growth will become more difficult to elucidate. The bottom line is that the fiscal partial equilibrium effects are not sufficient to get an accurate measure of the fiscal costs associated with population growth; instead, the general equilibrium effects could both be counteracting or reinforcing.

Economic Implications of Higher Life Expectancy

The macroeconomic implications of higher life expectancy are more straightforward than those of changes in fertility and population growth, but they are highly important in the case of Brazil, where life expectancy is projected to increase by as much as 11 percent over the period 2010–2050. If people expect to live longer, they are likely to increase their saving, simply in order to finance a longer life in retirement. These incentives will lead to an amplified second demographic dividend due increased capital accumulation.[27]

In an economic environment where the government plays a large role in economic policies, there will be additional partial equilibrium effects of increased life expectancy. For example, in the case of constant pensions for retirees, increased life expectancy will lead to higher contributions on the workers' part, all other things being equal. However, larger contributions are likely to produce distortionary saving behavior and thus lead to general equilibrium effects through the capital-labor ratio. The quantitative projections will strongly rely on how the Brazilian government decides to finance the fiscal costs associated with aging, that is, the government's policy response to aging, the focus of the remainder of this chapter.

Government Macro-Policy Responses: Three Scenarios

The Brazilian government faces a major policy dilemma in addressing the increasing financial burden associated with population aging. First, the government may decide to keep transfers, such as pensions and health benefits, unchanged. But this requires increasing taxes or debt. Second, the government may decide to reduce public transfers that depend on the population age structure in order to refrain from increasing taxes or debt or cutting other government programs. Third, the government may decide to abstain from changing either taxes or benefits but simply borrow on the basis of financial markets to finance the costs—thereby pushing the financing burden toward future generations.

Something has to give in this financial dilemma—even taking into account possibly high labor productivity in Brazil in the future.[28] In other words, in the general equilibrium framework, it is assumed that the Brazilian government has three instruments to use for tackling the financing burden associated with aging: taxes (social security contributions and health contributions); benefits (social security benefits and health benefits); and debt (public sector debt). The three policy scenarios of Debt-Financing, Tax-Financing, and Benefit-Financing will be analyzed and compared in turn—starting with the Tax-Financing scenario.

Policy Scenario I: Tax-Financing

It will become fiscally more expensive to have fewer tax payers and more retirees because the pension and health benefits bill will increase in size. The smaller number of workers due to historically low fertility would therefore need to finance such benefits—given that replacement rates and debt are assumed to be kept constant. As a consequence of the population aging, a larger fiscal burden will therefore arise under such policy assumptions. This is the "Tax-Financing" policy scenario.

Given that tax rates absorb the entire burden, leaving benefits and debt unchanged, it is possible to simulate the implications for the economy. The general equilibrium model by Jorgensen (2011), described in annex 7.3, is employed for this purpose, and the population projections fed into the model are illustrated in figure 7.5a, which comprises the projected trajectories for the population growth rate and life expectancy.

Figure 7.5   Possible Policy Responses to the Projected Population Growth and Life Expectancy

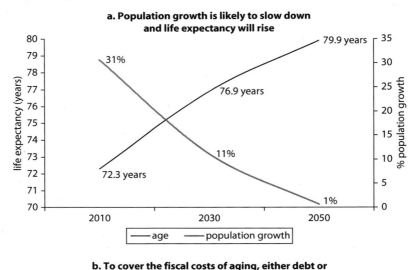

a. Population growth is likely to slow down and life expectancy will rise

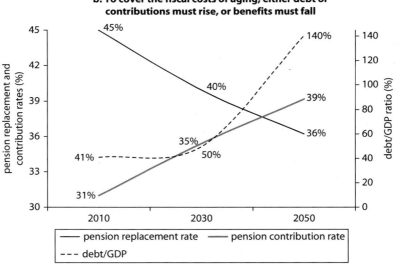

b. To cover the fiscal costs of aging, either debt or contributions must rise, or benefits must fall

Sources: UN Population Division (2008 rev.); Jorgensen 2011.

A key issue when interpreting the projected trajectory for the saving rate and other macroeconomic variables is the combination of the demographic factors that contribute to population aging. The fall in the population growth rate will generally reduce the saving rate, while the increase in life expectancy will tend to increase the saving rate. The rate of decline in the population growth rate is shown in figure 7.1a to decrease over time, so the life-cycle response of the general equilibrium model—in which workers save and retirees do not—will become smaller over time. However, the increase in the saving rate from longer life expectancy will also flatten out over time. The percentage changes are much larger for the reduction in population growth than for life expectancy. As a result, over the longer term, the saving rate is projected to fall.

Jorgensen (2011) finds that, in order to keep benefits constant, the social security contribution rate would need to increase by 8 percentage points from its current level of approximately 31 percent to 39 percent between 2010 and 2050 (figure 7.5b).[29] An open-economy version of the analysis has been made (referred to in the later section on "Robustness and Sensitivity"); the figure for an open economy that corresponds to figure 7.5b is presented in annex 7.5. The aggregate rise in the tax rate to cover constant health and social security benefits is 9.5 percentage points, consisting of 8 percentage points for social security contributions and 1.5 percentage points for health contributions.[30]

This choice of financing method will have macroeconomic implications. First, capital accumulation will be further crowded out by the 9.5 percentage points of higher taxes. This means that capital per worker will decline, as in figure 7.6b. There is a counteracting mechanism, however, since there will be fewer workers in the future, which will therefore increase the capital-worker ratio. Furthermore, higher life expectancy will have a tendency to reduce the saving rate (figure 7.6a) as well as the capital-worker ratio.[31]

In terms of wealth and welfare, the Tax-Financing scenario will yield a lower lifetime income mainly because increased taxes lead to lower income in people's working life (figure 7.7a). Also, as net income falls, the slightly increased saving rate will not increase aggregate saving sufficiently, but will reduce it slightly. This is evident from the evolution of capital per worker, which falls only a little over the next 20 years but falls faster after that. Consequently, income in old age also falls, reducing the size of lifetime income at an increasing rate. This reduced wealth accumulation corresponds to the simulated path for lifetime welfare in figure 7.7b.

The key message from the analysis of this Tax-Financing scenario is that capital accumulation, and thus wealth, will fall, which means that this policy choice will negatively affect the second demographic dividend. This will in turn reduce lifetime income. Altogether, raising taxes will negatively affect welfare.

Figure 7.6   Expected Saving Rate and Capital-Worker Ratio for the Three Policy Scenarios

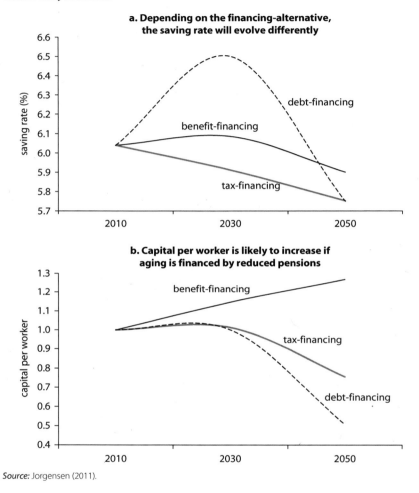

Source: Jorgensen (2011).

Policy Scenario II: Benefit-Financing

The results of the Benefit-Financing scenario are based on the same underlying general equilibrium model as the analyses of the other scenarios and therefore include the same demographic and macroeconomic dynamics. The only change from the Tax-Financing scenario is that contribution rates for pensions and health are now held constant and the corresponding benefits are now adjusted to the demographic dynamics. As more retirees enter both the pension and the health systems in the

Figure 7.7   Expected Lifetime Income and Lifetime Welfare for the Three Policy Scenarios

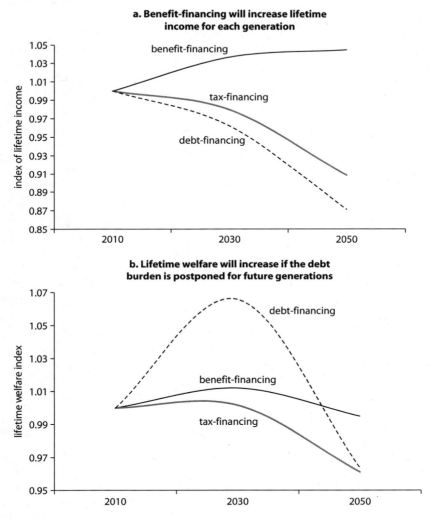

a. Benefit-financing will increase lifetime income for each generation

b. Lifetime welfare will increase if the debt burden is postponed for future generations

Source: Jorgensen 2011.

future, there will be fewer tax payers to contribute with an unchanged rate and there will be more retirees to be covered. Naturally, the replacement rate would need to fall, and the general equilibrium model estimates an approximate magnitude of such a decline in benefits.

The projections reveal that, in order for contribution rates to remain constant, the pension replacement would need to fall by 9 percentage points over the period 2010–50, from 45 percent to 26 percent. This would balance the government budget given that the debt-GDP ratio is held constant.[32] If pension benefits were reduced to the extent proposed by our simulations, there would be several beneficial effects on the economy. Regarding capital accumulation, there would be less crowding out of the current capital-worker ratio if taxes and debt were not increased. Furthermore, since lower population growth yields fewer workers and higher life expectancy leads to a higher saving rate (figure 7.6a), the capital-worker ratio is bound to rise (figure 7.6b).

When benefits are reduced to accommodate the fiscal pressure, the effect on lifetime income is an outright increase (figure 7.7a); lifetime income will tend to rise and lifetime welfare will follow the same pattern, though it will fall slightly toward the end of the simulation period. Pension reform with adjustments to the age of pension benefit eligibility could be considered, along with a reduction in the pension replacement rate, since such an indexation mechanism would potentially render the effective labor supply larger and the retirement periods shorter (Jorgensen and Jensen 2010).

Policy Scenario III: Debt-Financing

Under the Debt-Financing scenario, contribution and replacement rates are held constant and the entire fiscal burden of providing for more retirees by fewer workers will be covered by issuing debt. The debt-GDP ratio is seen to explode in figure 7.5b over the projected period 2010–50, when the population growth rate falls and life expectancy increases (figure 7.5a). In fact, debt-GDP is likely to rise by 99 percentage points from 41 to 140 percentage points.

Debt-Financing is likely to have devastating implications for capital accumulation and lifetime income (figure 7.6a and b).[33] Therefore the second demographic dividend will be negatively affected. Lifetime welfare, on the other hand, is seen to increase sharply as the current generation of workers realize that all costs associated with aging are merely postponed for future generations to pay off. Over time, however, future generations of workers would need to pay off the debt, then welfare would fall quickly as the debt-GDP ratio might have doubled or tripled by that time.

The bottom line of this Debt-Financing analysis is that current generations of workers are likely to gain in terms of welfare while leaving it to their children and grandchildren to pay off the debt. Ultimately, the choice of debt-financing will be detrimental to the economy and intergenerationally skewed in terms of welfare distributions. The main conclusion is that if the social security system is not to be touched, there is awaiting a massive bill for other sectors in the government budget to pay. Clearly, the second demographic dividend will be positively stimulated by a Benefit-Financing scenario, the result opposite of the two other alternatives considered. Capital accumulation will be promoted under the Benefit-Financing scenario, and this is likely to lead to enhanced wealth and welfare.

Further Policy Implications

Within the population aging debate, the main public finance concern is fiscal sustainability. This topic will not be dealt with explicitly here, but it is worth pointing out that tax policy may not be an appropriate strategy for the financing problem, since the life expectancy component of aging is likely to be somewhat permanent (Oeppen and Vaupel 2002; UN 2004). If population aging were not a permanent state, a tax-smoothing strategy (Barro 1979) could be an option to overcome the fiscal sustainability concerns, but with an aging population, some more structural policy measures are called for.

A sensible policy mix would consider the appropriateness of the generosity of the social security system in connection with a reform of entitlement ages to such transfers. The international experience, especially in Scandinavian countries, with longevity-indexed mandatory retirement ages, is ample—and, theoretically, thoroughly analyzed (for example, Jensen and Jorgensen 2008).[34] Effective labor supply is very likely to increase if the government decides to increase the statutory retirement age, because people are likely to stay in the labor force longer. Leisure may increase when the statutory retirement age increases, however. This is mainly because there will be less need to save since the retirement period will also be proportionally shorter (Jensen and Jorgensen 2010).

An additional implication of the increase in the retirement age is that lifetime leisure will fall, further increasing the demand for leisure during the working period. These mechanisms will counteract the increase in effective labor supply from the increase in the statutory retirement age, which is an important endogeneity issue that policy makers should be aware of. Consequently, if policy makers want to achieve a certain increase in effective labor supply from increasing the statutory retirement age, this increase must be even higher than initially presumed, since the endogenous reduction in the intensity of labor supply must be accounted for (Jorgensen and Jensen 2010).[35] This is exactly the opposite of what is intended by a policy rule of increasing the statutory retirement age in line with life expectancy.

Robustness and Sensitivity

Behind the general equilibrium results presented above lies the specific model assumption of a closed economy, where factor payments are endogenous and fully respond to changes in the capital-worker ratio. In reality, because Brazil is not a closed economy, the response of factory payments should be adjusted downward to some extent when considering the long-term implications of aging. Increased immigration and labor force participation, as well as an increasingly open capital account, would lead to such reductions in the magnitudes of factor payments.

The openness of the capital account, and whether domestic saving turn into domestic investments, are crucial questions. Rodrik (2000) argues that, as a matter of accounting necessity, investment has to be financed by saving from either domestic or foreign sources: "[I]n an economy investing, for example, 30 percent of its GDP, relying on foreign saving beyond this limit would imply running a persistent current account deficit in excess of 6 percent of GDP, which would be courting disaster" (Rodrik 2000).

When analyzing an open economy version of the general equilibrium model, the results remain broadly the same, depending on whether factor prices are assumed to endogenously change to a full extent (closed economy) or whether they remain constant (open economy). Table 7.3 testifies to the robustness of these results. The open economy version of figure 7.5b, with the various policy scenarios, is presented in annex 7.5.

The main difference in the simulations between the original general equilibrium model and the open economy version is the smaller reaction of the debt-GDP ratio in an open economy setting, which is due to a real interest rate that will not "explode" in size when capital accumulation is crowded out by debt issuance that reduces the capital-labor ratio to a major extent. In fact, the real interest rate will not change at all in an open economy setting, so the debt-GDP ratio will not be further inflated by higher interest rates on debt service. The "true" response, especially of the debt-GDP ratio, should be found in a hybrid of the closed and open

Table 7.3   Simulated Change in Policy Variables by 2050 (percentage points from 2010 value)

In order to finance the aging-induced fiscal costs:	Closed economy (percentage points)	Open economy (percentage points)
taxes would need to increase by:	9	8
or, pension benefits would need to be reduced by:	11	9
or, debt would need to increase by:	99	51

Source: Jorgensen 2011.

economy versions of the general equilibrium model, and will therefore lie between a 51 and 99 percentage point increase in the debt-GDP ratio by 2050.

The general equilibrium model is structured such that retirees do not save, while retirees in Brazil in fact save a lot out of their aggregate income, including pension transfers (see section on "Aging and Saving"). Bequests and reverse intrahousehold transfers from retirees to their working-age children should therefore also be incorporated into future research on this topic (Weil 1997). [36]

Heterogeneity in Economic Behavior

The high income inequality in Brazil is likely to have important consequences for the possibilities and incentives for saving and investment, as the poorest income groups face somewhat different economic circumstances and incentives than the non-poor. This section will analyze the implications of such heterogeneity for economic behavior, capital accumulation, and the second demographic dividend.

The poor part of Brazil's population is still in a situation with high, but decreasing, fertility and mortality rates (see section on "Aging and Saving").[37] Therefore fertility should be treated as an endogenous variable because poor people to some extent use children as an alternative means of saving for old age. In addition to the personal desire to have children to which humans may be genetically programmed (Dasgupta 1993), the motivation for having children can indeed be considered an economic one. Children can provide labor that will benefit the household; they can provide care for parents in old age; and they may be an instrument of altruism from parent to child (Barro and Becker 1989). Another motivation for having children is the expectation of receiving altruistic intrahousehold transfers from one's children after retirement (Ehrlich and Lui 1991; Jorgensen 2010a; Wigger 2002).

These mechanisms should be accounted for in the analytical framework by endogenizing fertility and altruistic intrahousehold transfers. A revised version of the general equilibrium model has therefore been developed in Jorgensen (2011). The result that improved health conditions will increase capital savings and economic growth (Chakraborty 2004; Jorgensen and Jensen 2010) may not hold when the economy is modeled with endogenous fertility decisions and altruistic transfers (Caldwell 1982).

Simulations for the effects on the household saving rate and per capita income are made by Jorgensen (2011) for projected increases in child survival (which increases the size of the labor force) and adult life expectancy (which increases the share of elderly in the population) over the period 2010–50. An increase in the child survival rate increases the number of dependents and reduces household resources. Furthermore, an increase in adult life expectancy encourages saving, as people expect to live longer. This implies that improvements in child survival should have negative effects on economic outcomes, while improvements in adult life expectancy should have positive effects.

Once three aspects are taken into account, child survival will have a net positive effect on economic outcomes compared to the direct negative effect on savings from adult survival. These aspects are (1) the negative fertility response to child survival, (2) the possibility of intra-household transfers, and (3) the possible compounding effect on capital savings from adult survival due to substitution for less expensive children as a savings mechanism. Brought together, the change in child survival and adult life expectancy rates will lead to an increase in the saving rate and in productivity growth, given the demographic projections for Brazil by the UN Population Division.

In this open economy version of the general equilibrium model, when fertility has declined to a certain level, there will be no altruistic transfers as retirees obtain more and more income through capital savings. When the economy reaches the point in the demographic transition where fertility has declined so much that the only motive for having children is the genetic motive, parents realize that they can no longer save child-rearing resources by switching to capital savings and away from having children as an old-age saving mechanism. After this point, an increase in public pensions will reduce the steady state capital stock in line with conventional wisdom.

However, while altruistic transfers are still operative, a rise in public pensions increases productivity growth and reduces fertility, therefore speeding up the process by which a country will go through the demographic transition. As a result, the savings motive for having children gradually disappears and workers only have children based on the "genetic motive." When adult life expectancy then increases further, the impact on capital savings will be positive, in line with existing literature (e.g., Chakraborty 2004; Jensen and Jorgensen 2008).

In conclusion, the economic dynamics among poor people suggest that saving rates are likely to increase as child and adult survival increases. However, this will depend on the degree of altruistic transfers from workers to their retired parents. Therefore, the estimates presented above should be adjusted upward, especially considering the generous pension system that is likely to reduce fertility rates among the poor. A complicating mechanism is the reverse transfers from retirees to their working-aged children that is evident among some groups in Brazil. Therefore, more research is needed in this area in order to determine the implications of PAYG pension benefits on fertility.

Annex 7.1: Private Saving Increases Cause Growth

Table A7.1   Private Saving Is Found to Granger Cause Growth

	Private saving and private investment (VAR regressions on Brazil)	Gross saving and gross investment (VAR regressions on Brazil)	Gross saving and gross investment (multicountry panel analysis)
Saving on growth	+***[+**]	+[+]	+**
Growth on saving	+[+]	+[+]	+**
Investment on growth	−**[−**]	−[−]	−**
Growth on investment	+*[+*]	+*[+]	+**
Saving on investment	+[+]	+[+]	+**
Investment on saving	−[−]	−[−]	+**

Source: VAR regressions, Jorgensen (2011). Results in brackets for difference estimations. Significance at 10%, 5%, and 1% levels is denoted by ***; **; *, respectively. The dynamic trivariate model by Attanasio, Picci, and Scorcu (2000) was OLS-based with a sample of 38 countries over the period 1960–94, controlling for simultaneity and country heterogeneity.

Table A7.2   The Old-Age Dependency Ratio Increases Private Saving

Step 1 Dependent variable: private saving rate	Coefficient (standard error)
Log of GDP per cap	−5.53* (3.03)
Private investment rate	0.89*** (0.20)
Public saving rate	−1.22*** (0.13)
Growth of old dependency rate	1.40* (0.82)
Real interest rate	0.02 (0.03)
Constant	52.36* (28.69)
R_2 (Phillips-Perron test)	0.87 (−16.93*)

Step 2 Dependent variable: change in private saving rate	Coefficient (standard error)
Δ log of GDP per cap	4.73 (8.50)
Δ private investment rate	0.96*** (0.20)
Δ public saving rate	−1.00*** (0.10)
Δ growth of old dependency rate	3.02* (1.52)
Δ real interest rate	0.04* (0.02)
Adjustment coefficient α	−0.42*** (0.16)
Constant	52.37* (0.35)
R_2	0.87

Source: Jorgensen (2011). Significance at the 10%, 5%, and 1% levels is denoted by ***, **, *, respectively. Data include 38 observations.

Annex 7.2: The Partial Equilibrium Model

This annex describes the main features of the partial equilibrium model by Jorgensen (2011) used to analyze the future implications of population aging in Brazil. The model is used for simulating the implications for the household saving rate when the population structure changes over the period 2010–50, combined with scenarios for the share of poor and rich households. The model combines age-specific saving rates, age-specific population projections, age-specific income distribution relative to the poverty line, and the household saving rate as the starting value for the projections.

Age-Specific Saving Rates

The information about income and consumption is available across age groups from the Brazilian POF survey (*Pesquisa de Orçamento Familiar*), where the household head is taken as the age-reference point when pairing age and saving rate. Only the age groups above 20 years are used; households below 20 years are relatively small in number and likely to provide unreliable estimates for the saving rate. Importantly, net income is adjusted by private pension contributions, and as a second scenario, also for public pensions.

The saving rate is found to differ across age groups between the share of the population above and below the poverty line. The POF 2002 gives similar results, so the latest available 2008 POF data are used. To make the comparison, this analysis uses the average of the preceding 10 years for each of the missing years. The equation below indicates how the weighted average of the saving rate is estimated, but the equation illustrates only how it is weighted by people in their youth, middle age, and old age. The estimation is, in fact, done by age. The second to fourth equations show how the saving rate is estimated based on income levels, where the fourth equation indicates the final weighting.

$$s = s_{children}\left(\frac{N_{children}}{N}\right) + s_{workers}\left(\frac{N_{workers}}{N}\right) + s_{elderly}\left(\frac{N_{elderly}}{N}\right)$$

$$s^{poor} = s_{children}^{poor}\left(\frac{N_{children}^{poor}}{N^{poor}}\right) + s_{workers}^{poor}\left(\frac{N_{workers}^{poor}}{N^{poor}}\right) + s_{elderly}^{poor}\left(\frac{N_{elderly}^{poor}}{N^{poor}}\right)$$

$$s^{non\text{-}poor} = s_{children}^{non\text{-}poor}\left(\frac{N_{children}^{non\text{-}poor}}{N^{non\text{-}poor}}\right) + s_{workers}^{non\text{-}poor}\left(\frac{N_{workers}^{non\text{-}poor}}{N^{non\text{-}poor}}\right) + s_{elderly}^{non\text{-}poor}\left(\frac{N_{elderly}^{non\text{-}poor}}{N^{non\text{-}poor}}\right)$$

$$s = s^{\text{poor}}\left(\frac{N^{\text{poor}}}{N}\right) + s^{\text{non-poor}}\left(\frac{N^{\text{non-poor}}}{N}\right)$$

Population Projections

The population is incorporated for each age and over the period 2010–50 based on the medium fertility variant from the UN Population Division (2008 rev.). The data are available on a five-year interval by age, so Sprague-multipliers are used to interpolate for each age. The age-specific population projections are combined with the age-specific share below the poverty line in order to divide the population into a non-poor and poor segment by age group.

Inequality Measure

The share of the population below the poverty line is calculated based on the Brazilian PNADE household survey data for the available years: 1995–2007 (except 2000). As inequality scenario 1, the average annual percentage change in the share below the poverty line is used as the future percentage trend change in the share below the poverty line; scenario 2 is a fairly pessimistic scenario with regard to inequality since it is based on zero change in the share below the poverty line. Note that the share below the poverty line is also estimated at an age-specific level, where the share that is poor is seen to shift downwards as the projected share below the poverty line is reduced over time.

Simulation

The combination of age-specific saving rates, population projections, and inequality levels is used for projections of the weighted average of the saving rate. 2006 is used as the initial year for the projections based on IBGE Estimates for Families' Saving. The saving rate levels are used in the simulations; however, for the final analysis, the percentage changes in the saving rate are used to project the aggregate family saving rate as it was reported by IBGE at 4.84 percent in 2006. This is because the levels are based on a sample of households in Brazil and may not necessarily be representative of the whole population of non-poor and poor households.

In the simulations, the new rich (the share of the population that would still have been poor if the poverty headcount rate had not fallen) are not assumed to save with the full amount as the rich population segment. Instead, this analysis assumes that the simple average of the age-specific saving rates for the rich and poor population segments applies to this "intermediate" group. Therefore, it is assumed that the transition from high to low saving rates is phased in line with improvements in the poverty headcount.

Annex 7.3: The General Equilibrium Model

This annex describes the main features of the general equilibrium overlapping generations (OLG) model used by Jorgensen (2011) to analyze the future implications of population aging in Brazil. Its purpose is to simulate the effect on key macroeconomic variables given the projected changes in population aging (population growth and life expectancy) from 2010 to 2050.

The model builds on Jorgensen and Jensen (2010) and features the decisions made by households, firms, and the Brazilian government, as well as the associated economic developments over the life cycle of a representative agent and firm. Within this demographic-economic framework it is possible to analyze the behavioral and economic implications of population dynamics. The government can then respond to aging with various parametric or structural policies in order to meet its objectives.

An OLG model is appropriate to use in the context of aging because it incorporates the endogeneity of key variables, which a partial equilibrium model does not do. Therefore, the model addresses the weaknesses of the partial equilibrium model of saving presented in this chapter. On the other hand, the weakness of the stylized version of the deterministic OLG model applied here is that it cannot incorporate some key features specific to Brazil, such as endogenous bequests and the complexity of the social security system. However, it will deliver estimates of the overall direction of the economic implications of aging in Brazil, since the model is calibrated in line with what are considered suitable magnitudes of parameters for Brazil. Key structures of the model relating to population aging are as follows.

Demographics

The population grows at a certain rate, which falls when the population ages. Life expectancy (that is, the length of the retirement period) is incorporated since aging encompasses both changes in age-structures and in longevity. The population is assumed to either be working or retired.

Households

The representative agent maximizes utility subject to consumption in their working and retirement periods, respectively. In addition, an increase in life expectancy is assumed to lead to higher lifetime utility.

$$U = \frac{c_{1,t}^{1-\sigma}}{1-\sigma} + \phi_t \frac{c_{2,t+1}^{1-\sigma}}{1-\sigma}$$

where U is lifetime utility; $c_{1,t}$ is consumption in the generation t's working period; $c_{2,t+1}$ is consumption in the retirement period of the same generation t; σ is the inverse elasticity of substitution; and ϕ_t is the (relative) length of the retirement period for generation t, incorporating also the discount rate (Jorgensen and Jensen 2010).

Out of labor income, workers decide how much to save and consume, given their mandatory contributions to health and pension systems (the two systems most directly fiscally affected by aging); workers' saving leads to investment in this closed economy, which in the next generation period is assumed to be transformed into physical capital used for production; retirees consume the principal and interest on their savings in addition to the pension and health benefits. The intertemporal budget constraint, featuring the relative prices on intertemporal consumption as well as lifetime income, is shown as:

$$c_{1,t} + \frac{\phi_t}{R_{t+1}} c_{2,t+1} = \left(1 - t_1 - t_2 + \frac{\varphi\phi_t}{R_{t+1}}\right)w_t + h\left(1 + \frac{\phi_t}{R_{t+1}}\right)$$

where R_t is gross real interest earnings in period t; w_t is the real wage rate; h is public health expenditures; t_1 is taxes devoted to the public pension system and debt; t_2 is taxes devoted to the public health system and debt.

Firms

Firms employ labor and capital to produce output according to a Cobb-Douglas production function, from which the wage and real interest rate is generated. So, when labor supply falls due to historically lower fertility, the return to labor supply, which is now the more scarce production factor, increases and the return to capital falls.

Government

The Brazilian government manages a pay-as-you-go (PAYG) pension scheme, where workers contribute and retirees receive benefits, and a health system, where workers contribute and both workers and retirees receive the benefits. Both systems depend crucially on the number of

workers contributing and the number of retirees (and workers) benefit-
ting. In addition, the government is able to issue debt (domestically). As
a result, in each period, the government finances pension and health
expenditure as well as interest payments on debt and amortization of
previous period debt. Related to aging is the fact that public debt is essen-
tially the debt of taxpayers, so the fewer taxpayers (workers) there are to
bear the debt-burden of previous generations, the less sustainable a given
level of debt-GDP ratio. The government budget constraint is stated in
the following equation, where the left side is tax revenue and debt in
period t, which finances the expenditures on the right side, which is the
reimbursement of last period debt with interest and the public pension
benefit for retirees and health care expenditures (all denoted in units of
effective labor):

$$(t_1 + t_2)w_t + b_t = \frac{b_{t-1}R_t}{(1+n_{t-1})(1+g_{t-1})} + \frac{\varphi\phi_{t-1}w_t}{1+n_{t-1}} + h\frac{1+n_{t-1}+\phi_{t-1}}{1+n_{t-1}}$$

where b_t is public debt as a share of GDP per worker; φ is the share of
real wages received as a public pension annuity; n_t is the exogenous
population growth rate; and g_t is the exogenous technology growth rate
between periods t and $t+1$.

Calibration
The model is calibrated for Brazil with the following data: Time periods of
the model are assumed to be 20 years; as evident from figure 7.5a, the
population growth rate equals 56 percent (growth rate over the period
1970–1990, UN Population Division [2008 rev.]. In order to calibrate for
life expectancy, the length of the model's first period is normalized at
unity, while the length of the second period equals 61 percent (estimated
as the share of total life spent in retirement: average retirement age equals
57.83 [Queiroz and Figoli 2010]; average entry-age into the labor force is
13.3 [da Silva Leme and Málaga 2001]; life expectancy equals 69.3 (average life expectancy at birth over the period 1998–2088 [UN Population
Division (2008 rev.)]). The share of capital in output equals 18 percent
(average gross capital formation over the period 1990–2010; IMF WEO).

For the base year 2010, the simulation of the general equilibrium
model assumes a debt-GDP ratio of 41 percent (Banco Central do Brazil);
the contribution rates to the health system are residually estimated based
on 1.46 percent for health benefits (based on health spending relative to
GDP over the period 1984–2009 [Tafner 2010]); the contribution rate to

the social PAYG pension system is calibrated to 31 percent (11 percent from workers and 20 percent from employers [Queiroz and Figoli 2010]). The average replacement rate for pensions, weighted by the share of the population receiving pension benefits at various rates, is estimated to be 45 percent.

The replacement rate to public servants is assumed to be 95 percent, since older public servants participated in a plan of virtually 100 percent replacement rate, while younger generations receive slightly less. The replacement rate for non-public servants is estimated residually based on pension payment data for the two groups. The weighted average is constructed based on the share of the population is each group; the effective weighted average is found to equal 45 percent (data from DATAPREV, SUB, Plano Tabular da DIIE, and Ministerio da fazenda). Productivity growth is assumed to follow output growth and equals 168 percent (growth over the period 1988–2008); discount rate equals 0.9.

Simulations

The model simulations start in 1990, so the past 20 years of demographic transition are taken into account in projecting the economic implications from 2010–50. The model is simulated in Matlab using Dynare software (Jorgensen 2006). The results should be interpreted as the economic implications over generational periods of 20 years; that is, over the periods 2010–30 and 2030–50. The projections are based on 20-year projections in population growth and life expectancy (UN Population Division [2008 rev.]).

Annex 7.4: The Reduced-Form General Equilibrium Model

The methodology for estimating the first and second demographic dividend follows Lee and Mason (2004) and Mason and Lee (2010). The method is also described in Queiroz and Turra (2010), but the key equation for separating the aggregate demographic dividend into the first and second dividends is from Bloom and Williamson (1998). The methodology is briefly described here.

Estimates of the first demographic dividend use age profiles of income and consumption combined with population age distributions. The results for Brazil by Queiroz and Turra (2010) were estimated using Brazilian profiles for 1996. This cross-sectional profile is assumed constant during the period of analysis (1970–50). The demographic bonus gives rise to two demographic dividends: the first is measured by purely demographic factors, while the second is an economic measure.

To estimate the second dividend, Queiroz and Turra (2010) follow Mason (2005) and apply several simplifying assumptions: The ratio of capital to labor income at ages 50 and older is assumed to represent the wealth accumulated over the individual life cycle; age patterns of consumption and labor income are assumed not to change over time; and consumption and income levels are allowed to increase by 1.5 percent per year. To estimate the present values of consumption and labor income, an interest rate of 3 percent is further assumed. An elasticity of labor income with respect to capital is assumed to equal 0.5. The first and second dividends are formalized in Mason (2005) and Queiroz and Turra (2010). If the effective number of consumers is denoted by N and the effective number of producers by L, then

$$N(t) = \sum_a \alpha(\alpha)P(\alpha,t),$$

$$L(t) = \sum_a \gamma(\alpha)P(\alpha,t)$$

where $P(\alpha,t)$ is the population of age a at time t, and $\alpha(\alpha)$ and $\gamma(\alpha)$ are age-specific coefficients reflecting relative levels of consumption and production. Output per effective consumer (Y/N) is given by

$$\frac{Y_t}{N_t} = \frac{L_t}{N_t}\frac{Y_t}{L_t}$$

where Y_t is the total output. The effective number of producers (consumers) is the population weighted by the age income (consumption) profile (Cutler et al. 1990; Mason 2005). The support ratio (N_t/L_t) is given by the ratio of effective producers to the number of effective consumers. By taking the natural log of both sides and deriving with respect to time, Mason (2005) as well as Bloom and Williamson (1998) obtain rates of growth according to:

$$\dot{y}^{n(t)} = \dot{L}(t) - \dot{N}(t) + \dot{y}(t)$$

The rate of growth in output per effective consumer $(\dot{y}^n)$ is the sum of the rate of growth of the support ratio, $\dot{L}(t) - \dot{N}(t)$, and the rate of growth of output per worker $\dot{y}$. The first dividend is then defined as the rate of growth of the support ratio, while the second dividend operates through productivity growth by inducing the accumulation of wealth and capital deepening. Mason (2005) shows that the rate of growth of productivity is proportional to the ratio of capital to labor income when both capital and transfer wealth grow at the same rate (that is, when there are no changes in intergenerational transfer policy).

The relationship between life cycle wealth, capital, and economic growth can be clarified further by assuming that output depends on capital and effective labor only, and that the production function is Cobb-Douglas. It can be shown that growth in output per worker is proportional to the growth in the ratio of capital to labor income, $\dot{k}$, according to

$$\dot{y}(t) = \frac{\beta}{1-\beta}\dot{k}(t)$$

where β is the elasticity of output with respect to capital (Solow 1956). Note that capital deepening in this formulation is measured as an increase in capital relative to labor income, rather than capital relative to labor. A more general formulation of the production process that incorporates human capital does not alter estimates of the effect of capital deepening (Mankiw, Romer, and Weil 1992).

Annex 7.5: Open-Economy Implications for Policy Scenarios

Figure A7.1   An Open-Economy Version of Policy Scenarios in Figure 7.5b

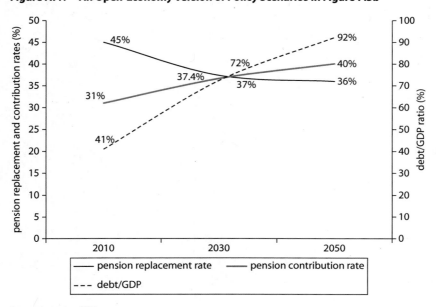

Source: Jorgensen 2011.

Notes

1. Chawla, Betcherman, and Banerji (2007) analyze the LCH and potential saving responses to population aging in Eastern European and Central Asian countries and reach similar conclusions.

2. The second demographic dividend arises as the low dependency ratio (the demographic bonus) leads to a larger share of prime savers in the economy, thus boosting savings. Such a higher saving rate, combined with higher future saving due to an expectation of increased longevity, will lead capital accumulation to enhance growth through a higher capital-labor ratio (the section "The First Demographic Dividend" provides a more elaborate discussion of this topic).

3. Bloom, Canning, and Fink (2009) deal with such issues in a broader context; and the institutional settings for harvesting the demographic dividend is not incorporated (Bloom and Canning 2003; Bloom et al. 2007). These and other excluded issues remain for future research on the economic implication of aging in Brazil—though chapter 5 touches on labor participation, and chapter 6 adopts an institutional perspective on the socioeconomic implications of aging.

4. Building on Brazilian data from IPEA (National Institute for Applied Economic Research), a vector auto-regression (VAR) analysis is performed by Jorgensen (2011) to study whether gross or private saving positively (Granger) causes economic growth over time (see annex 7.1, table A7.1). In a separate VAR model in which public saving and the old-age dependency ratio are included in the equation system, the result still holds. A key reference for this interrelation between saving and growth in a panel setting is Attanasio (2000). The findings for Brazil are comparable to those by Attanasio.

5. The findings are robust for the measure of saving being either gross or private. Cumulative impulse response functions from the VAR model further support the positive growth implications over time of an increase in private saving (Jorgensen 2011). There is one important caveat to this analysis, however: The data on public and private saving in Brazil are not as reliable as one would hope. The period 1984–94 is somewhat unreliable, because the public and private savings were not available from IPEA for that decade, and this is the period where public and private saving display a spike. The IMF is the available source for public saving within this period. On the other hand, Morandi (1998) finds a similar though smaller spike in private saving, and Oliveira, Beltrão, and David (1998) find a similarly small spike within this period.

6. Bosworth, Burtless, and Sabelhaus (1991) estimate the average saving rate for retirees in the United States, correcting for the pension adjustment suggested by Miles (1999), and find that the traditional measure of the unadjusted savings rate was 14.9 percent, while the measure that was adjusted by private pensions was 1.8 percent.

7. Meredith (1995) estimated that a 10 percentage point increase in the old-age dependency ratio could reduce the saving rate by around 9 percentage points, while a 0.1 percentage point drop in the young-age dependency ratio would lead to an increase in the savings ratio of about 6.1 percentage points. Also, simulations by Miles (1999), based on a model that assumes that LCH holds, found that the private savings rate in European economies could fall from 15.9 percent (of GDP) in 1990 to around 4.5 percent by 2060. Roeger (2006) furthermore finds that life expectancy of the population in European countries is projected to increase by around five years over the next four decades, but that the positive effect on domestic savings is not likely to offset the impact of the increasing old-age dependency ratios in this region.

8. Jorgensen (2011) uses an error-correction model to address this question. The problem with a single equation error-correction model could be a simultaneous equation bias if the causality between private saving and one of the other variables runs both ways, which could explain the negative coefficient of GDP per capita in the long-run relationship. An alternative is to use Johansen's approach of vector error-correction, but this is not pursued due to the small number of yearly observations. The study by Jorgensen (2011) also attempted to include in the error-correction model the terms of trade, money supply (M2), and the inflation rate, but these estimations did not produce significant results.

9. This approach avoids double-counting the precautionary saving motive; inflation is significantly positively related to saving.

10. A further neglected issue is that reductions in income inequality may lead to a larger middle class that generally saves more. One reason why poverty decompositions usually reveal that inequality increases poverty may be due to the saving channel; the higher the inequality, the lower the average private saving rate. So, high inequality may reduce saving, which reduces growth and increases poverty.

11. The above evidence on the saving-growth and aging-saving relationships has been purely empirical. The evidence suggests that the old-age dependency ratio is not likely to have had a negative effect on private saving over the time period covered (1970–2008). This might also be the case in the future, but such projections would always be subject to the Lucas critique, that is, that parameters used in projections may change if exogenous shocks or policy reforms appear.

12. The measure that excludes public pension benefits is equivalent to evaluating the LCH relative to labor income.

13. The "non-poor" and "poor" are classified according to the $2 PPP (Purchasing Power Parity) per day national poverty line.

14. As figure 7.3b illustrates, the trajectories for the population across different age groups will display parallel shifts when the poverty headcount is reduced, for example, by one percent.

15. The partial equilibrium model is described in annex 7.2, including a description of the data used and a discussion of the assumptions for simulations.

16. If public pensions are excluded from income, the main finding, that the saving rate is likely to increase, will be overturned. On that account, two robustness scenarios were performed in figure 7.4b—whether public pensions should or should not be counted as income, which alters the main finding that the saving rate is likely to increase. As figures 7.2a and b illustrate, the saving rates evolve in line with the LCH if public pensions are not included. Such a saving pattern would generate a weighted average of the saving rate that would fall over time when the population ages. It is the authors' view, however, that these scenarios are not particularly credible, so while we present the implications for illustrative and transparency purposes, we choose to rely on the income measurement that includes public pensions—and, thus, rely on the saving profiles that result in a slight rise over time.

17. Moreover, macroeconomic responses to aging that endogenously affect growth, such as reductions in the availability of labor in production, were also not taken into account by the partial equilibrium model.

18. The miracle economies of the Eastern and Southeastern Asian Tigers provide compelling and consistent evidence that the demographic dividend was an important contributor to that region's economic success (Birdsall, Kelley, and Sinding 2001; Bloom and Williamson 1998; Mason 2005; World Bank 1993). Bloom and Williamson (1998) use econometric analysis to conclude that about one-third of the Asian Tigers' increase in per capita income was due to the demographic dividend; while Mason (2005) uses growth accounting methods to estimate that the dividend accounted for one-fourth of the region's growth.

19. The effective number of consumers is the number of consumers weighted by age variation in consumption needs (Mason 2005).

20. The first dividend contributed to almost 30 percent of the observed economic growth in Brazil 1970–2010, according to Queiroz and Turra (2010). Mason (2005) estimates the first dividend to be 20 percent for the United States and about 10 percent for India during the same period.

21. The pro-growth effect of capital accumulation and wealth is the source of the second demographic dividend, but this wealth can take different forms (Mason 2005). One possibility is that retirees will rely on transfers from public pension and welfare programs or from adult children and other family members. A second possibility is that individuals will accumulate capital during their working years and that this capital will serve as the

source of support during the retirement period. Both of these forms of wealth can be used to fill in the life cycle deficit at older ages, but only capital accumulation influences economic growth—an issue that is incorporated in the general equilibrium model applied in the following section. If capital is invested in the domestic economy, the result will be capital deepening and more rapid growth in output per worker. If capital is invested abroad, the result will be an improvement in the current account and an increase in national income. In either case, per capita income will grow more rapidly than it would otherwise. It is important to note, however, that accumulation of capital does not need to be as high as when working-age population is growing at rapid rates. Since there are fewer effective producers, the amount of capital necessary to keep the capital-labor ratio constant is reduced.

22. For example, from 2000 to 2005 GDP per effective consumer growth rate was one-half of what the demographic dividends would predict.

23. The estimations by Mason (2005) Queiroz and Turra (2010) of the first and second dividend both assume that the cross-sectional profiles of consumption persist into the future. In a sense, it is assumed that the costs or benefits of aging are anticipated and shared across generations in the same manner as they are at present. Capital accumulation could rise, transfer programs could expand, families could provide more support, and the elderly could adjust their needs to the demographic realities. Alternative scenarios are definitely possible. The estimation presented here does not capture the costs that these possible generational crises would impose on societies. On the contrary, developed countries studied by Mason (2005) will have a small or even negative contribution from the demographic dividends to economic growth.

24. A general equilibrium model has its own advantages and disadvantages compared to the partial equilibrium model and the reduced form model, because the demographic changes are usually more broadly defined than in a general equilibrium model to the detailed accounting in a cohort-component demographic model used in the partial equilibrium analysis, and market structures are usually quite crudely defined compared to reality.

25. The general equilibrium model is described in annex 7.3, including a description of the data used and a discussion of the assumptions for simulations.

26. There is a large body of literature on the subject of demographic change and viability of social security arrangements (Auerbach and Lee 2001; Campbell and Feldstein 2001; Cutler et al. 1990), but this is not the focus here. Furthermore, Weil (2006) finds that the distortion created by taxes needed to fund PAYG pension systems is a key channel through which a higher dependency ratio affects aggregate output and welfare.

27. In Brazil, a higher capital-labor ratio is beneficial for welfare since consumption and income will approach the optimal level. The capital-labor ratio can also be too high and may "steal" all the consumption possibilities of households and thus eventually reduce welfare.

28. Furthermore, it is not likely that the envisaged future oil windfalls will "take care" of the problem, since such commodity revenues are often associated with low saving and investment incentives (Papyrakis and Gerlagh 2006) or an outright curse for the economy (Sinnott, Nash, and de la Torre 2010). There are also likely to be important trade-offs in terms of intergenerational distributions of enhanced consumption possibilities in light of expected pre-salt oil and gas windfalls. Jorgensen (2010b) finds that the optimal allocation of oil windfalls is strongly affected by the long-term economic implications of population aging, and that aging is a key driver of a policy rule for the efficient and equitable allocation of pre-salt windfalls.

29. The system for social security contributions is, naturally, more complicated than simply the two rates referred to. However, to make the general equilibrium model tractable, it is assumed that the contributions to the social security system can be reasonably replicated by an aggregate 31 percent contribution rate (annex 7.3).

30. This increase in the pension contribution rate assumes that the health system balances such that fewer workers also finance the health expenditures of more retirees and fewer workers. The contribution rate for the health system consequently does not rise as much.

31. These dynamics are all interdependent over the projected period; as the saving rate starts falling, the steepness of the decline in the capital worker ratio would also increase.

32. This reduction in pension benefits is accompanied by the need for a simultaneous reduction in the health benefit rate, as the model has been formulated.

33. If domestic public debt increases, the capital stock will be crowded out even further, thus worsening the current situation where "only" the generous social security system in Brazil neutralizes the incentive to save.

34. Proposals for using the retirement age as a policy instrument are found in de la Croix, Mahieu, and Rillares (2004) and Andersen, Jensen, and Pedersen (2008).

35. This could also be interpreted as an endogenous drop in the voluntary early retirement age, financed by workers' own savings.

36. The growing tendency for elderly people to live alone in Brazil might lead to a reduced prevalence of the bequest motive, which is an issue that should be taken into consideration in future research on this topic.

37. "Poor" is defined in this section as living below the $2 PPP national poverty line.

References

Acemoglu, D. 2010. "Theory, General Equilibrium, and Political Economy in Development Economics." *Journal of Economic Perspectives* 24 (3): 17–32.

Andersen, T. M., S. E. H. Jensen, and L. H. Pedersen. 2008. "The Welfare State and Strategies Towards Fiscal Sustainability in Denmark." In *Sustainability of Public Debt*, ed. R. Neck and J.-E. Sturm, 161–191. Cambridge, MA: MIT Press.

Attanasio, O. P., Lucio Picci, and A. E. Scorcu. 2000. "Saving, Growth and Investment: A Macroeconomic Analysis Using a Panel of Countries." *The Review of Economics and Statistics* 82 (2): 182–211.

Attanasio, O. P., and M. Székely. 2000. "Household Saving in Developing Countries: Inequality, Demographics and All That—How Different Are Latin America and South East Asia?" IADB Working Paper 427, Inter-American Development Bank, Washington, DC.

Auerbach, A. J., and R. D. Lee (eds.). 2001. *Demographic Change and Fiscal Policy.* Cambridge, UK: Cambridge University Press.

Bailliu, J., and H. Reisen. 1997. "Do Funded Pensions Contribute to Higher Savings? A Cross-Country Analysis." OECD Technical Papers 130, Organisation for Economic Co-operation and Development, Paris.

Barro, R. J. 1974. "Are Government Bonds Net Wealth?" *Journal of Political Economy* 82 (6): 1–46.

Barro, R. J., and G. Becker. 1989. "Fertility Choice in a Model of Economic Growth." *Econometrica* 57: 481–502.

Birdsall, N., A. Kelley, and S. Sinding. 2001. *Population Matters: Demographic Change, Economic Growth and Poverty in the Developing World.* New York: Oxford University Press.

Bloom, D. E., and D. Canning. 2003. "Contraception and the Celtic Tiger." *The Economic and Social Review* 34 (3): 229–47.

Bloom, D. E., D. Canning, and G. Fink. 2009. "Population Aging and Economic Growth." World Bank Commission on Growth and Development, World Bank, Washington, DC.

Bloom, D. E., D. Canning, G. Fink, and J. E. Finlay. 2007. "Demographic Change, Institutional Settings, and Labor Supply." Program on the Global Demography of Aging Working Paper 42, Harvard School of Public Health, Cambridge, MA.

Bloom, D.E., D. Canning, and J. Sevilla. 2003. *The Demographic Dividend: A New Perspective on the Economic Consequences of Population Change.* Population Matters: A RAND Program of Policy-Relevant Research Communication. Santa Monica, CA: RAND Corporation.

Bloom, D. E., and J. G. Williamson. 1998. "Demographic Transitions and Economic Miracles in Emerging Asia." *World Bank Economic Review* 12 (3): 419–55.

Bosworth, B., G. Burtless, and J. Sabelhaus. 1991. "The Decline in Saving: Evidence from Household Surveys." Brookings Papers on Economic Activity 1, Brookings Institution, Washington, DC.

Caldwell, J. C. 1982. *A Theory of Fertility Decline*. New York: Academic Press.

Callen, A.D.-G., and C. Thimann. 1997. "Saving in Southeast Asia and Latin America Compared—Searching for Policy Lessons." IMF Working Paper 97/110, International Monetary Fund, Washington, DC.

Campbell, J., and M. Feldstein. 2001. *Risk Aspects of Investment Based Social Security Reform*. Chicago: University of Chicago Press.

Chakraborty, S. 2004. "Endogenous Lifetime and Economic Growth." *Journal of Economic Theory* 116: 119–137.

Chawla, M., G. Betcherman, and A. Banerji. 2007. *From Red to Gray: The 'Third Transition' of Aging Populations in Eastern Europe and the former Soviet Union*. Washington, DC.: World Bank.

Corbo, V., and K. Schmidt-Hebbel. 1991. "Public Policies and Saving in Developing Countries." *Journal of Development Economics* 36 (July): 89–115.

Cutler, D. M., J. M. Poterba, L. M. Sheiner, and L. H. Summers. 1990. "An Aging Society: Opportunity or Challenge?" *Brookings Papers on Economic Activity* 21 (1): 1–74.

Dasgupta, P. 1993. *An Inquiry into Well-Being and Destitution*. New York: Clarendon Press.

Dayal-Gulati, A., and C. Thimann 1997. "Saving in Southeast Asia and Latin America Compared: Searching for Policy Lessons." IMF Working Paper WP/97/110, International Monetary Fund, Washington, DC.

de la Croix, D., G. Mahieu, and A. Rillares. 2004. How Should the Allocation of Resources Adjust to the Baby-Bust?" *Journal of Public Economic Theory* 6 (4): 607–36.

De Nardi, M., E. French, and J. B. Jones. 2009. "Why Do the Elderly Save? The Role of Medical Expenses." NBER Working Paper 15149, National Bureau of Economic Research, Cambridge, MA.

De Serres, A., and F. Pelgrin. 2002. "The Decline of Saving Rates in the 1990s in OECD Countries: How Much Can Be Explained by Non-Wealth Determinants?" OECD Economics Working Paper 344, Organisation for Economic Co-operation and Development, Paris.

Doshi, K. 1994. "Determinants of the Saving Rate: An International Comparison." *Contemporary Economic Policy* 12 (1): 37–45.

Edwards, S. 1996. "Why Are Latin America's Savings Rates So Low? An International Comparative Analysis." *Journal of Development Economics* 51 (1): 5–44.

————. 1995. "Why Are Saving Rates So Different Across Countries? An International Comparative Analysis." NBER Working Paper 5097, National Bureau of Economic Research, Cambridge, MA.

Ehrlich, I., and F. Lui. 1991. "Intra-Household Trade, Longevity, and Economic Growth." *The Journal of Political Economy* 99 (5): 1029–59.

Fletcher, K., C. Keller, P. K. Brooks, D. Lombardo, and A. Meier. 2007. "Safe to Save Less? Assessing the Recent Decline in Turkey's Private Saving Rate." IMF Selected Issues Paper 07/364, International Monetary Fund, Washington, DC.

Graham, J. W. 1987. "International Differences in Saving Rates and the Life Cycle Hypothesis." *European Economic Review* 31 (8): 1509–29.

Gregory, P., M. Mokhtari, and W. Schrettl. 1999. "Do the Russians Really Save That Much? Alternative Estimates From the Russian Longitudinal Monitoring Survey." *The Review of Economics and Statistics* 81 (4): 694–703.

Haque, N. U., M. H. Pesaran, and S. Sharma. 1999. "Neglected Heterogeneity and Dynamics in Cross-country Savings Regressions." Cambridge Working Papers in Economics 9904, University of Cambridge, Cambridge, UK.

Jensen, S. E. H., and O. H. Jorgensen. 2010. "Reform and Backlash to Reform: Economic Effects of Ageing and Retirement Policy." World Bank Policy Research Working Paper 5470. World Bank, Washington, DC.

Jensen, S. E. H., and O. H. Jorgensen. 2008. "Uncertain Demographics, Longevity Adjustment of the Retirement Age and Intergenerational Risk-Sharing." In *Uncertain Demographics and Fiscal Sustainability*, ed. S. J. Alho, S. E. H. Jensen, and J. Lassila, 239–257. Cambridge, UK: Cambridge University Press.

Jorgensen, O. H. 2010a. "Health, Demographic Transition, and Economic Growth." World Bank Policy Research Working Paper 5304, World Bank, Washington, DC.

Jorgensen, O. H. 2010b. "Should Oil Finance Aging in Brazil? Efficiency and Equity Implications of Oil Windfalls and Population Aging." Unpublished working paper, World Bank, Washington DC.

Jorgensen, O. H. 2011. "Macroeconomic and Policy Implications of Population Aging in Brazil." World Bank Policy Research Working Paper 5519, Background paper prepared for the Workshop on Aging in Brazil, Brasilia, April 6–7, 2010.

Jorgensen, O. H., and S. E. H. Jensen. 2010. "Labor Supply and Retirement Policy in an Overlapping Generations Model with Stochastic Fertility." World Bank Policy Research Working Paper 5382, World Bank, Washington, DC.

Koskela, E., and M. Virén. 1992. "Inflation, Capital Markets and Household Saving in the Nordic Countries." *The Scandinavian Journal of Economics* 94 (2): 215–27.

Kotlikoff, L., and L.H. Summers. 1981. "The Adequacy of Savings." NBER Working Paper 627, National Bureau of Economic Research, Cambridge, MA.

Lee, R., and A. Mason. 2006. "Back to Basics: What Is the Demographic Dividend?" *Finance & Development* 43 (3).

Loayza, N., K. Schmidt-Hebbel, and L. Servén. 2000. "What Drives Private Saving Around the World?" World Bank Policy Research Working Paper 2309, World Bank, Washington, DC.

Mankiw, N., G. D. Romer, and D. N. Weil. 1992. "A Contribution to the Empirics of Economic Growth." *The Quarterly Journal of Economics* 107 (2): 407–37.

Mason, A. 2005. "Demographic Transition and Demographic Dividends in Developed and Developing Countries." Unpublished working paper, Department of Economics, University of Hawaii at Manoa, and Population and Health Studies, East-West Center, Honolulu, HI.

Mason, A., and R. Lee. 2010. "Introducing Age into National Accounts." NTA Working Paper 10-02, National Transfer Accounts Project, Honolulu, HI. http://www.ntaccounts.org/web/nta/show/WP10-02.

Masson, P. R., T. Bayoumi, and H. Samiei. 1998. "International Evidence on the Determinants of Private Saving." IMF Working Paper 95/51. International Monetary Fund, Washington, DC.

Meredith, G. 1995. "Demographic Change and Household Saving in Japan." In *Saving Behavior and the Asset Price Bubble in Japan: Analytical Studies*. IMF Occasional Paper 124, 36–45. International Monetary Fund, Washington, DC.

Miles, D. 1999. "Modelling the Impact of Demographic Change upon the Economy." *The Economic Journal* 109 (452): 1–36.

Modigliani, F., and R. H. Brumberg. 1954. "Utility Analysis and the Consumption Function: An Interpretation of the Cross-Section Data." In *Post-Keynesian Economics*, ed. Kenneth K. Kurihara, 388–436. New Brunswick, NJ: Rutgers University Press.

Morandi, L. 1998. "Stoque de Riqueza e a Poupança do Setor Privado no Brasil—1970/95." Texto para discussão 572, Instituto de Pesquisa Econômica Aplicada, Rio de Janeiro.

Nerlove, M., and N. L. Raut. 1997. "Growth Models With Endogenous Population: A General Framework." In *Handbook of Population and Family Economics*, ed. M. R. Rosenzweig and O. Stark, vol. 1, part 2, 1117–74. Amsterdam: Elsevier BV.

Oeppen, J., and J. W. Vaupel. 2002. "Broken Limits to Life Expectancy." *Science* 296 (5570): 1029–31.

Oliveira, F. E. B. de, K. I. Beltrão, and A. C. de Albuquerque David. 1998. "Previdência, Poupança e, Crescimento Econômico." Texto Para Discussão 607,

Interações e Perspectivas, IPEA, Instituto de Pesquisa Econômica Aplicada, Rio de Janeiro.

Ozcan, K. M., A. Gunay, and S. Ertac. 2003. "Determinants of Private Savings Behaviour in Turkey." *Applied Economics* 12 (35): 1405–16.

Paiva, C., and S. Jahan. 2003. "An Empirical Study of Private Saving in Brazil." *Brazilian Journal of Political Economy* 12 (1): 121–32.

Papyrakis, E., and R. Gerlagh. 2006. "Resource Windfalls, Investment and Long-Term Income." *Resources Policy* 31 (2): 117–28.

Poterba, J. 1994. "The Impact of Population Aging on Financial Markets." NBER Working Paper 10851, National Bureau of Economic Research, Cambridge, MA.

Queiroz, B. L., and M. G. B Figoli. 2010. "The Social Protection System for the Elderly in Brazil." Background paper prepared for the Workshop on Aging in Brazil, World Bank, Brasilia, April 6–7, 2010.

Queiroz, B. L., and C. M. Turra. 2010. "Window of Opportunity: Socioeconomic Consequences of Demographic Changes in Brazil." Unpublished NTA Working Paper, National Transfer Accounts Project, Honolulu, HI.

Rodrik, D. 2000. "Saving Transitions." *World Bank Economic Review* 14 (3): 481–507.

Roeger, W. 2006. "Assessing the Budgetary Impact of Systemic Pension Reforms." Economic Papers 248, European Commission, Economy and Finance.

Schrooten, M., and S. Stephan. 2005. "Private Savings and Transition: Dynamic Panel Data Evidence from Accession Countries." *Economics of Transition* 13 (2): 287–309.

Silva Leme, M. C. da, and T. Málaga. 2001. "Entrada e Saída Precoce da Força de Trabalho: Incentivos do Regime de Previdência Brasileiro." *Revista Brasileira de Economia* 55 (2): 205–22.

Sinnott, E., J. Nash, and A. de la Torre. 2010. "Natural Resources in Latin America and the Caribbean. Beyond Booms and Busts?" World Bank, Washington, DC.

Solow, R. M. 1956. "A Contribution to the Theory of Economic Growth." *Quarterly Journal of Economics* 70 (1): 65–94.

Stokey, N. 1979. "Do Bequests Offset Social Security?" Discussion Paper 376, Northwestern Center for Mathematical Studies in Economics and Management Science, Evanston, IL.

Tafner, P. 2010. "Public Expenditure Review for Health, Education and Social Security in the Context of Population Aging in Brazil." Background paper prepared for the Workshop on Aging in Brazil, World Bank, Brasilia, April 6–7, 2010.

UN (United Nations). 2004. *World Population in 2300*. New York: United Nations.

Weil, D. N. 1997. "The Economics of Population Aging." In *Handbook of Population and Family Economics*, ed. M. R. Rosenzweig and O. Stark, 968–1014. Amsterdam: Elsevier Science.

———. 2006. "Population Aging." NBER Working Paper 12147, National Bureau of Economic Research, Cambridge, Massachusetts.

Wigger, B. U. 2002. *Public Pensions and Economic Growth*. Heidelberg: Springer-Verlag.

World Bank.1993. *The East Asian Miracle: Economic Growth and Public Policy*. New York: Oxford University Press.

Index

Boxes, figures, notes, and tables are indicated by *b*, *f*, *n*, and *t* following page numbers.

A

"Absolute Bonus," 206–7
Academia da Cidade program, 133, 135
accidents. *See* external causes of health
        problems; road accidents
Ackerberg, D., 187*b*
Acre (Brazil), fertility in, 51
Active Aging: A Policy Framework
        (WHO), 141
active aging concept, 141–45, 161*n*6
adult population
    change in size of, 5–10, 57, 59
    survival of, 262
age curves, creative, 168
Age-Friendly Cities Global Network, 142
age-period-cohort (APC) analysis, 21
age-productivity profile, 169–73, 176, 179
Age Rule program, 107, 117*n*14
aging index, 8, 10, 10*f*
aging-saving transmission channel, 232
"*agiotas*" (established financial sector), 241
Alagoas (Brazil), life expectancy in, 48
"alternative scenario"
    for education spending, 208
    for health care spending, 218
Amadeo, E. J., 178

Annual Relation of Social Information
        Survey (RAIS), 183
APC analysis (age-period-cohort), 21
Araujo, T., 24
Argentina
    education evaluation in, 175
    life expectancy in, 7, 121
    as "pro-aging" country, 17
Asian Tigers, Eastern and Southeastern,
        274*n*18
Attanasio, O. P., 235, 239, 272*n*4
Aubert, P., 186*b*
Australia, budget projections in, 199

B

Banerji, A., 272*n*1
Batista, Anália S., 148
Bay, G., 205
Becker, Gary S., 22, 25, 174
Belgium, unused labor capacity in, 78
Beltrão, K. I., 272*n*5
Benefício de Prestação Continuada (LOAS-
        BPC or BPC), 89–91, 90*f*, 90*t*, 101,
        106, 107, 162*n*9
Benefit-Financing scenario, 33, 233,
        256–58, 259

283